MW01124308

Unequal Foundations

Perspectives on Justice and Morality

Carolyn Hafer
Series Editor

Books in the Series

Unequal Foundations

Inequality, Morality, and
Emotions across Cultures

STEVEN HITLIN

SARAH K. HARKNESS

OXFORD
UNIVERSITY PRESS

OXFORD
UNIVERSITY PRESS

Oxford University Press is a department of the University of Oxford. It furthers
the University's objective of excellence in research, scholarship, and education
by publishing worldwide. Oxford is a registered trade mark of Oxford University
Press in the UK and certain other countries.

Published in the United States of America by Oxford University Press
198 Madison Avenue, New York, NY 10016, United States of America.

© International Society for Justice Research 2018

Library of Congress Cataloging-in-Publication Data
Data Names: Hitlin, Steven, author. | Harkness, Sarah K., author.
Title: Unequal foundations : inequality, morality, and emotions across
cultures / Steven Hitlin, Sarah K. Harkness.
Description: New York, NY : Oxford University Press, [2018] |
Series: Perspectives on justice and morality | Includes bibliographical references
and index.
Identifiers: LCCN 2017028980 | ISBN 9780190465407 (hardcover : alk. paper)
Subjects: LCSH: Equality—Cross-cultural studies. | Income
distribution—Social aspects—Cross-cultural studies. | Moral
conditions—Cross-cultural studies. | Moral development—Cross-cultural
studies. | Ethics—Cross-cultural studies.
Classification: LCC HM821 .H58 2018 | DDC 305—dc23
LC record available at https://lccn.loc.gov/2017028980

9 8 7 6 5 4 3 2 1

Printed by Sheridan Books, Inc., United States of America

For E.

CONTENTS

Unequal Foundations

Introduction

"If there is one fact that history has irrefutably demonstrated, it is that the morality of each people is directly related to the social structure of the people practicing it."

—EMILE DURKHEIM, *1925*[1]

INTRODUCTION

Freedom has long been considered one of the guiding principles of the United States. The Bill of Rights focuses on a range of American values, but current concerns over economic inequality were not a priority for the country's founders. The idea that "all men are created equal" is taken for granted as an assumption about human nature. It is not set out as a goal for Americans to achieve; the focus is on equality of opportunity, not equality of outcome. Freedom here means the freedom to fail, yet Americans systematically underestimate how many people fail to achieve the American Dream, and how a only a few people have acquired such a large part of the pie (Norton & Ariely, 2011).

In the early part of the 21st century, America has one of the largest spreads of economic inequality in the world. At the time of this writing, almost 42% of the country's wealth is held by the richest 1%, a level of inequality that has risen since the middle of the last century (Pikkety, 2014; Semuels, 2016). In 1944 Franklin Delano Roosevelt suggested a second bill of rights, hoping to enshrine the concept that all Americans had a right to a job, a home, and the opportunity to enjoy good health and have adequate medical care. That this proposal was unsuccessful suggests that the American Experiment focuses a good deal more on the freedom that people have than the resources and lack of opportunities that might constrain that freedom. From a sociological perspective, this serves to perpetuate the current social order. The notion that people are created equally, and what happens to them in life is a result of their own efforts (with perhaps a dash of luck involved), is a bedrock belief in American society.

In contrast, China has approximately as much economic inequality as the United States but with a very different belief system about the nature of the individual and the amount of freedom the public should have vis-à-vis the government. Most social psychological theories that compare the East versus the West consider China and the United States to operate very differently, shaping citizens who have fundamentally distinct ways of perceiving the world, social obligations, and the nature of morality. Even though their levels of economic inequality are similar (we will go into detail about this in Chapter 8), the United States and China supposedly have little in common, culturally. However, we argue that, in a fundamental way, the structure of inequality in these two distinct countries shapes individual worldviews in similar – previously unanticipated -ways.

We argue that the level of inequality in a society molds fundamental societal beliefs about the nature of the world, represented in the moral emotional reactions we experience while interacting with others. More specifically, we suggest that the cultural environments of more unequal societies shape people to have harsher negative moral judgments. Members of more equal societies instead often experience positive, community-uplifting, empathetic moral reactions, reflecting the less structurally unequal nature of their social world. Societal inequality is baked into our emotions, and an environment filled with moral emotional sanctioning maintains steep social hierarchy, which then recreates and reinforces the same sanctioning in the future in a feedback cycle.

How you have learned to feel about the world traces from forces that you are probably only dimly aware of, ranging from parenting choices made before you were sentient to patterns embedded in the very economic structure undergirding societies. While many of these forces are outside of easy measurement, we will explore the affective meaning embedded in cultural languages as a prime tool for the transmission of these expectations (that we all internalize) about the world in which we live. By learning a language, you are learning a host of meanings, feelings, and expectations for how the world is and how it should be. You become acculturated first to how people in your family, then eventually in your nation, see the world. Perhaps you do not agree with each and every "average" feeling in your society, but you are certainly aware of them, and you know when your own opinions, beliefs, and emotions diverge from what "typical" people feel. The fundamental nature of a language as experienced by those in a society—the shared feelings, expectations, and understandings that make what we refer to when we talk about an "American" way of being—allude to a coherent-in-the-abstract people. In practice, there is certainly variation within every society; the "public" is a complicated and multifaceted entity. However, to be a member of a society is to understand how the majority thinks and feels about a range of issues and objects and to be part of a shared definition of the components of a society. This fundamental understanding is embedded in our language, the definitions children learn, and, more importantly, the semantic understandings we develop about what words and situations mean and feel like.

We, the authors, are both professional sociologists, concerned with the ways that societies operate and how individuals fit into larger social institutions. In our field, there has been a lot of research about how individuals are shaped by a society that existed before they were born and will continue after they die. Terms such as *norms, values,* and *beliefs* capture the non-physical aspects of the social world communicated across generations, and why we can be broadly certain that the world we experience when we wake up tomorrow will be similar to what we know today. Certainly external shocks can shift this, but short of revolution or natural disaster, even societies that experience terrorist attacks or tragic accidents more or less bounce back to their "regular" state at the national level, if not immediately within the particular community that experiences the social or natural disaster. Fundamental beliefs pertaining to what a mother is or what it means to instruct someone are part of the everyday minutiae of our lives, and these cultural meanings are very stable (Heise, 2007). Ideologies and belief systems are difficult to change, for both individuals (we are quite attached to the ways that we see the world) and society writ large. Our book presents a necessarily simplified overview of some of this work linking individuals to their place in society, a core sociological tenet being that your normative beliefs, values, and behaviors are shaped by your location within the broader stratification system of your country.

We are also both social psychologists, trained in various traditions to theorize and measure how social structures, groups, ideologies, and moral codes shape individuals, including how people think, feel, and behave. The distinction between sociological and psychological ways of gathering and presenting evidence may only be of interest to a small minority of people, but as a shorthand, scholars on our end of the divide begin with the proposition that society exists prior to the individuals who comprise it. While we all have free will (to some extent, we don't have equivalent resources or opportunities based on a variety of factors), the very language shaping our understanding of ourselves and others is provided for us. We do not make up our own cultures, our own ideologies, or our own meanings (Patterson, 2014). Occasionally groups of people can change the wider society, and certainly technological innovations shape the patterns of interaction and language and culture shift over time. But the most common direction of influence is from macro society down to the individuals who are socialized to fit into that society. For many people in our corner of social science, the interesting questions involve how and when people interact in ways that perpetuate current social arrangements, how even well-meaning people might unconsciously mirror systems advantaging men, Whites, the well-to-do, and so forth. We are who we are because of where we were (Hitlin & Pinkston 2013); we are shaped by our circumstances and experiences.

MORALITY

One central thread for how people understand the world as it is, and as it should be, involves the moral substrate of a society. This involves the sorts of moral understandings that we develop as we learn our culture. Within our nations, we develop values and moral beliefs reflecting how people "should" act, a standard by which we can judge ourselves and others. Sociologists have long considered morality to be a core aspect of social life, although direct interest in the topic has waxed and waned in the past century. Within the past decade, however, interest in morality has steadily increased, especially as cognitive and social psychological disciplines highlight the importance of emotions for understanding moral development, moral action, and the power of moral codes to circumscribe individual behavior. Morality binds societies together, forming the core of what it means to be part of a shared culture. It is a key component of those aspects of society captured in the "generalized other"—the internalized conception of what other members of one's society think and feel—and forms the basis for evaluating social action. Research in this tradition demonstrates considerable cross-cultural variation in moral attitudes, emotions, and behavior, supporting the claim that individuals from different societies differ aggregately on important dimensions.

This book aims to tie a few often-disparate traditions into a broad umbrella to build an intentionally strong claim addressing a notable missing piece of the academic literature linking individual functioning to social inequality. Work in sociology has demonstrated, using a variety of methodologies and theoretical presuppositions, that the values we have, the beliefs we hold, the objects we find important, and the behaviors that seem "proper" are all shaped in major ways based on whether we grew up at the top, middle, or bottom of our society's stratification hierarchy. This is old news, although many of the details are still to be filled out.

We build on this, however, to add societal inequality as a core aspect for structuring individual experiences of language, emotion, and morality that, perhaps surprisingly, has not been explicitly addressed with respect to academic research linking society and the individual. All societies have some degree of stratification, and people at the top of the system largely tend to have more resources and advantages than those lower on the scale. Sociology (and some cognate social sciences) has spent much time also exploring how the *degree* of stratification in a society on the one hand and, on the other, how people's position in this stratification hierarchy shapes their beliefs and actions; yet somehow these two established traditions have not been systematically synthesized. That is, we know less about how people's beliefs and actions are shaped by the *level of inequality* in their society. Does growing up and living in an exceedingly unequal society affect the behaviors and emotions of its members differently than experiencing the world through the lens of a more equal one? Examining this kind of social structure is surprisingly rare, even within the social psychological research tradition examining the effects of structure on individuals: the Social Structure and Personality tradition (see McLeod & Lively 2003 for an overview).

Thinkers tracing back to Adam Smith, a forefather of economics, linked inequality with moral functioning, although in ways that might surprise those who focus only on his misunderstood notion that the "invisible hand" will fix society's inequities. Smith expected that people's "natural" ability to imagine how others would feel would temper the drive for success that capitalism would unleash. He felt that sympathy was a fundamental human trait that would necessarily constrain a thirst for acquisition. People would never take the raw pursuit of money to its logical conclusion because that would mean blocking core human feelings of sympathy. Without sympathy, capitalism's advantages would only accrue to a select few, who could use these advantages to consolidate power. For Smith, sympathy alone is necessary but cannot ensure balanced societal outcomes; the notion of an "impartial spectator" was his answer (Halteman & Noell, 2012). He imagined what a supposedly unbiased member of society might think about contemporary American inequality and the emotional reactions that people would have as a result. This impartial spectator represents the standard for societal appropriateness. If a person feels wronged, this triggers strong emotional reactions, but their limited point of view makes it hard to adjudicate if they are correct in these feelings. Smith felt that, while sympathy was vital for keeping people in check, we also need to consider what an impartial spectator might think about people's feelings, to decide if they were valid, or too extreme. Emotions, coupled with society's judgment, were the pivot around which Smith's theory—properly understood—revolved.

Smith was aware, however, that in practice people may or may not listen to these internal and social voices. He worried that if too few people got too rich, others might find this supposedly natural moral sense distorted, offering too many excuses for immoral behavior by those at the top and being too dismissive of those at the bottom. "Thus, it is precisely the presence of extreme economic inequality, and the distortion of our sympathies that attends it, that allows—perhaps even encourages—the rich to spurn the most basic standards of moral conduct. If they were nearer to the rest of society in terms of wealth and hence status, their incentives would be quite different" (Rasmussen, 2016, p. 8). He thus linked individual emotional experience not just to social position, but also to the type of social structure delimiting the possible positions. All modern societies have some amount of stratification; the extent of this spread has a great deal to say about how people experience the world and what they find moral or immoral.

Our theory, developed in more detail in Chapters 5 and 6, hinges on understanding how inequality at the societal level filters into everyday interaction and individual emotional experience. Sociology has long been, in many ways, the study of inequality, and this focus has more recently been picked up across academic domains (economists now are quite concerned with a topic that we have been exploring for over a century) and is fundamental to current political and policy debates. The causes of societal inequality are largely outside of our scope (see Kus, 2016 for one overview), although we will touch on this in the next chapter, but we are demonstrating ways that the structure of society alters how individuals learn to interact and interpret the world. Thus, while we cannot say much about why China and the United States have large levels of economic inequality, we can suggest how this fact plays out in everyday life and in ways that might help perpetuate those distinctions. Morality, we will suggest, is an often overlooked mechanism within this process.

MORALITY AND SOCIETY

Understanding the ramifications and development of moral codes was a major concern for classical sociological theorists (Hodgkiss, 2013). For

Durkheim and writers of that era, "social" and "moral" were interchange-able terms (Jahoda, 2007); in fact Durkheim chose to use the word "social" to keep his work more in line with Comte's ideas, although he preferred "moral" to capture the sense of a nation's social fabric (Lukes, 1985). We might also speak of members of a particular society as developing some commonality of habitus (Bourdieu, 1977; Elias, 1996), an implicit, embodied understanding of the norms, moral codes, and expectations of that society. Recently, Abend (2014) terms this the "moral background," meaning the underlying normative structure setting the stage for what members of a society locate within the moral domain. This is not to say all individuals and subgroups in a society are identical, but that it is a meaningful unit of social analysis to examine aggregate understandings of various nation-states.

This book examines these structural underpinnings of morality and makes the strong claim that societal inequality drives different experi-ences of moral emotion. Specifically, the moral reactions in societies with greater levels of economic inequality are harsher, more sanctioning, and generally more divisive than those of more equitable societies, which are more communal, understanding, and uplifting. We support our argu-ment first theoretically, with an overview of the highly discussed topic of inequality as it relates to interaction and social psychological analysis, before offering a novel, empirical way of analyzing cross-cultural variation in moral reactions to social events. We draw on insights across sociology and psychology, most concretely affect control theory (Heise, 1979, 2007), to compare five advanced industrial societies to empirically explore the implicit understandings, feelings, and meanings that people within a cul-ture share as their national "habitus" and moral emotional background. Ultimately, we develop a theory linking individuals' moral emotions to national inequality.

A quick note: the study of morality is distinctly *not* the study of reli-gion. Certainly most religious faiths claim some sort of special insight into what is and is not moral, although commonalities in moral belief across societies might suggest that these religions capture some essential issues of human social organization. Most religions and secular moralities tend to largely agree on basic moral tenets: be kind to others, do not commit harm. Religion is often linked to moral codes that maintain moral order, but other institutions within a society can also channel the development of morality. However, "morality is not dependent on religion and religion is not confined to defining moral teachings" (Bader & Finke, 2010, p. 243). There is no evidence that religious people commit moral acts more frequently than the non-religious, although they do report more intense moral emotions when they do commit immoral acts (Hofmann et al., 2014).

Using society as a unit of analysis is a staple of cross-cultural work in sociology and psychology, with a number of traditions performing similar links between societal-level analyses and individual functioning. Scholars like Shalom Schwartz (2013) provide extensive evidence for examining countries as meaningful cultural units, in his case with a well-established, widely influential theory of cultural values (see Schwartz, 2014 for a recent overview and update; also Hitlin & Piliavin 2004). Other approaches include the political scientists Ronald Inglehart's Modernization thesis (e.g., Inglehart 1997; Inglehart & Baker, 2000) and Hofstede's (2001) Cultural Dimensions theory. The key is that cultural and/or structural forces are systematically explored through examining the individual values, beliefs, and perceptions held by people within those societies.

We build on this tradition through a novel measure of emotions. As we will lay out in more detail in the book, moral emotions are visceral reactions to events that break or exemplify our moral norms, and these emotions in turn guide societally defined appropriate action (Blasi, 1999). Our emotional apparatus is shaped by, and well-attuned to, the strongly held shared expectations held by members of a society. Emotions are in many ways signals about interaction, telling us how the interaction is unfolding. Of particular importance, emotions guide our impressions of whether our experiences are outside of the realm of what we originally expected, and, if so, in what ways (e.g., Hochschild, 1983; Heise, 2007). Moral emotions are perhaps the most fundamental subset of these potential reactions, windows into how interactions are proceeding with respect to the core tenets of a society, the fundamental expectations that we have—often non-consciously—about what "should" be happening, how people in these situations and roles "ought" to behave. Violations of these standards are experienced quite strongly, and trigger intense emotional reactions, positive and negative.

Thus, morality involves the shared cognitive and emotional understandings binding a society together. For our disciplinary progenitor Durkheim, morality is a source of solidarity with the group, the pressures in society that fight against pure egoism and put us in touch with concerns about others (Fournier, 2013). Emotions are privately experienced but socially shaped and channeled. "History, culture, and therefore, personal ideology also influence the prevalence of certain feelings as well as the interpretations imposed on them" (Kagan, 2007, p. 47). Smith's ideas allow us to enter inequality into the mix as an understudied factor shaping these personal ideologies.

Merging theory on inequality and recent criminological ideas (Garland, 2013) with psychological treatments of emotions (Fiske, 2011), we argue that societies with greater economic inequality enact harsher moral judgments of people who are often "above," "below," or "outside" of one's place within the social and economic hierarchy; whereas societies with less inequality exhibit greater compassion, sympathy, and praise toward other people who are, given the relative equality, more often economically similar to themselves. We link structural economic realities to cultural beliefs to individual moral reactions across five countries, showing how our theory offers a link to social structure that improves on cross-cultural categorizations, including the popular-but-overstated East versus West distinction, as well as more recent approaches focusing on cultural "looseness" (Gelfand et al., 2011).

We discuss inequality further in Chapter 2 as a growing factor in popular and political discussions and summarize a bit of the sociological state of knowledge about how inequalities operate in society and are linked with important national outcomes (trust, crime, health, and so forth; see Lareau, 2011; Pikkety, 2014; Silva, 2013; Young, 2004; Wilkinson & Pickett 2011). A market economy can be an effective tool for distributing goods, but Sandel (2012) suggests that we have moved too far in this direction, shaping and ultimately distorting our social relations along a model of economic market expectations. This can lead, he suggests, to inequality and corruption.

Much academic work on language involves studying the words, meaning, and the construction of language itself (see Maynard & Turowetz, 2013 for a sociological overview). We are introducing a novel sociological approach, focusing on what the meaning of words conveys about that society. We can learn a good deal about the way a society is structured, as we attempt to demonstrate, through understanding how language is constructed and used. A measure of shared culture is the backbone of what Guibernau (2007) considers national identity, something that creates bonds of solidarity among members of a community and renders it distinct from others. "Through their emotions, people comment, to themselves if not to others, on what the interaction that is occurring says about themselves in a given scene, and they also comment on the overall stories that they are constructing as they shape a path through life" (Katz 1999, p. 324).

PLAN FOR THE BOOK

This book has two major parts. First, we will spend a few chapters explaining what social science has determined about our core concepts: inequality, morality, and language. Given the volume of work about each of these topics—many excellent scholars have dedicated their careers to advancing just one subsection of each of these areas—we are only providing overviews of each as they inform our general development of a theory linking societal inequality to individual emotional experience. We hope through citations that the interested reader can learn more for herself about any of these areas that spark interest; we find value in bridging such a wide range of topics in the service of our empirical project, while acknowledging that we are likely to give few of these areas the depth of treatment they deserve.

We then turn to our original empirical project, examining the fundamental meaning of interaction using affect control theory and its

computerized instance, *Interact* (found at http://www.indiana.edu/
~socpsy/ACT/interact.htm), as a tool for understanding the moral culture
of the United States, China, Germany, Japan, and Canada. After explaining the theory that *Interact* is based on, and how the methodology works,
we present a series of simulations uncovering patterns across our five case
studies. Ultimately, we will discuss how these analyses support our broad
contention that the level of economic inequality of a society is baked into
its cultural scripts for interaction and language.

We will try to be clear throughout our discussion that these analyses
are just a preliminary step toward support of our theory. There are limitations to all social science, and our limitations are notable, and they will be
discussed as we encounter the empirical portion of the book. However, we
suggest that there is great utility for social science in taking clear positions
on the complicated nature of social reality (see Mirowsky's 2013 call for
more scholars to take the risk of being "precisely wrong"). The first half
of the book spells out what we believe to be the reasonable thesis that we
develop in Chapters 5 and 6 (but mostly 6). The second demonstrates that
our data fit with this theory.

Thus, our conclusions will be taking a stronger position than warranted
by the data, insofar as it is rather difficult to convincingly measure and
track over time all of the core constructs we attempt to weave together.
We consider this a strength; our biases certainly were not factored into the
development of *Interact*, thus lending credence to our linking of theory,
method, and results. Consider this first chapter an acknowledgment, then,
that the subsequent chapters may be making strong claims that outpace
what our data will allow us to conclusively correlate. We have reasons
for confidence in our theory and results; it is up to the reader to decide
whether this thesis is adequately supported and worth pursuing in future
studies with different methods.

NOTE

1. The quote continues: "The connection is so intimate that, given the general charac-
    ter of the morality observed in a given society, . . . one can infer the nature of that
    society, the elements of its structure and the way it is organized."

2

A Primer on Inequality

One of sociology's biggest contributions is an interrogation of broad social structures, including the consequences and continuation of social inequalities. We begin setting the stage for our project in this tradition by outlining some key issues of economic inequality across societies (McCall & Percheski, 2010; Neckerman & Torche, 2007). We discuss a bit of what it means to have inequality in society and what that looks like in practice. Specific to this project, we spend more time than many sociologists typically do discussing how such inequality gets internalized to shape beliefs about right, wrong, and possible futures for people at the top and bottom of those unequal systems, with a focus on social psychological mechanisms of inequality (see McLeod, Lawler, & Schwalbe, 2014 for a collection of relevant papers; also Buttrick & Oishi, 2017 for a review). We conclude with some prominent ideas that link structure, culture, and the individual (work by Giddens, and Sewell), often

captured in the notion of "structuration," a theory about how these unequal social systems get reproduced across people and time.

Income inequality is a seemingly ubiquitous feature of modern
societies—American political debates have become more and more suffused with discussions of inequality over the past decade—though in reality, inequality varies quite a bit across nations. When scholars speak about
income inequality, they could reference the inequalities found between
entire nations—how much inequality exists in Germany as opposed to
China, say. There is, for instance, far more between-nation inequality than
within nation inequality (Atkinson & Brandolini, 2008; Firebaugh, 2000).
Scholars could also be referencing how disparities in economic resources
between two people affects stratification processes, such as determinations
of where one falls in the social class hierarchy and how much prestige each
actor may have as a result of their resources. Participants in social systems
get more or less rank, status, or credit for being higher or lower in that
society, and these processes are at the root of much social psychological research on inequality. When we discuss inequality here, we mean the
overall amount of income disparities endemic to particular nations—the
level of economic inequality within the society writ large.[1]

Societies can be arrayed according to their relative levels of income
inequality, with some societies experiencing exceedingly more inequality than others. This degree of inequality is important for everyday social
interactions—of which morality is a huge component because it affects the
form and contours of our daily experience. Some societies are relatively
equal; the people at the top of the system have more money and wealth
than others, but not nearly to the extent of highly unequal societies. Such
nations tend to concentrate incomes and wealth to comparatively few
people, who may amass as much money as the rest of the society, as in the
notion of the "1%" in current American political discourse.

Traditionally, sociologists have focused either on the nature of inequality across societies or how being relatively deprived or advantaged within
a society affects outcomes such as health and occupational attainment.
Being higher up in a system affects your life, as we know from decades
of sociological study. But being higher up in a drastically unequal society

may have different effects than being at a greater advantage in less unequal societies; this latter formulation is less explored. No matter where you fall in the economic hierarchy, the level of inequality changes the fabric of your culture and thereby affects us all. Inequality is a large component of the backdrop or foundation against which we find common ground. It is always "in the air," so to speak, and, as we will later argue, gets "under the skin" to affect cultural meanings, our language, norms, and social action. But before we get too far down that road, we first want to delve into a discussion of what this inequality looks like, how it is measured, and how societal-level inequality shapes various outcomes.

MEASURES OF INEQUALITY AND TRENDS

To begin, we first consider various ways of measuring income inequality. Generally, there are three broad ways to examine the level of inequality within a country (McCall & Percheski, 2010). The first category includes measures of the percentage of income held by a certain portion of the society, like the top quartile. The second category comprises comparative measures examining the ratio of incomes from two percentiles of the population, like the 90/10 ratio that compares the incomes of the 90th percentile to the 10th percentile. Finally, there are what McCall and Percheski (2010) term the "one-number summary statistics" (p. 332) providing an overarching summary of the level of income inequality throughout a society, as opposed to at a single point in the income distribution as in the prior two categories of measures.

These summary statistics include such measures as the Theil, Atkinson, and Robin Hood indexes, and, perhaps most famously, the Gini coefficient. The Robin Hood index, for instance, is aptly named, as it measures the amount of income you would need to "rob" from the rich and "give" to the poor to reach complete equality. We will instead largely focus on the widely used Gini coefficient here, which is equal to 100 (or sometimes scaled to 1) if all of the income in a country went to one person and 0 if everyone in a society makes the same amount of money. Thus,

higher Gini coefficients indicate greater inequality. We will be using the
Gini for our analysis because large organizations such as the World Bank
provide this measure for various nations and across time. The Gini coefficient is highly associated with many of these other measures (including
the Thiel, Robin Hood Index, and income share of the top quartile), so
we could have selected, say, the Robin Hood index and found similar
patterns (Evans, Hout, & Mayer, 2004).

Using these statistics, we are able to compare changes across time and
compare the relative inequalities of various countries. As a quick note,
although the measures are standardized, direct comparability is hampered
by the quality of the data sources used to produce the statistics. As one
striking example, the Chinese government stopped releasing public Gini
information from 2000 to 2012 (Hu, 2012). The granularity of the data
also affects comparability. For instance, there may be inconsistencies in
whether data are reported on the value of fringe benefit packages, like
stock options, which can dramatically increase the incomes of top earners,
thereby affecting these statistics. Nevertheless, the general trends are still
informative, and even with these imperfections, the Gini is standard for
these sorts of cross-cultural comparisons. We will turn repeatedly to the
idea of "structure," and the Gini is an efficient measure of the economic
structure of a society.

What do these trends show us? First, let us examine the range of
income inequality (indicated by that Gini coefficient) in the Organization
for Economic Cooperation and Development (OECD) countries, plus
China. Figure 2.1 presents the most recent Gini coefficients available for
each of these countries as reported by the World Bank. These coefficients
range from a low of 23.1 in the Czech Republic to a high of 50.5 in Chile,
which is closely seconded by Mexico at 48.1. The United States is also in
this upper-end of the range (41.1), along with Israel (42.8), China (42.6),
and Turkey (40.2) for these most recent data. After that, there is a sharp
decline in inequality, with the remaining countries' Gini coefficients in the
upper 20s to mid-30s. There are two main takeaways from this: (1) There
is a large amount of variation in income inequality even among countries
that have bound together (e.g., OECD countries), and (2) there is a clear

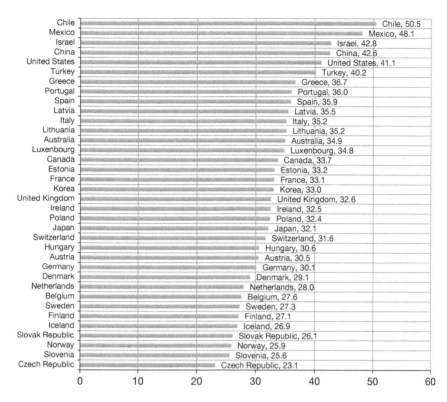

Figure 2.1 Gini Coefficient among OECD Countries and China (2008–2013, Most Recent Reported)

division between countries with higher income inequalities, from Chile through Turkey, and the remaining countries. These are notable differences, as even a slight increase in Gini coefficient may represent billions of dollars in a society being funneled toward the "haves."

While examining a snapshot of Gini coefficients is informative for comparing a wide variety of countries, looking at trends in particular countries over time tells us a bit more about how income inequality—and the related social structure—has changed. For this work, we focus on five countries: the United States, China, Germany, Japan, and Canada, and you can see the trends in their Gini coefficients in Figure 2.2 (we note here that these five countries are the basis for our empirical exploration in the latter third of this book). Inequality in total incomes has, at a minimum, slightly increased in the last several decades within this particular subsample. This

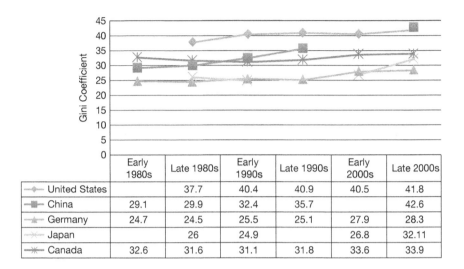

Figure 2.2 Trends in Gini Coefficients by Country

is especially apparent in China and the United States. In the United States, for instance, the level of income inequality today has not been seen since immediately prior to the Great Depression. Saez (2015) reports that the income shares of the top 10% in the United States are currently between 49 and 50%, with most of the income growth going to the top 1%, who are taking home a little over 20% of current incomes. Labor market and entrepreneurial earnings have largely driven this shift (Piketty & Saez, 2003; see also Volscho & Kelly, 2012). Earnings for median households, however, have remained stagnant since the mid-to-late 1990s (McCall & Percheski, 2010). Indeed, some researchers find that the disparity between the lower and middle portions of the economic distribution has even decreased since 1990 (McCall & Percheski, 2010; Western, Bloome, & Percheski, 2008). We can thus think of a Gini coefficient as a snapshot in time, but a trend in coefficients tells us even more about the nature of that society's inequality.

This rising Gini for the United States is really the result of a decades-long trend as wage inequality has been growing steadily since the mid-1970s (Morris & Western, 1999; Neckerman &Torche, 2007). This basic increase has also been observed in Canada, Ireland, the United Kingdom, and Australia (Brandolini & Smeeding, 2009; Kenworthy, 2007). France, interestingly, actually experienced a decline in inequality over this same period (Brandolini & Smeeding, 2009). Income inequality in China is a little more difficult to gauge as there are debates among Chinese scholars and governmental officials as to the exact statistics, but their level of inequality is higher than even that of the United States and has been steadily increasing over the past few decades (Hu, 2012; Rabinovitch, 2013; Xie & Zhou, 2014).

CONSEQUENCES OF INCOME INEQUALITY

Considerable efforts have been spent identifying the multitudes of important national trends associated with income inequality. As Evans et al. (2004) and Neckerman and Torche (2007) note, research in this area generally falls into two main camps: the first focuses on how changes in income inequality affect individual-level variation, such as mortality rates. Broadly, if we know a relationship exists between individual-level income and some outcome of interest, then changes to the overall distribution of incomes in a population will then shift this relationship in predictable ways. If people with more money are healthier, then a society experiencing an increase in their number of wealthy citizens (i.e., greater income inequality) would also see greater resulting health disparities.

The second camp instead focuses on whether the environmental or contextual effects of inequality alter population-level outcomes at the neighborhood, state, or country-level. This type of research treats inequality as producing what is called an "externality," where living in places with certain aggregate levels of inequality blanketly affects everyone in that area. Inequality becomes something that is "in the air" affecting outcomes even if people are relatively advantaged by their personal earnings. For example, Vagero and Lundberg (1989) note that those with greater incomes tend to live longer than those at the bottom of a country's income hierarchy; however, when comparing Sweden (a country with relatively low income inequality) to England and Wales (countries with higher inequality), the mortality-income relationship in Sweden is much flatter and those with the highest incomes in England and Wales actually have higher mortality rates than Swedes at the bottom of their income distribution. Context matters.

While much scholarship is of the first kind, linking individual location in the society with individual outcomes, less social psychology is involved with this second kind. We are mainly concerned in this project with these contextual effects, although it should be mentioned that it is entirely possible to do research in both camps, even simultaneously in one research project.

And what are some of inequality's contextual effects? Evidence suggests that societal inequality is related to various health outcomes, education, violence, and imprisonment (Neckerman & Torche, 2007; Wilkinson & Pickett, 2011). For health, macro-levels of inequality appear to decrease life expectancy for everyone in that society, while increasing incidences of infant mortality, mental health problems, drug and alcohol addiction, and obesity (see Wilkinson & Pickett, 2006, 2009). One way to think about this is that in highly unequal countries, even those who are relatively economically advantaged do not have the health returns to their individual incomes that those with similar relative incomes have in more equal societies. The nature of the structure matters alongside the more conventionally studied aspect of one's location within that structure. Having more is typically better than having less, but having more in an unequal society does not carry the same advantages as having more when living in a more equal society.

Others have found a contextual effect between inequality and happiness (Alesina, Tella, & MacCullouch, 2004; Delhey & Kohler, 2011; Oishi, Kesebir, & Diener, 2011; Wilkinson & Pickett, 2011), suggesting that more equal areas are also generally happier. In addition, recent work by Burkhauser, De Neve, and Powdthavee (2016) argues that higher national levels of income inequality allow for lower subjective well-being and a greater frequency of experiencing negative emotions such as anger, sadness, and worry. Interestingly, this is even though inequality was not found to affect the frequency of positive emotional experiences (although happiness was not included in this measure).

This work is not without debate, however, as some researchers claim there is actually no association between aggregate levels of inequality and these health outcomes, although proponents of contextual effects take issue with the data sources and model specification of these more critical studies (see Babones, 2008; Eckersley, 2015; and Lynch et al., 2004 for an overview; Beckfield, 2004; McLeod, Nonnemaker, & Call, 2004; Wilkinson & Pickett, 2006). Tellingly, however, in support of our contention that national-level structure is important, Babones's (2008) cross-national, longitudinal study of inequality and health finds that individual incomes explain no more than a third of the variation in individual health outcomes. He states, "there is a strong, consistent, statistically significant, non-artifactual correlation between national income inequality and population health" (p. 1614), although he concludes that causality is difficult to assess because population-levels of inequality tend to remain fairly stable over time, necessitating even broader datasets. Similarly, Wilkinson and Pickett (2006) find that among 155 papers examining this relationship, over 70% find a negative relationship between national levels of inequality and population health—as inequality goes up, health is depleted.

Similar relationships are found between inequality and educational outcomes. Siddiqi et al., (2007) compare reading literacy among 22 OECD countries, finding that higher levels of reading literacy tended to be found in countries with lower inequality. In an analysis of children's educational attainment in the United States, Mayer (2001) finds that in states with higher levels of inequality, educational attainment was similarly unequal: rich children experienced increases in their attainment, while poor children's attainment was lowered. Just a 2% increase in a state's Gini coefficient resulted in 0.192 fewer years of schooling for low-income children and 0.372 more years of schooling for high-income children. As Mayer concludes, even these seemingly small disparities can compound to create even more inequality for future generations.

Finally, we touch on violence and imprisonment's relation to income inequality. Edwin Sutherland (1947) was perhaps the first to note that crime rates are lower in more egalitarian societies. From neighborhoods (Hipp, 2007) on up to major metropolitan areas (Hipp, 2011), states (Kennedy et al., 1998), and countries (Lynch et al., 2004; Pickett, Mookherjee, & Wilkinson, 2005; Wilkinson & Pickett, 2006, 2011; Wolf, Gray, & Fazel, 2014), research tends to find that crime rates are higher in areas with greater inequality, though perhaps more so for violent crime as opposed to property crime (Kelly, 2000; Messner, Raffalovich, & Shrock, 2002). While some theories of crime suggest that having fewer resources, known as "material deprivation," is enough to increase the propensity for criminal activity, this latter finding suggests that something more is going on behind this trend than just material deprivation, as one would suspect property crime to be more affected in that case. Relative deprivation, not just materially having less, is a major part of the potential comparison processes people use when viewing the world within situations possibly presenting opportunities for criminal behavior. Interestingly, countries with strong social welfare programs are better able to lessen the negative effects of inequality on homicide rates (Messner et al., 2002; Savolainen, 2000).

Incarceration rates are also positively associated with national-level inequality (Wilkinson & Pickett, 2011; Western, 2006). Once incarcerated, prisoners tend to be treated more harshly in more unequal societies. Wilkinson and Pickett (2011) point out that in Japan—a society with low rates of inequality and low imprisonment—prisoners are treated with leniency and are generally trusted by criminal justice officials and the public to reform their ways if they express regret and a desire to change. This compares strikingly to the highly punitive nature of the United States' prison complex, which has been condemned by Amnesty International, the Human Rights Watch, and the United Nations.

POSSIBLE EXPLANATIONS

Why do we see these trends? One common counterargument to the inequality story is that a true lack of material resources (like feeble living arrangements and food insecurity) and poverty are really driving these population differences in health, happiness, and so forth, as opposed to the breadth of the income distribution. Scholars like Wilkinson and Pickett

(2006; 2011) and Oishi and Kesebir (2015) argue, however, that when you examine associations between national incomes per person (typically measured as GDP per person; a proxy for overall living standards and poverty) and life expectancy or happiness, there is a sharp rise in these positive outcomes as countries go from being extremely poor to modestly wealthy. But the association then levels off, becoming essentially flat as countries become increasingly prosperous. For example, they report (2009) that the life expectancies between the United States and countries like Portugal, Greece, and New Zealand are not that different, even though the United States is at least twice as wealthy. Further, Wilkinson and Pickett (2011) demonstrate that national incomes per person are unrelated to child well-being and their index of health and social problems (composite measure of trust, mental illness/addiction, life expectancy, infant mortality, obesity, children's educational performance, teenage births, homicides, imprisonment rates, and social mobility). Instead, some of the most economically rich countries, like the United States and the United Kingdom, fair much worse than poorer countries on these outcomes.

This still leaves us with the question of "why?" with many theorists pointing to social psychological processes of status competitions, emotions, trust, and social alterations (e.g., Buttrick & Oishi, 2017). First, humans attune to inequality as social beings from an exceedingly early age. It is something compelling us to take notice and contend with. Even by age ten, children understand and apply principles of equality (Damon, 1984); however, some work suggests at this early stage, "children are sensitive to inequality, then, but it seems to upset them only when they themselves are the ones getting less" (Bloom, 2013, p. 80). Several theorists of morality posit that equality/inequality are foundational to moral judgments. Piaget's work, for example, suggests two types of morality, the first based on domination (from parents to children), the second on equality, a wider morality (Ossowska, 1970). And as a basis of morality, equality relationships are one of the four types of moral motives found across cultures (Rai & Fiske, 2011). Concerns about equality may therefore be fundamental to our moral systems, a point we will return to in later chapters.

Greater inequality also creates more divisions within a society—more subgroups fractioning the whole. As Wilkins, Mollborn, and Bó (2014) point out, work on modern hunter-gatherer societies, which have little inequality due to a lack of surplus goods, demonstrates that they are highly cooperative and communal with few social divisions (Wiessner, 2002). When resources accumulate and are unequally distributed, with a select few amassing considerably more than others (no matter how "fair" or "earned" the distribution may have been), this creates a situation perfect for the creation of socially meaningful, lasting divisions.

Work on status construction theories (Harkness, 2017; Ridgeway, 1991; Ridgeway et al., 2009) demonstrates that when certain types of people come to possess more material resources or other scarce rewards (like luxury goods or credentials from elite institutions) and these people also share some defining trait, the situation is likely to create a new status group based on that distinction. This new "rich" group will then enjoy the benefits of higher status and prestige: they will be listened to more often, turned to for advice, seen as more distinguished, deferred to more often, and put into leadership positions. For instance, it may be that the status of new immigrant groups is largely impacted by the occupations, including their associated incomes and prestige, in which they cluster or are most visible (Berger & Fisek, 2008; Fernandez-Kelly, 2008; Silventoinen et al., 2007). Once these divisions are created, they give rise to the often-implicit biases of discrimination, prejudice, and stereotyping, and perhaps even stigmatization against those at the bottom of the hierarchy (Fiske, 1998; Link, Phelan, & Hatzenbuehler, 2014).

As these processes continue, more and more status groups are formed, creating further divisions between the "haves" and the "have nots" that feel natural and true—divisions that are socially legitimate and to be respected. This creates a vicious, reifying cycle wherein more and more resources and privileges flow to the "haves" because those at the top *and* bottom of the hierarchy view those above them to be worthy and "better." These become very powerful cultural beliefs. Wilkins et al. (2014) describe this naturalization process eloquently:

Through naturalization, humans come to understand differences to be normal, immutable, and reasonable—and often, just—explanations for social inequality. By making difference moral, processes of naturalization make it more difficult for people to fight for change; change becomes associated with perversion and immorality. Naturalization conveys the idea that things have *always been like this*, and should therefore be sustained . . ..failing to conform . . . renders a person not only unnatural or abnormal but also possibly culturally unintelligible. (p. 136)

But even when we mutually agree on the hierarchy's form and divisions, this still can be quite stressful for those behind others, as well as stressful for those above to maintain their position (Dickerson & Kemeny, 2004). Such widespread status competitions may be detrimental to a society's well-being. Though the pressures to maintain one's position can be deleterious, many have argued that having relatively lower social status is particularly stressful. This may be because those at the bottom of the hierarchy do not have as much control over their personal and professional lives (Marmot, 2004) and because they feel disrespected, devalued, and inferior (Charlesworth, Gilfillan, & Wilkinson, 2004; Wilkinson & Pickett, 2006). Violent behavior, in particular, is often brought on by feeling disrespected (Wilkinson, 2004).

Emotion research details similar responses, as people in more disadvantaged economic positions experience more negative and less engaged emotions (Foy et al., 2014). Indeed, people in low-status positions are seen as less good and others feel coldly about them (Cuddy, Fiske, & Glick, 2007). As Foy and colleagues (2014) point out, even just interacting with a low-status person can "tarnish one's reputation" (p. 298).

This sense of relative deprivation and competition can appear even when basic living standards are met. When we come out behind and generally lacking compared to others—whether to those close to us in the social pecking order or to valued positions we aspire to and desire—this generates a sense of being "less than," leading to lower self-esteem, dissatisfaction with one's current lot, and perhaps even alienation. Adam Smith even noted this basic truism of the material ways we live our lives:

> By necessaries, I understand not only the commodities which are indispensably necessary for the support of life, but whatever the custom of the country renders it indecent for creditable people, even the lowest order to be without. A linen shirt, for example, is, strictly speaking, not a necessary of life . . ..But in the present times . . . a creditable day labourer would be ashamed to appear in public without a linen shirt, the want of which would be supposed to denote that disgraceful degree of poverty which, it is presumed, nobody can well fall into without extreme bad conduct. (pp. 869–870)

Adam Smith recognized the stigmatization of poverty and the desire to appear respectable to the point of it being a basic necessity for life. Keeping up appearances, however, is expensive and time intensive—resources few can easily afford. This is especially true for the vast majority of people, since doing so becomes increasingly expensive as one moves up the social ladder. More rungs on the ladder mean more Joneses to compare oneself to. These comparisons do not simply disappear as one moves out of poverty; instead we are constantly comparing ourselves to others and ascertaining our relative personal worth (Festinger, 1954).

Class-based comparisons also generate class identities and evaluations (Hout, 2008), further drawing boundaries around socioeconomic groups. This solidifies notions of "us" versus "them," thus heightening social closure and exclusion (Milkie, Warner, & Ray, 2014) and making the social class hierarchy even more divisive (DiMaggio & Garip, 2012). The more unequal a society is, the more class closures are formed. This divisiveness leads to exclusionary social networks, reduced engagement with others (a loss of social capital), and lower trust, all of which may be particularly damaging to our social fabric (Uslaner, 2002; Putnam, 2000). When we are able to trust others, we form connections with people and through these connections gain information, material resources, services, collective engagement, and efficacy. All this leads to greater reciprocity, interdependence, solidarity, and donation of time and money to helping others, thus making our communities stronger (i.e., social capital; see Cook, 2014). Without trust, strangers do not have the opportunity to become our acquaintances or friends and we lose all the benefits these potential connections may have provided while our communities experience a loss of civic engagement.

Political scientist Robert Putnam (2000) notes that levels of social capital and inequality are interlinked, with more equal societies having greater community involvement. He notes that through the 1950s and 1960s, civic engagement was at a high and American inequality was at an all-time low for that century. As inequality started rising in the mid-1960s/early-1970s, our social capital began to erode. Eric Uslaner (2002) argues and finds empirically that instead of being reciprocally linked, levels of economic inequality directly affect trust (see also Rothstein & Uslaner, 2005). And trust matters for a number of outcomes. For example, recall the findings of Oishi et al. (2011) that happiness decreases with increased inequality. They also found that lower levels of trust explain a large part of this relationship such that more inequality reduces trust, which then reduces happiness.

Thus, we begin to trace the relationship between macro-inequality and individual functioning. As we will spell out in greater detail, these links have been widely established between social structure and the ways people think, feel, and behave who fill the roles within that structure. Less work has linked the level of inequality in that structure all the way down to individual psychology, though the paths suggested here underlie the theory we will develop in this book, that morality is a pivot for explaining and measuring the ways that society is structured.

STRUCTURE AND CULTURE

Inequality is a structural feature of social life, and its consequences enormously affect the initiation, form, and consequences of our daily interactions. But these processes are not constructed de novo every day. Instead

they become enmeshed into the very cultural meanings and understandings of our social world so that they become normative knowledge readily available to be passed on through the generations and reenacted daily.
Despite the influence on situational creativity and novelty appearing in
some social theories, it is fairly self-evident that most interactions proceed
along roughly expected lines, within unspoken boundaries about what
behaviors and words are appropriate and what are out of bounds. Walking
into a restaurant or library in a new city in a country you are familiar with
is not a particularly stressful situation; you should have a rough schema
for what to expect, and you and those you interact with will, most of the
time, operate within intuitively understood parameters.

As we teach these meanings to others and act on them, we recreate and
solidify this culture for successive generations and reproduce the very
inequalities that initially helped give rise to the whole system. We will
suggest how this works in the next few chapters, but keep in mind that
these "hidden" factors—things we cannot see like structural inequality
and culture—are bound together. Giddens (1976, 1984) and Sewell (1992)
perhaps most famously theorized links between structure and culture,
moving beyond more static conceptualizations and viewing these two
aspects as being fully distinct. Theirs is a "dualist" argument about structure, as social structures have both a material quality (e.g., resource distributions and behaviors) and are full of cultural knowledge and schemas
for action. Resources and schemas are inextricably linked: "Nonhuman
resources have a material existence that is not reducible to rules of schemas, but the activation of material things as resources, the determination
of their value and social power, is dependent on the cultural schemas that
inform their social use" (Sewell, 1992, p. 12).

Because the world is mutually constituted by both resources and cultural meanings and logics, and these resources and logics mutually rein-
force one another, the system itself remains inherently stable. There is, of
course, room for agency in this system—we are not merely robotic cogs
in the machine, or potatoes in a sack (to use Marx's coin of phrase; Sewell,
1992). Money is not the only form of material resources in this system,

and the processes guiding and adjudicating these different structures may affect change, such as when political systems deregulate industries or societies become more technologically driven. Existing schemas may compete with each other, such as when American meritocratic beliefs are put up against the reality of deadened mobility, and individuals or subcultures may have different interpretations of certain cultural rules (see Swidler, 2001). Resource accumulations can also be somewhat unpredictable. In these moments, people can develop and utilize entirely new sets of schemas to create novel overriding structures, particularly in these disruptive junctures (Swidler, 1986). This can even cause change to the broader resource distributions and culture in these moments.

On the whole, however, the study of society focuses on the patterned, recurrent forms of behavior, beliefs, and feelings enacted by individuals, but shaped distally by these cultural and structural forces. Traditionally, the economic organization discussed here is studied in a different way from the moral and normative cultural belief systems that might serve to legitimize them; moral concerns are only recently starting to become embroiled with the conceptualization of economic markets (e.g., Fourcade & Healy, 2007). We will endeavor to spell out, and then present empirical analyses consistent with, the notion that societal levels of inequality can be identified in the moral, emotional reactions internalized by adherents of those societies.

CONCLUDING REMARKS

We hope that this brief walk through inequality theory and research has provided necessary glimpses into what the distribution of income inequality currently looks like in various nations, what some of the contextual consequences of this inequality are, and some of the reasons put forth as to why we see such detrimental outcomes for public health and well-being as societies become more unequal. On one level, these inequalities represent differential access to resources—money, power—serving to advantage some over others. People with more education and financial wherewithal are linked to having better health, for example. However, we are focusing on the more social psychological aspects of these processes—the ways unequal economic systems filter down into the behaviors, beliefs, feelings, and understandings that people have that consequently reproduce those systems. Inequality creates legitimated social divisions leading to constant comparisons and competitions between various points along the hierarchy—however steep the hierarchy may be. More equal societies have fewer points of comparison and more similarities. It is easier to "keep up with the Joneses" and stay in good social standing.

Unequal societies, however, have many points of comparison, no matter one's place in the distribution. Coming up short gets "under the skin" and leads to feelings of inferiority, disengagement, a diminishment of self-esteem and efficacy, more negative emotions, increased stress, and lowered trust—all while the system remains socially valid, legitimate, and largely uncontested (but see a review of inequality and social movements by Snow & Owens, 2014). Even in the face of modern political movements aimed at reducing such inequalities, like Bernie Sanders's recent political campaign, change is slow if ever to come and the resistance to such political movements is strong. "Socialist" is certainly still an epithet in modern American culture.

Further, these structural inequalities are wrapped up in and help to constitute our cultural meanings and rules for interaction, as the structuration theorists point out. So not only do unequal structural arrangements cause harm, but they also affect the cultural information that is passed down through our generations to recreate these very inequalities for decades, if not centuries to come. We learn to act toward people, objects, and ideas through our culture, and these cultural meanings are imbued in the language we develop. It is this point—that structure informs culture and culture affects structure—that is crucial for understanding how societal levels of inequality affect moral codes of action and reaction. The often overlooked issue is that these ways of understanding the world have a moral component; we do not just learn that the world "is" a certain way, but many of these structural and cultural forces shaped us toward believing that the world "should" be that way.

NOTE

1. There are other forms of inequality that we will sideline, here. Ethnic, religious, urban vs. rural are all ways that societies may be organized with vastly disproportionate members in one or another social group.

3

The Social Scientific
Study of Morality

The study of morality has reemerged as an important topic across the social sciences over the past 15 to 20 years—a resurgence based in part on the development of new research methods such as fMRI (functional magnetic resonance imaging) brain studies, alongside easier access to online samples of potential subjects. The original concerns of the progenitors of sociology, economics, and psychology revolved a great deal around moral codes, expectations, norms, values, and such phenomenon. Interest waned in the latter half of the 20th century for a variety of reasons (Spates, 1983), but this is fortunately changing, with the subject of morality becoming more prominent again within psychology and sociology (Hitlin & Vaisey, 2013; Greene, 2012; Haidt, 2012).

We should be clear at the outset that the study of morality is about how individuals, groups, and cultures develop, use, shape, internalize, and experience moral codes. This scientific study is distinctly not, as we practice it, prescriptive. That is, we do not claim special knowledge about how individuals or societies *should* act. We simply aim to understand how they operate in practice. Some scholars (notably Smith, 2009; Sayer, 2011) do suggest that the philosophical distinction between "is" and "ought" is overstated, that social science can, in fact, point us in the right direction for improving personal and societal moral codes. We take, in contrast, the professional Weberian directive to attempt to articulate and then set aside our own values—neither of us is advocating for *more* inequality within societies or that particular types of moral emotion reactions are somehow better for societies—and follow the data where it leads us. We leave it to theologians, politicians, and increasingly celebrities to tell you how people should behave. We want to understand better how people actually behave, and how society shapes and enforces that behavior, largely through its members internalizing a shared sense of right and wrong.

After introducing some basic concepts and definitions, this chapter involves two parts. First, we will discuss the classic conceptions of morality found within the work of important social theorists—largely, but not fully. from sociology. Then, we will provide an overview of ways that different traditions (e.g., Kohlberg, Durkheim, Social Intuitionist Theory) have studied and conceptualized morality at both the micro and macro levels, including the observation that much of the work takes a micro, person-centric approach to morality. Later, we will make the argument that understanding a society's moral codes tells us a great deal about the organization of that society, but for now, let us begin with an overview of the main concepts and findings about the nature of human morality. Because of the sheer volume of theory and research, the empirical portion of this chapter focuses largely on what is known as the "micro" aspects of moral functioning within both psychology and sociology. Chapter 4 will focus on the more "macro," societal-level constructs as we build toward our own theory.

DEFINITIONS

Morality is one of those terms that carries a lot of weight because of how flexibly it can be used to appeal to a variety of topics. People examining areas as diverse as education, race, poverty, workplaces, culture (another loosely defined term), and crime have all mentioned how important morality is for understanding these phenomena. To make it more complicated, morality can appeal to understandings shared by an entire nation all the way down to teaching children to share toys. Many different definitions of morality exist, ranging from Abulof (2015) suggesting that societal members have deep ontological fears about survival (mortality), leading members of a society to focus on moral feelings and a collective sense of belonging to governing relations between people in order to maintain social systems (Kurtines, 1984).

Morality is so taken for granted, so ingrained into the fabric of social relations, that it can be a difficult subject to identify, much less explain. Especially since much of morality is unstated and implicit, people are actually pretty poor at articulating their moral codes (Vaisey, 2009). Competent members of a group or society are those who just "know" how to behave and what actions or ideals might mark them as outside of the mainstream for that particular category. They agree on what Durkheim carved out as the "sacred" objects—physical or immaterial—that a group privileges. That might be something like the American flag or a college's mascot, the notion of "freedom" that is central to the American story, or the high esteem that many people hold for their grandparents. Certain properties are imbued with a force centralizing the sense of "us-ness" that forms a collective. This has a moral weight attached, even if we cannot always explain it.

Some scholars suggest that morality is locatable when it is violated. Classically, the theorist Goffman (1983) suggests that social space is, in fact, a moral arena (Rawls, 1987); the implicit understandings that people share involve powerful—if unarticulated—notions of propriety and respect for society. Fiske and Rai (2014) argue that ruptures of morality are so damaging that they motivate interpersonal violence, as morality is a core part of regulating relationships. According to their argument, moral understandings between people are so important that their violation can trigger violent reactions, and in some cases this violent behavior is justified and accepted. More abstractly, Black (2011) argues that morality is identified when "social time" moves, when the understandings that a society takes for granted shift, something that can be quite upsetting to people. He suggests that conflict happens when people increase or decrease the amount of intimacy, inequality, or diversity in their relationships or in society, perhaps as evidenced by current debates over issues like gay marriage. Krebs (2011) argues that morality derives from those forms of conduct that let certain groups survive evolutionary pressures over others; we understand morality through those evolved aspects of modern conscience.

Broadly speaking, we focus on morality as multi-leveled, dynamic orientations toward understanding right and wrong, desirable and undesirable thoughts, feelings, and actions. Morality operates at the levels of individuals, groups, cultures, and nation-states and includes those external standards appearing to people as self-evidently true and binding (Taylor, 1989; Joas, 2000). At the individual level, moral action involves self-regulation (Bandura 1991), suggesting individuals have at least some control over their actions, even if many of our responses, thoughts, and feelings are less under our control than we think (more on that later). Morality involves drawing boundaries around those objects, ideals, and behaviors that are considered noble or wrong in society (Hitlin 2008); the ideas of "should" and "should not" capture the proactive and inhibiting elements of moral life (Bandura, 1999).

Morality is not reducible to religion (Bader & Fiske, 2013), altruism (Penner et al., 2005; Piliavin, 2008), or the broad and well-studied category of prosocial behavior. Traditional understandings of moral behavior are often conflated with altruistic actions, those helping others at a cost to oneself, or the notion that actions that are good for society are properly moral. There is a good deal of overlap in these situations; we consider moral exemplars to be those who dedicate their lives to helping others (Colby & Damon, 1992), and we laud those who uphold the standards of society. However, not all societies advocate actions (slavery is the extreme example) that should be supported, and altruism can have many motivations (Willer et al., 2010), including the desire to gain social standing (e.g., Willer, 2009) and build a reputation as a good person. Morality is an umbrella term for these sorts of conventionally "good" actions, as well as the process of drawing lines around the range of potential human actions. People can draw on moral reasoning and justification to exculpate a wide range of activities. The key issue is that morality is experienced as binding, largely through emotions (e.g., justice, shame), and forms the basis for our overall argument. By 'binding', we mean that people experience certain pushes, pulls and taboos as self-evidently true, beyond argument. Violations of this implicit binding force are judged as immoral.

Morality is both a source of cohesion and conflict (Turiel, 2002); psychologist Jerome Kagan (1994 [1984]) suggests that the capacity for moral judgment is distinctively human. These capacities, rooted in a sense of empathy, trace back to our evolutionary animal cousins (de Waal, 2009). There is no single, top-down moral code in a society (Zigon, 2008), one of the issues in the famous sociological work by Talcott Parsons (1951) that was often interpreted as a totalizing model of society that left scholars quite unsatisfied (Joas & Knobl, 2009) and squelched the study of morality for a half decade (Hitlin & Vaisey, 2013). Morality, understood broadly to capture the explicit rules of a society and the powerful, often emotional and inarticulable, internal experiences of its members, is a prime locus for our endeavor to link large-scale collective phenomena with the experiences of the individuals who are part of those societies.

Philosophical quests for a unified theory of morality, anchored in utilitarianism ("the greatest good for the greatest number") or deontological rules (actions are judged by their intentions to follow moral laws), seem misguided when one is presented with the array of possible moral systems found across disparate societies. The idea that any society has a single unifying moral rule is an error; most societies have conflicting ideals, and different moral goods may be in conflict for particular people. The value of being a good parent can conflict with the value of being a strong employee (Blair-Loy, 2010), and morality is about how people adjudicate these conflicts, not about a single "right" answer. The issue for social scientists is that moral judgment and interpretation are part of the human condition (Prinz, 2007), part of living in a social community. People who seem to lack moral emotions are viewed to be quite outside of the realm of typical human interaction, often labeled as sociopaths (or children, who have not learned the rules yet). For Haidt (2012), one of the most important recent scholars on the topic, "morality is the extraordinary human capacity that made civilization possible" (p. xii).

A BRIEF PRIMER ON MORALITY AND SOCIAL THEORY

The recent scientific resurgence of interest in the topic of morality is not the first intellectual engagement with intertwined issues about the nature of society, the individual, right, and wrong. Philosophers have been debating these issues throughout recorded history, and religious thinkers even before that. Regular people, societal leaders, and young children are all concerned with what is considered normal in their social environment, what is considered laudable, and especially what will get you shunned from the group. To be social is to be aware of moral codes, and human beings are inextricably social. For our purposes, we will focus briefly on the classic social thinkers whose work directly shaped the current fields of sociology and economics. For these scholars, morality largely involved creating social solidarity and maintaining social order, thus balancing the place of the individual within a world of expectations and social requirements. Within our home discipline of sociology, a discussion of theory and morality necessarily revolves around the work of Emile Durkheim.

Durkheim and Weber

For Durkheim (1858–1917), morality is part and parcel of social life. Groups of people, early tribes in his theorizing (although the anthropological work he based some of his ideas on has proved to be incomplete), practiced intense, repeated ritual interaction that heightened emotions and brought members of the group together. Broadly speaking, the process through which societal values and rules becomes fundamental to the individual is through this collective energy. The sacred nature of moral values, in addition to other totems, represents society; challenges to these sacred principles and objects imply challenges to the very group itself (Rosati & Weiss, 2015). Like the more widely known Freud, Durkheim sees people as having a rather inborn set of self-concerns, if not pure selfishness, kept in check by the power of society. For Durkheim, this control largely works through a process of making things sacred, and thus it becomes experienced as less coercive and more desirable than Freud's psychological id/ego/superego model. The self cannot be a source of morality; morality must, for Durkheim, be anchored in something higher (Hookway, 2015).

Durkheim articulated the ways that individuals, previously largely considered as atomistic, rely on society for almost all of their development. His focus on "social facts," things existing outside of and apart from individuals yet coercive over them, helped establish a social science of society. Society has the power to define the world as experienced by its members, and Durkheim believed that moral codes were a prime aspect of this capacity. To act against the strictures of a society will both trigger massive approbation by its members and signal the emotional force that holds that collective together.

Thus, for Durkheim, morality was not a particular set of values or prescriptions but a type of rule (Powell, 2010). The philosophical quest to determine what is moral does not reflect the social scientific enterprise to determine what particular groups and societies consider moral. For Durkheim, moral facts are the objects of scientific study and are recognizable by their form, the violations of which trigger powerful feelings among its members. That substrate binding groups, families, organizations, and societies is captured in the often implicit notions of sacredness, a self-evident (to its adherents) understanding that some things just are not done. Classically, Durkheim argued, these feelings became instantiated in material totems (sacred animals or flags) representing the group. Modern society, perhaps particularly Western, has partially shifted the focus of the sacred away from the group's totems and toward individuals.

Today we consider people—and their senses of self (Goffman, 1959)—as sacred objects due largely to the power of religion. In concert with societal emphasis shifting to the importance of the individual (evidenced in documents such as the Bill of Rights and the Magna Carta), religious traditions also enshrined the lone person as having sacred worth. Over time, as society became larger and more complicated, these religious roots became superfluous (Joas, 2013) even as the focus on the individual as sacred remained. Modernity has shaped individuals as beings of prime importance, something worthy of respect in ways not always found in other historical eras. This suggests, however, that a privileging of the individual over society could lead, as Durkheim feared, toward an imbalance within the forces of solidarity holding society together. The answer was not simply to redesign structures constraining individuals; the issue was how to make morality desirable, not just something that felt obligatory to the members of a society (Hodgkiss, 2013). Morality, which evolves in modern society largely outside the realm of groups trying to intentionally shape it, is necessary for society to exist, since moral rules lead people to care about solidarity with groups and not simply their own individual goals (Shadnam, 2015).

The common criticism that Durkheim focused on society as having one unified moral system misrepresents his work, which is often dismissed as naively considering just the view of morality held by those in power. As society was growing more complex, Durkheim noted that "co-present" moral spheres, potentially different ways of conceptualizing moral problems, would lead to a sort of dissonance (Kenny, 2010) and (like some of the pragmatist thinkers, notably Dewey) that individual competence at adjudicating moral issues would become an important skill. Thus, increasingly complex social order leads potentially to more complex moral thinking.

Moral emotions, for Durkheim, are experienced when people meet or violate societal expectations. The moral outrage that group members experience and direct toward rule-breakers lays bare the bonds of society. These reactions are sanctions toward the rule-breaker that attempt to keep such people from acting too narrowly in their own self-interest

(Durkheim, 1965 [1912]; Lukes, 1985). Emotions, as we will discuss, indicate instant feedback about how actions or ideas violate or uphold a particular social regime. Durkheim largely discussed these micro-processes obliquely, as he was more concerned with the macro-social orders that develop and the admittedly fuzzy historical processes that he hypothesized led to current social-moral arrangements.

Max Weber was another early, influential sociological thinker whose work is cited for linking macro structures to individual behavior. His views of morality suggested that individuals internalized culturally prevalent values about right and wrong that in turn motivated action by helping people choose between competing goals. Various beliefs provide information for people, thus becoming a "psychological motive force" (1930 [2001], p. 259) that compels adherents to those beliefs to act in prescribed ways. Weber's overall work highlights the multifaceted nature of society and describes how competing social forces, ideologies, and groups battle over defining action and how individuals struggle to make decisions in the face of these constraints (Weber, 1930 [1905]). Weber was less focused on morality at a societal level, instead suggesting that morality involves "clouds of probability" in individuals' subjective beliefs that help actions become mutually predictable (Powell, 2010). Morality involves Weber's ideal type of action, which he termed "value-rational," not rational in a calculating means-ends sense, but rational given a particular constellation of presuppositions (Shadnam, 2015).

Weber did offer a focus on what today would be considered the cultural factors that influence shifts in human societies over time, specifically his famous thesis linking the Protestant work ethic to the global spread of capitalism. In short, he considered humans as having some basic drives, but the urge to gain wealth was tempered, he felt, by the urge to enjoy life (through spending money on luxuries of life). Elements of Puritanism that seeped into certain societies reinforced a different moral ethic of working to gain and build capital: "Puritanism established a mechanism for the ongoing reinvestment of capital" (Radkau, 2011, p. 186), thus the belief system motivated a particular approach to money that turns out to be quite useful for accumulating vast stores of wealth. Over time, this religious influence faded, and the general approach (ethic) toward earning and reinvesting money grew alongside the spread of the capitalist system. Working hard and accumulating wealth become morally acceptable, if not laudable, shifting individuals' orientations toward balancing work, wealth, and leisure.

Theories about the Individual

Other social theorists have engaged these issues of morality and society, and we briefly turn to those whose work is more expressly about the individual as a social actor and theorize about how moral concerns fit into the process of situated behavior. John Dewey, the noted philosopher, suggested three potentially contrasting characteristics of moral experience (Fesmire, 2014): demands of communal life, individual goals, and social approbation. Fesmire suggests that these map onto different philosophical theories of morality that one is often presented in a college course on ethics: deontological theories of justice (Kant, where rules apply no matter what the outcomes), consequentialist theories (utilitarianism, where the outcomes adjudicate if something is right or wrong), and virtue theories (e.g., Aristotle, where societal ideals, rather than rules or consequences, are intended to guide behavior). In contrast with many of the philosophers of morality, who are more invested in prescribing action rather than describing it, Dewey suggests that a sophisticated moral life requires balancing these approaches. Using imagination and reflecting on the consequences of past actions while encountering new ones become skills people develop for dealing with moral (and social) issues. We cannot, without knowing context, simply tell people how they should always act. Through trial and error, and perhaps through watching others (either in one's life or mediated through fiction or the media), we develop a sense of how to handle situations tantamount to other artistic or athletic sorts of skills, a "feel for the game."

In this, Dewey's views dovetail a bit with Adam Smith, the patron intellectual for much of economics, who concluded that morality required the capacity to develop appropriate emotional sensitivity. This ability to develop the proper form of sympathy toward others was necessary for people to adjudicate moral claims properly (Thacher, 2015). We cannot simply apply pre-given rules, but we need to have an emotional capacity to understand the plight of others, else the invisible hand—Smith's more selectively applied concept that somehow strips his theory of its moral basis (Halteman & Noell, 2012; Rasmussen, 2016)—will not function. While the philosopher Kant felt that emotion was to be ignored with respect to moral action (actions only arising from a sense of duty were properly moral for Kant), Smith believed that emotion was a fundamental aspect of human functioning and thus instrumental for moral understanding and behavior. People cannot develop their own moral standards; like Dewey, Smith thought that one must appeal to the community (Thacher, 2015) to help determine what is properly moral. Presaging elements of our argument, the social structure of that community might, for Smith, distort the "natural" human drive toward sympathy that he believed would temper the Invisible Hand. Smith thought that the "disposition to admire, and almost to worship, the rich and the powerful, and to despise, or, at least, to neglect persons of poor and mean condition" is "the great and most universal cause of the corruption of our moral sentiments" (Smith 1982 [1759], p. 61, quoted in Rasmussen, 2016, p. 7).

Emotion was core to these early theorists, the power of the feeling of "oughtness" to motivate action was quite strong. Simmel (1908) highlighted how society benefitted from individuals being socialized into following predictable moral codes, although the nature of modern society meant that people would often be presented with multiple possible moral actions, leading to dilemmas and an early sense that people contained multiple selves (Levine, 2010). The forefather of sociological social psychology, George Herbert Mead, suggested a similar notion of multiple selves existing as the individual psyche reflects the various roles and groups that a person becomes enmeshed in. These ideas were important for demonstrating that older ways of conceptualizing a society influencing an individual were quite simplified, and they papered over the number of competing forces, ideologies, groups, and situations that a competent member of modern society was forced to juggle.

Contrary to many of these theorists' focus on the internal aspects of moral functioning, Erving Goffman's influential approach to social analysis emphasized the public display of the individual when acting within circumscribed social situations. Goffman felt daily life involved a strange mix of cynicism, ritual, and trust (Manning, 1992). This trust involves the fact that other people will play their parts, and the accordant rituals, within established understandings. There is a moral dimension to the pressures that we all feel to act appropriately, and Goffman (1959, 1967) highlighted the processes people use to present certain images and the potential moral appropriation we are subject to if these performances fail (Rawls, 1989). Individuals feel the feedback of others, and their own internalized senses of what is appropriate for that situation within that society, and attempt to present competent versions of the appropriate role. Failure to do this leads to moral feelings of shame and embarrassment, to be discussed shortly. Goffman focuses on the rules and the tactics people use to live up to them, less on the internal experiences that people have during this process, suggesting scholars should study the pressures in a situation more than the people (Rawls, 2010).

This is an admittedly cursory overview, largely an acknowledgment—not a thorough engagement—of some of the major scholars whose work framed the very problems we hope to address. Building off of some of these ideas, with newer tools that were unavailable to these thinkers, we attempt in this book to link the societal expectations for moral behavior that our tool measures (through the experience of moral emotions) with the likely internal experiences that members of a culture would experience. The through-line for all of these particular thinkers is that the individual is not the cause of their moral worlds; we are products of environments that shape our very ways of seeing and experiencing the social world. We can certainly be critical in our reflection about these ways of being in the world; this is one of the goals of the system of higher education that employs us. But to understand people's worlds (moral and otherwise), we need to also understand the environments that shape them and the situations they encounter.

EMPIRICAL SOCIAL PSYCHOLOGICAL
RESEARCH ON MORALITY

For a long time, psychological work on moral functioning drew a strong distinction between cognition and emotion. Current models, based in part on advances in neuroscience, suggest that this is a false distinction, that even "logical" functioning in normal brains involves emotional signals and triggers (e.g., Damasio, 2003). We will provide a short overview of this logic by discussing a couple of the major perspectives on moral psychology and offering a cursory overview of the role of neuroscience in these understandings. We will then talk a bit about what constitutes a moral emotion, central for our theory as developed in subsequent chapters, and discuss social psychological research on how these ideals/feelings/thoughts translate into behavior. The history of these ideas leads quite nicely to current understandings of morality: we have at least two major moral systems in the brain (Dinh & Lord, 2013), known as the dual-process model.

Rationalist Perspective

Much of the work at the individual level in the past 20 years has stemmed from psychologists becoming engaged with classical philosophical questions. The latter half of the 20th century involved the cognitive revolution in psychology, with a strong focus on the mental processes that lie between stimuli and responses, followed by a strong counter-focus on emotional processes. For a while, the focus was on moral judgment and moral reasoning, slowly giving way to the empirical reality that people do not always act in the manner that they think they will. The original rationalist perspective has given way to what we group together as "social intuitionist" perspectives (Haidt, 2001; Haidt & Bjorklund, 2008), which are starting to get some sway in sociology (Vaisey, 2009; Lizardo et al., 2016).

Classic psychological work on moral reasoning traces back to Kohlberg's (1971) influential operationalization of classic ideas from Piaget (1932 [1960]) and, even before that, Immanuel Kant (1785 [1959]). Kant's philosophical theory has motivated centuries of Introduction to Ethics courses through instantiating the idea that rational decisions are the peak form of moral action. Kant distrusted human emotional reactions to ethical dilemmas, advocating a purely logical standard (the Categorical Imperative, for those who remember their mandatory philosophy course) for adjudicating proper action. The key was to decide whether the proposed decision would be viable as the basis for a universal morality. I may want to steal a piece of cake while my significant other is not looking, but according to Kant, a world in which we all steal when people are not looking is an untenable one, therefore I should not steal. My emotions are irrelevant; Kant believed that true moral actions only stem from logical inquiry. All of the ideas that Smith and Dewey later developed, discussed earlier, were too ephemeral, Kant would argue, on which to base any sort of social system. Kant's views suffused into a variety of approaches suggesting that there is a single, unified moral code in the world based in logical (i.e., unemotional) concerns with justice, harm, and fairness.

Kohlberg (1971, 1981) developed a typology of moral development within this tradition, theorizing that children believe in right and wrong solely on the basis of being told by authority figures how they should behave. Kohlberg based these ideas on the work of Piaget (1932) and a bit less famously on Dewey (Gibbs 2003). As we develop, Kohlberg held, we learn that right and wrong can be based in community standards, often encapsulated in family expectations. We stop stealing because honest behavior will gain the esteem of significant others, not just because we are afraid of them. Some people, in Kohlberg's scheme, reach even higher levels of moral development, finding right and wrong to be anchored in the universal principles advocated by complex logical ethical systems like those suggested in Kant's writings. We find these abstract principles to be valid not on the basis of the authority of others or care for others, but because they are logically and self-evidentially true. Only 1–2% of the world's population develop this justice-orientation, the highest stage of

Kohlberg's scheme, which is a point of contention in the eyes of many critics, including the largely debatable finding that women almost never made it to the top (Jaffee & Hyde, 2000). Empirical work with children has not really supported this scale (e.g., Killen, 2007; Smetana & Tuirel, 2003), especially the gender-bias in its development (Gilligan, 1982; Jaffee & Hyde, 2000), and it found some strong cross-cultural limitations (e.g., Shweder et al., 1990).

Although the details of Kohlberg's approach have not stood up well to scrutiny, they were quite generative for other people's research (a good thing), and the ideas that harm and injustice motivate moral reasoning have spread to other influential approaches (Nucci, 1981; Nucci & Turiel, 1978, Turiel, 1983). Developmentally, these scholars argued, children learn that stealing is wrong, for example, by viewing the pain it causes others; thus emotions are the motivational foundation for the logical principles people develop as they age. Subsequent cross-cultural research suggests thay this focus on harm/justice as a core moral principle is found across cultures, including North America (Turiel, Hildebrandt, & Wainryb, 1991; Tuirel, Killen, & Helwig, 1987), Korea (Song, Smetana, & Kim, 1987) and Nigeria (Hollow, Leis, & Turiel, 1986). This involves expanding the notion of "harm" to include issues such as burning national flags, which are more symbolic than physical (an unwitting echo of Durkheim's notion of the sacred, discussed earlier). Later work, again stemming from psychological scholars, has expanded the range of moral principles and reduced the hypothesized percentage of pure logical reasoning underlying moral psychological functioning.

Social Intuitionist Perspective

Much of the recent resurgence in studying moral functioning can trace back to work of Jonathan Haidt (2001), who argued persuasively that the "rationality first" crowd had things backwards. Haidt (2012) argues that Kant is the wrong philosopher for understanding moral judgment. Rather, he argues, Hume and the Scottish philosophical tradition properly placed the focus on emotionality, first. Rather than reason logically to decide the moral thing to do, Haidt suggests, we have instantaneous, non-conscious reactions that communicate what we want to do and what we find properly moral. These emotional systems are faster than our logical brains, and thus set out the "right" answer before we realize we have made an evaluation. Only then do our logical systems weigh in, most often to justify whatever intuitive reaction our bodies and minds have already chosen. Moral judgment is the result of implicit processes, not conscious evaluation (Haidt, 2008; Haidt, Koller, & Dias, 1993; Nussbaum, 2005; Sayer, 2005). Hume is widely quoted as saying "reason is, and ought only to be the slave of the passions" (1739 [1978], p. 451). This model opens up the possibility, which is more discussed in sociology than in psychology, in which nationality, culture, social class, and a host of other factors developmentally shape intuitions outside of the realm of logical inquiry. To become a member of any of these groupings is to deeply internalize their ways of perceiving the world, and this happens outside of conscious deliberation.

Haidt's work offers intriguing examples of times that one's intuitive, emotional reaction overshadows any logical reasons for an emotion. One example occurs when researchers (Haidt et al., 1993) ask respondents to judge whether certain actions—which did not cause harm to others— were immoral, such as eating your dog after it has been killed in a car accident or cleaning a toilet with your country's flag. If the Kantians are right, actions logically causing no actual harm will not be judged as moral violations. But that is not what Haidt and colleagues discovered. Individuals have intense emotional reactions to these hypothetical stories, reporting strong, instantaneous verdicts that these situations are morally wrong. Yet they have trouble articulating why this is so, since these vignettes do not directly speak to issues of harm. The majority of respondents felt disgust, and that reaction, alone, made things immoral even when conventional reasons would not suffice as explanations. People just "knew" these things were wrong. Haidt (2006, 2012) suggests that human beings reason like lawyers, building a logical-enough case toward a predetermined end, in this case the emotionally guided end. This contrasts with Kant's ideal that we all think like scientists, following our data to its logical conclusion. In contrast, here your gut reaction tells you something is wrong, motivating the search for logical-enough sounding reasons to support that reaction; most people hold onto the moral judgment even when all logical supporting reasons are removed (Haidt, 2001).

We will discuss moral emotions in more detail, specifically in relation to our theory, in subsequent chapters. Note for now, however, that evidence suggests that this gut reaction is shaped by our cultural and structural positions (discussed in next chapter). Another relevant upshot of Haidt's work is the role of disgust in contributing to a large swath of moral judgment. This can happen even if the feeling of disgust is irrelevant to the question at hand. Schnall, Haidt, Clore, and Jordan (2008) induced disgust in participants as they reacted to a series of morally questionable situations like those just described. They did this by exposing them to a bad smell (a "fart spray") or working in a filthy room. Participants who worked in a disgust-inducing environment were more likely to form harsher moral decisions to events having nothing to do at all with the state of the room. Just having the visceral feeling is enough to trigger moral responses, even when the feeling is unrelated to the logical issue at hand.

Evidence from Neuroscience

Additional evidence that moral processing is largely implicit and emotion-driven comes from neuroscience, which has for a decade or so begun to explore these philosophical issues with modern technologies. These non-Kantian ways of experiencing the world through emotion and intuition are what give morality its power (Turner, 2007). Emotions, recent evidence tells us, turn out to be vital for even logical decision making. Led by Antonio Damasio (1994, 1996; Damasio, Tranel, & Damasio, 1991), teams of neurologists have developed the Somatic Marker Hypothesis that internalized feelings resulting from past decisions and actions are stored in the brain. These somatic markers are either consciously or unconsciously recalled when facing stimuli that are similar to those past experiences. Somatic markers are tagged to various choices we are presented with, and thus the implicit, non-conscious aspects of the intuitionist model shape the fundamental ways we process information. These markers try to keep us from experiencing negative outcomes (Damasio, 1994), perhaps through anticipating negative feelings (e.g., embarrassment), and this process leads a person to ignore that potential in favor of others not coded with negative aspects. Moral processing of difficult options is an especially propitious time for drawing on these somatic markers; they operate like traffic signals (Damasio, 1996), telling us whether to go, stop or turn when faced with choices.

Morality, then, is found emotionally within the brain to both bond people positively together and draw boundaries between the self and those one finds morally abhorrent (Firat & Hitlin, 2012). Evidence for this construction of somatic markers comes from studies of people who have damaged ventromedial prefrontal cortexes (VMPFC) and other associated areas of the brain, including the ventrolateral cortex (OFC/VL), critical areas for processing emotions. Damage to the VMPFC or OFC/VL hinders the formation of somatic markers linked to new experiences that will influence future choices (Damasio et al., 1996), although people with such damage are often quite typical with respect to intelligence. People with recent damage (that forms lesions) to these areas have knowledge of the moral rules and norms of their society; they simply have emotional processing disruptions. Their reasoning does not include the anticipated emotional ramifications somatically attached to potential courses of action (Bechara, Damasio, Damasio, & Anderson, 1994; Camille et al., 2004; Lough et al., 2006). Behaviorally, such individuals typically act well outside of social norms. Even though they can articulate the prevalent standards of their society, they apparently do not feel bound by them. Patients with such damage are typically motivated for immediate personal gain regardless of the social cost, sometimes extending to behaviors like stealing and violence (Anderson et al., 1999; Anderson, Damasio, Tranel, & Damasio, 2000).

Damage to such regions likely impairs the typical functioning of the moral emotions of shame, guilt, pity, and pride (Anderson et al., 1999; Koenigs et al., 2007) that we will discuss in detail in Chapter 5, and forms the indicators for our empirical project in the second half of this book.

People with this kind of damage have lost the ability to place themselves in the role of another, a core aspect of social interaction (Mead, 1934), and thus they fail to understand other people's feelings (Blair & Cipolotti, 2000; Koenings et al., 2007; Lough et al., 2006; Shamay-Tsoony et al., 2003). People with VMPFC lesions appear to accept moral violations as acceptable, drawing on utilitarian conclusions from which typically functioning individuals emotionally recoil (Blair & Cipolotti, 2000). Put differently, they apply coldly logical solutions (that Kant would endorse) that might involve harm to others, relying almost entirely on the rational parts of the brain but making decisions that typically functioning humans find disturbing (see for reviews Marazziti et al., 2013; Moll, Oliveria-Sousa, Zahn, & Grafman, 2008). Some sociological work (Firat & Hitlin, 2012; Franks, 2010) has begun to explore these moral processes from a wider perspective, but this is relatively new and requires a great deal of theory and research in the future.

Recent advances in neurology (e.g., Immordino-Yang, Yang, & Damasio, 2016) focus on the role of culture in the experience of emotion. Evidence suggests that culture shapes how people express emotions, offering support for the classic sociological ideas about how we learn about our experiences based largely on how we interact with others and their treatment of us. Imoordino-Yang et al. (2016) suggest that people learn the strength of feelings, and the content of what emotions feel like, based on the cultural messages they learn about expressing emotion. These messages about the display of emotion in turn shape the actual internal experience and articulation of that feeling. Adolescents in China and the United States, according to this fledgling research, internalize cultural messages that shape the very experience of moral emotions largely through messages about how expressive people are "supposed" to be (although this varies a bit based on personality, as well).

Ultimately, we will move away from this hard-core psychological and neurological focus on emotions and morality. These processes are implicit within all of the theories and models we will discuss in the next few chapters, as well as our own contribution later in the book. The evidence in this section supports our general contention, although being sociologists, we find ourselves swayed by critiques (Churchland, 2011; Moll et al., 2005) suggesting that the necessary controls needed for studies like those discussed earlier distort moral emotions away from everyday processing. The ways people process information morally within a laboratory or an fMRI machine are likely to diverge from how we handle everyday situations. Much of the psychological work on emotion captures what Abend (2011) calls "thin" emotions and ignores the "thick" sorts of feelings (e.g., righteousness, loyalty, fanaticism) that comprise a full moral life. We hope that our measure of emotions takes a step toward applying the study of morality within a wider engagement with social life.

Moral Emotions

We have to this point collapsed a lot of things—most non-conscious processes, really—into a broad conception of "emotions." We will return to the topic of emotions later when we discuss how morality indicates facets of a society. Broadly speaking, however, moral emotions locate people within social relationships (Rai & Fiske, 2011) or concern the welfare of others or of society as a whole (Haidt, 2003). Even self-oriented moral emotions, like shame, represent how people perceive themselves to be acting in accordance with the real or perceived judgments of others. "A moral emotion is one that is aroused in reference to cultural codes that contain evaluative content" (Turner & Stets, 2006, p. 556). People feel emotions that signal how they are acting in accordance with important societal and situational norms and values. There is a wide range of potential emotions that we will discuss shortly; typically, however, psychological research on moral emotion has dealt with a fairly truncated set of potential emotions (Abend, 2011).

Morality does not work without "teeth" (Turner, 2007); negative emotions form the basis for individuals' monitoring and constraining of their behavior. Moral emotions allow instantaneous feedback about how our or others' behavior supports or violates local moral systems (Blasi, 1999; Owens & Goodney, 2000). Prominent sociological accounts (e.g.,

Goffman, 1959; Stets & Carter, 2011, 2012) suggest that moral emotions provide feedback for how well an interaction is proceeding along the lines of agreed-upon meanings and identity standards. Much like the somatic markers discussed earlier, the real and anticipated feedback of interaction partners or imagined audiences can trigger emotions—or the guilt of negative emotional repercussions—like fear or shame that we are highly motivated to avoid. Emotions are the information that guides us toward perceived positive interactional outcomes and away from possible negative ones. Our society, obviously, defines and communicates what those positive and negative situations might be.

Ultimately, we are closer to the position of those (e.g., Smetana, 1995; Walker, 2000) who suggest that, in contrast with the rationalist theories discussed here, the world presents itself to people in ambiguous ways that we respond to based on our habits of moral interpretation. This process of context→interpretation→response unfolds within the field of action (see work by the pragmatists) and traces back to ideas from Dewey: the best that social science can do is artificially carve up this process into analytically discrete concepts and constructs. "What we will actually do in a moral situation necessarily flows from the reality we have previously constructed and the habits of moral reasoning and moral interpretation we have previously developed" (Walker, 2000, p. 153). Emotions are critical in decision making in many ways because of their spontaneity; they are experienced as "sincere" (Blasi, 1999). These processes occur rapidly and without deliberation (Bargh & Chartrand, 1999).

BRINGING THE STRANDS TOGETHER: SOCIOLOGY, DUAL-PROCESS MODELS, AND CULTURE

As sociologists, we are interested in how these implicit, emotional reactions are shaped by cultural and structural forces that are in play well before we are born and become competent members of a society. The current movement in psychology has started to become incorporated into sociology in a few subfields, whether focusing on evolutionary patterns of brain development (Massey, 2002), social psychology (Hitlin, 2008), or how individuals use culture (Vaisey, 2009). Consistent throughout this work is the automaticity of information processing, shaped by emotion and also subject to conscious influence in the right circumstances. These are collectively referred to as dual-process models of cognition (Chaiken & Trope, 1999; Evans, 2008; Greene et al., 2004).

Put simply, our automatic, unconscious mental processes filter situations and information before we are even consciously aware that it is happening. Many of our judgments about the world are emotional and automatic; although we like to believe we are in control of our actions, much of our behavior is "decided" before we are consciously aware of what is going on or how we will act. We do not have as much free will as we think we do; we have what Ramachandran (2007) refers to as "free won't." We can stop some of our impulses from leading to action, but we are less able to generate those impulses without serious training, discipline, and engagement (Haidt, 2006). We can stop ourselves from eating the cake, and we can want to not want to eat the cake (e.g., Frankfurt, 1971), but is much harder to train our automatic systems to not want the cake. Cakes are tempting. We have these two mental systems operating at once, each one shaped by our involvement in larger groups and cultural milieus. They may or may not agree with each other, as we can literally be of "two minds" about many moral issues.

For a long time in sociology, especially in the growing subfield of the study of culture, people were thought of as having "toolkits" of potential responses available as they went through life (Swidler, 1986; see also Boltanski & Thévenot, 1999; DiMaggio, 1997, 2002). Writing in response to a movement in sociology that gave "norms" explanatory power over our behavior, Swidler suggested that people are not just following these rules blindly, but can make strategic choices about their potential behavior. We do not just blindly follow social rules; different societies, and different groups within those societies, provide potential ways of acting, and when presented with a situation we pull out a "tool" that will serve to help solve a current problem. Recent engagement with this influential model has incorporated what we know now about dual-process psychology to suggest that the logical-sounding reasons people give for their actions are more justifications than accurate representations of why people do things (Vaisey 2009). Swidler (2001), in advancing this classic perspective, finds that people are quite inconsistent in the reasons they give for past behavior, drawing somewhat haphazardly on cultural scripts to narrate stories of the past. These stories, sociologists are suggesting, are not the causal forces of action. Rather, they are conscious attempts to make sense of past and future behavior, post hoc explanations for explaining their own, or others', behavior.

Vaisey's newer articulation of these ideas suggests that the toolkit of available stories cannot be the only cause of action, rather people internalize cultural messages at the implicit, emotional level. Sometimes we "choose" things without really knowing why or being strategic in any narrow, calculating sense. Some options just feel right, and when pressed, we may not be able to articulate why. Following the currently ubiquitous ideas of Bourdieu (1984, 1990), the ideologies of a group or society become internalized, automatic guides for behavior, much like the arguments within the social intuitionist model of morality and the somatic marker hypothesis. Bourdieu (1900) refers to these internalized habits that unconsciously guide behavior, tastes, and preferences as *habitus*. Other scholars have expanded this into the sociology of morality, showing how it becomes deeply embedded often outside of conscious articulation (Ignatow, 2009; Ignatow, 2010; Winchester, 2008). People do not internalize all cultural messages to the same depth. The most internalized messages are the ones that most influence the implicit processes that drive automatic behavior and judgment (D'Andrade 1995; Vaisey, 2009), largely through the emotional heft of the present makes things seem self-evidently true.

Lizardo and colleagues (2016) offer an umbrella for how sociological work like ours can borrow from the burgeoning psychological literature on dual-process models, which they say are largely uncontroversial in that field (see also Dinh & Lord, 2013). The larger framework that people have emotional and rational subsystems in the mind, and both are shaped through cultural influences, is fairly well-established. Psychologists largely agree on ideas captured in the notions of "fast and slow," "hot and cold," or "conscious and unconscious" mental processes, as we have outlined here in the history of social theory. They suggest this larger framework is more profitably broken down into four processes when considering how culture enters the individual: learning, remembering, thinking, and acting. These are four phases of the acculturation process. Future work might develop our empirical analysis along these lines to specify how moral systems become internalized and shape action.

Thus, dual-process functioning captures an important element of the ways that cultural ideologies—and, we will argue, societal inequality—become internalized. We will discuss the kinds of ideologies we have in mind in Chapter 4, but at this point we want to simply establish that these processes allow an empirically validated link between macro structures and individual functioning that is useful for developing a sociology of morality (e.g., Hitlin & Vaisey, 2013; Powell, 2010). This dual-process model of having two intertwined brain systems, one more deliberative and one more automatic, can account for a wide range of cognition and behavior, thus highlighting emotions as a core aspect for social interaction. This calls for a theory of how societal forms channel the internalization of meaning and emotion, thus shaping how individuals respond to the world. There are some universal capacities for emotion—the basic range of emotions appears to be circumscribed, a notion we will engage shortly—but the content and the stimuli for these emotions can be differentially shaped across the world.

4

The Difficulty of Studying
Morality Across Cultures

M any English speaking readers are likely to come from a similar, Western background as the authors, that is, from an environment that is rather focused on the individual. In America, especially, our students are trained to think about people as isolated individuals, responsible for their successes and blameworthy for their failures. It is difficult, for those of us who try to teach people to view the world from a sociological lens, to put that view of the individual in greater context to understand that an extreme focus on the individual reduces other powerful forces in their lives to afterthoughts. People are shaped by their environments, and while we do make choices, we may not make as many unique choices as Americans are taught to believe. We are quite patterned—sharing a racial category, a social class background, a region of the country—and these social locations tell us a decent amount about how any individual in those categories will see the world and behave. Not perfectly, of course, but while we are taught to view our children each as special snowflakes, when we look at people in the aggregate, we need to understand more than just individual idiosyncratic personalities.

Thus, in this chapter we turn to a more macro-oriented approach to understanding the intersection of morality and culture. Individuals make moral decisions, but they do not do so in a social vacuum. Building off our brief discussion of Durkheim's writings about social structure as an influence on morality, we turn now to more modern discussions of the ways society influences individual moral functioning, along with some theories about the forms of potential moral beliefs and priorities that exist across cultures. Some theories treat different cultures as if they developed in isolation; others offer evidence to suggest that overarching patterns of structural societal features, like economic growth, shape moral imperatives (e.g., Inglehart & Baker, 2000). We provide a broad overview of these ideas in the process of building toward our own focus on societal inequality as an understudied aspect of how the individual is socialized.

Influential models linking culture to individual psychological functioning have been less concerned with the emotional processes underlying these ties. Oddly, even though psychology and sociology both engage the topic of culture, scholars too rarely cross boundaries to learn from each other's work (DiMaggio & Markus, 2010). An incorrect stereotype suggests psychologists focus more on the micro processes we outlined in the last chapter, and sociologists supposedly focus more on the macro aspects of societal functioning. In reality, however, a sizable portion of sociology is concerned with individual and small group actions in concrete situations, while a significant subset of psychology focuses on the role of cultures around the world. However, the practical lack of communication between the fields—not a total absence, but certainly not the exchange that would be desirable—hinders both fields. Within sociology, we suggest many of these cultural models are missing a refined social psychology of the sort we set forward later in this book, and even broader disciplinary calls to explore "mechanisms" (Reskin, 2003; Gross, 2009) would benefit from some of the bridging work at the micro end of our field. For our purpose, we build off the consensual notion, discussed in the previous chapter, that implicit, emotionally driven, culturally shaped moral intuitions are a vital motivating force for situated behavior. Having established that individuals operate through interrelated conscious and unconscious systems fueled by both emotion and cognition, we need to have a fuller understanding of the environments shaping these systems—particularly in ways that are not immediately evident to either members of those societies or the social scientists trying to make sense of them.

Sometimes scholars downplay the fact that the things we study today (poverty, education, politics) are part of an ongoing life course: our actions today are partially related to things that happened to us previously, our environments shape what we experienced, and historical events shape everyone of a certain age at a certain time (e.g., Elder et al., 2015). We are born with very little understanding of what is happening around us, leaving culture to fill in our potential capacities for social life as we age. Babies are born with the capacity for the range of human moral intuitions, beliefs, and emotions, but, like language, we are channeled into the ethical codes learned within particular societies, families, and social groups (Huttenlocher, 1994; 2009; Moll et al., 2003). Babies learn to distinguish between "good" and "bad" between ages 2 and 3 (Kagan, 1994), a socialization process that makes affect and emotions a salient feature of social life (Bloom, 2013).

Human capacities for making sense of our social worlds evolved within a certain range of potential processes (we can only sense time in one direction, for example). Evolution, often mistakenly understood to be a simple survival of the fittest, occurs within social groups, a position even Darwin suggested, although he did not follow up on it (Kinder & Kam, 2009). Primitive people were no more likely to live in isolation than people alive today. Evolution, then, is itself strongly shaped by social processes (Turner, 2007, 2010). Some scholars suggest these evolutionary pressures shape individuals into beings specifically designed to thrive within group life (e.g., Greene, 2014; Krebs, 2011; Sunar, 2009), with cooperation being a key feature to groups' survival in a dangerous world. While not fully established, such a view is consonant with modern understandings of the primacy of group identification (e.g., Brewer, 1991) and the proposition we hold today that humans are inextricably attuned to social cues and are fundamentally tribal (Berreby, 2005).

Those capacities facilitating group life, gaining security and social acceptance, are hypothesized to be as important to human evolution as being able to conquer enemies from other tribes. We are admittedly cursory in our treatment of the anthropological forces shaping modern humans, but we do want to highlight the aspects of group life, suggested by classic scholars (e.g., Durkheim, discussed in Chapter 3), suggesting that the density of group life and the resultant social structures shape individual psychological capacities. For Durkheim, as societies became more complicated, people's contributions to their groups became more specialized and human capacities for abstract logic, mathematics, and thinking became more advanced. More recently, McCaffree (2015) suggests a similar link between religious belief and individuality, suggesting that agrarian societies typically believed in polytheistic deities that were relatively uninterested in the lives of individual people. As societies became larger, monotheistic deities were more likely to emerge that "were quite interested in the individual behaviors and beliefs of peasants" (McCaffree, 2015, p. 45). Thus, the modern primacy of self can be linked to the ways that society is organized, including the size and economic capacities of a group. We are largely agnostic on these processes here, but merely want to highlight how important social organization is to such shifts over time.

Moral intuitions are a large part of the ways individuals learned to coordinate (Martin, 2011) and learning to channel and inhibit antisocial tendencies to support groups was key to human development (Boehm, 2012). The sorts of issues that human groups need to deal with—coordination, trust, safety, resource acquisition—are universal (Schwartz & Bilsky, 1987; Brown, 1991, 2004). Cultures may build on these evolved tendencies by highlighting certain potential ideals over others, forming the basis for what we consider distinct societal understandings of the world captured in various terms such as "culture," "ideology," "habitus," and "nationality." This capacity keeps humans from being coldly rational, thus enabling us to coordinate in "large cooperative groups, tribes and nations without the glue of kinship" (Haidt, 2012, p. xiii). We gain pleasure from fitting in with others, from comradery and a sense of fellowship. We internalize social expectations for our roles in groups and society, and we derive significant self-worth from fulfilling them. We only know who we are, as we will discuss more in subsequent chapters, through the reflected feedback we get from others. When that feedback adheres us to our groups, we have positive feelings. Being shunned, excommunicated, or put into solitary confinement are among the harshest punishments people can experience.

This is not to say that all people like to follow rules, or that all of the norms humans internalize are identical across societies, or even within any one society. Some nations privilege religion, others prioritize money. Some societies treat the genders more equally and have a wider understanding of the possible genders, while others are rigidly stuck believing that all men are alike, as are all women, and that there are only two genders. We know a good deal about the values on which different societies place the highest priority, and certainly they do not all agree. Within any country, people with more or less power or resources may also subscribe to different priorities than the powerful; social movements and revolutions involve large numbers of such people coordinating in how to change current social systems. The differing cultural foci vary across societies and time (Zerubavel, 1997), and even particular societies can shift regarding values or priorities that are in tension over time in response to such movements or other historical changes (Inglehart & Welzel, 2005).

Moral beliefs are quite fundamental to a society. They are neither fixed nor fully random, however. Societal changes in moral codes are typically slow, given the power of such beliefs to structure what people expect, and we do not like our worlds to feel tenuous (Abulof, 2015). Weber believed, for example, that modernity involved a predictable shift in moral codes over time. Where once the "individual" was not the primary foci of legal or political concern, modernity involved a pattern of institutions attempting to extend the dignity and interests of individuals as widely as possible (Boudon, 2008). This is something increasingly done in what we will discuss as "individualistic" societies (Sastry & Ross, 1998). Thus the evolution of moral codes can unfold along predetermined lines rather than randomly.

For reasons that are partly historical, partly chance, and well beyond our ability to discuss causally, different societies develop different moral priorities. Broadly speaking, the emotions and intuitions prominent in a society become reinforced and are then felt more strongly and with more nuance than other potential feelings (Higgins, 1996). This is similar to how children learn to vocalize the sounds of their native language yet the ability to make other sorts of vocalizations lessens as they age. If you are raised to care deeply about your family lineage and this is reinforced through your intimate family, social media, peers, and educational institutions, you will internalize that as one of your core priorities. Religion operates similarly; in most human societies the next generation is raised to be as adherent to a faith—often a single dominant faith within a nation—as the prior generation. And while religious and moral content may differ across societies, "[o]ne may venture to propose that certain phenomena seem to be cross-culturally prone to become the target of moralization, such as lifestyles, sexuality, people's characters and accomplishments, death and dying, and, in general, sacred and religious dimensions of behavior" (Bergmann, 1998, p. 289).

As with the acquisition of language, this emotional sense of a society's morality develops largely in childhood and adolescence, which are periods of high neural plasticity when the mind is open to being filled in with a society's content (though neural plasticity persists throughout our lives, arguably to a lesser degree as we become more set in our ways). Colloquially, we understand that it is easy for children to learn multiple languages, as their minds are primed to learn. It is harder to learn new languages as we age, perhaps like moral codes, and as we develop our language shapes us. Once internalized, these codes become self-evidently true, in part because they are deeply felt, and thus guide future interaction. We develop values and then typically select people and situations that allow us to affirm those values (Alwin et al., 1991); we are less likely to purposefully put ourselves in positions to challenge and uproot our core senses of right and wrong. It can happen; some people study abroad in college, or move away from a religious community, but these are notable pursuits precisely because most of us unconsciously gravitate toward paths of lesser resistance. In the American context, for example, this balkanization by political leanings has shaped residential patterns such that people are increasingly unlikely to be living next to somebody from a different political persuasion or to socialize with such folks. Taken at the aggregate, cultures thus reproduce themselves, with the potential for shifts and variation, but those will occur when many people and groups shift their standards, not simply because of any one individual.

Other forms of evidence, including a qualitative study of Japanese children who spent some of their childhood in the United States, support the notion of early learning shaping later functioning by demonstrating different patterns of moral socialization. Children who spent the earliest part of their lives in the United States did not maintain American norms upon returning to Japan, while those who encountered US moral norms during a sensitive developmental period between the ages of 9 and 15 internalized them deeply through imbuing them with emotional content (Minoura, 1992), thereby becoming indistinguishable from American adolescents of the same age. Thus, we view these processes (see also Chapter 3) as underlying the links between societal options and individual experience. We fill in our universal capacity to judge things as right or wrong with the particular content our families and societies of origin offer us. Over time, such ways of perceiving the world are unconsciously shaping who we spend time with, how we judge others, and what feels comfortable and right. Unless something distinctive changes us, or we work very hard to change our internal wiring, as it were, our lives will unfold within the boundaries of the moral codes we believe in. Or if we violate them, and most people will at some level, we feel guilt or shame and try to repair the social damage; if the offenses are so great as to violate criminal law in modern societies, we may even be imprisoned as a result.

While this capacity is universal, the content is culturally specific. We now turn to a broad overview of theoretically influential models about the range of potential moral experience across societies, the macro patterns in moral codes that eventually filter down into individual choices, beliefs, and judgments.

FORMS OF CULTURAL VARIATION

Various arguments, captured notably in sociology Ralph Turner's (1976) classic paper, argue that modern society is shifting from a dominant focus on rules to one more based on emotions and intuitions. Where ideal authorities in society once came from social expectations embedded in institutions (family, work, education), the argument is that modernity represents a notable shift toward internal (not external) criterion for deciding how one should act, with America being the key exemplar of this process. We leaned on outside sources, once, to help us understand right and wrong, what is acceptable and what we needed to avoid, and how we were expected to act. These days, supposedly, the locus for deciding what to do has shifted to internal markers. Not feeling like doing something is more valid today as an excuse than it once was, when people acted more based on their social roles. We felt "real," in Turner's terms, when we lived up to societal expectations. The shift toward intuitions as a valid basis for making decisions is relatively new.

While a bit overstated—much of sociology exists because we can understand people based on the institutions they belong to, and social psychology focuses a great deal on how situations shape our behavior well beyond idiosyncratic personalities—the general trend toward the individual is a theme across a number of social theorists, for good and ill. These shifts reflect forces exemplified in the American context, with its apparent shift toward an individualism present since its founding (Woodard, 2016). American society was seen as revolving around four sorts of moral cultures (expressive individualist, utilitarian individualist, civic republican, and biblical) even as each of these are particular variants of an American characterological concern with individualism (Bellah et al., (1985 [2007]). This classic work demonstrates the rise and eventual decline of morality based on norms of community and biblical strictures toward what the authors identified as an increasing emphasis on individualism, findings mirrored over time in studies of college students (e.g., Twenge, 2006; Twenge et al., 2008).

In psychology, perhaps the most widely utilized cross-cultural paradigm relates to this focus on individualism by suggesting it is a product of a particular set of cultural traditions. This involves the ubiquitous distinction between Eastern and Western cultures: the individualist/collectivist dimension (Hofstede, 2001; Markus & Kitayama, 1991; Triandis, 1995). According to this tradition, East and West are separated by cultural forces shaping, even in the most basic ways, how people experience the world. Members of these two types of cultures fundamentally perceive the world in different ways (Nisbett, 2004; Nisbett et al., 2001), with Easterners being holistic thinkers—paying more attention to the entire situation and using fewer analytic categories and formal logic—than Westerners, who are viewed as more analytic thinkers (Kagan, 2007), most interested in ideas that transcend concrete settings.

An example comes from Kondo's (1990) ethnography of an American living in Japan, articulating the nature of purportedly collectivist thinking. She reports that many workers receive formal ethics training that highlights the importance of family and teams over the individual, a message reinforced in many different ways at work, including group punishment for the violations any individual might make. These interactions, she argues, instantiate the goal of group reliance and subordination of the individual. The locus for deciding what to do, right and wrong, comes from outside in Eastern ways of perceiving, while people in the West putatively will listen more to internal voices.

Religious traditions are thought to account for some of these differences, or at least to have shaped the paths that East versus West have developed over the past few thousand years. Eastern notions of reality and morality emphasize duty and social goals, while Western culture is more focused on the prevalence of personal rights and independence (Bedford & Hwang 2003). A Confucian notion of selfhood is inextricably bound up with one's family and ancestors, thus is a broader notion of the self than typically highlighted in the West, wherein groups and family membership supposedly do not carry the same motivational value (Markus & Kitayama, 1991).

Empirical evidence for this popular distinction is mixed. Some find evidence that Eastern versus Western approaches to perceiving the world are valid (Grimm et al., 1999), while others find the distinction overly simplistic (D'Andrade, 2008; Oyserman, Coon, & Kemmelmeier, 2002). The distinction is rarely explicitly linked with moral functioning, although we can apply some of the conclusions from how guilt and shame—the paramount moral emotions to be discussed in more detail later on—are discussed in each culture. Collectivist cultures define the self by privileging conformity to the social order, focusing on people's interdependence. This suggests that shame is more likely to occur, as shame is considered to be a reaction to a loss of face and violates core aspects of the self (Babcock & Sabini, 1990; Bedford & Hwang, 2003; Niedenthal, Tangey, & Gavanski, 1994). Western, individualistic nations are thought to be more prone to guilt than shame, an emotion triggered by having done something wrong in a particular setting (causing harm to another). Guilt does not implicate the self in the same way as shame, thus the experience of moral violations is supposedly seen less as a result of one's essentially flawed character (Wong & Tsai, 2007). We will return to this point in more detail later on.

A few other influential models focus on how features of a societies' structure and culture influence moral functioning. Inglehart (1990, 1995, 2006), with a series of colleagues, has advanced the Modernization thesis, modeling a structural shift based on a nation's level of economic development. Briefly, Inglehart draws on the World Values Survey (http://www. worldvaluessurvey.org/wvs.jsp) over time to demonstrate that less economically advanced nations report attitudes privileging law and order and economic stability, while more economically advanced nations—with economic certainty more established—value issues of quality of life, a society-level counterpart to Maslow's famous hierarchy of needs. Once people (or society) feel their basic security is established, they are free to worry about higher-order concerns. A powerful aspect of the Modernization thesis involves the empirical demonstration that, accounting for cultural history (Inglehart & Baker, 2000), countries shift from valuing security (what he terms "materialist") toward valuing overall quality of life ("postmaterialist") as their Gross Domestic Product rises. The more economically advanced a country becomes, with the exception of the United States, the more its values shift in a postmaterialist direction. While countries with different traditions have different ultimate concerns, this general trend toward higher order values appears evident around the world. Also with the exception of America, the more economically advanced a nation gets, the less religious it becomes (Nevitte & Chochrane, 2006). America has a particular set of contradictory internal traditions (Baker, 2005; Hewitt, 1989; Woodard, 2016), with some elements moving in the same pattern as the rest of the world, but with a substrate of religiosity that largely maintains an influence, in contrast to world patterns of economic development.

Another established tradition involves the explicit study of values (Schwartz 1992 et al., 2012; Bilsky, 1987, 1990). Having examined all literate nations in the world, researchers find that people consistently recognize the following ten values, each defined in terms of its motivational goal:

Hedonism: self-centered sensual gratification

Stimulation: encourage risk taking and adventure

Self-Direction: autonomous thought and action

Universalism: tolerance and concern for welfare of all others

Benevolence: preserve and enhance welfare for those one frequently contacts

Conformity: self-restraint, subordinating one's inclinations to others' expectations

Tradition: traditional and religious activities

Security: stability, safety, and harmony of society, relationships and self

Power: status and prestige, control people and resources

Achievement: competitive personal success

When analyzed, these ten values can be represented in a circular fashion with neighboring values (like hedonism and stimulation) showing similar importance, and people (and societies) that privilege one portion of the circle (like achievement/power) tend to be less concerned with the values placed on the opposing side (universalism/benevolence). A variety of empirical measures (Schwartz et al., 2001; Oishi et al., 1998; Pakizeh et al., 2007) support this basic structure, with societies falling along the two dimensions (self-enhancement vs. self-transcendence, and conservation vs. openness to change) that can be discerned from these ten values. These values represent different concerns groups have in order to survive; they are all important to some level.

Countries are often coded, then, based on the important values within their boundaries (e.g., Roccas & Sagiv, 2010). Some recent work (Fischer & Schwartz, 2011), however, finds more value consensus across nations than within (see also Longest et al., 2013), suggesting that issues such as class and gender might shape values more directly than nation (with the exception of conformity, see also work by Kohn, 1983). For our purposes, this suggests that measures of values may not tell us as much about what is distinctive about a society as other measures, such as the one we introduce in Chapter 7. Societies have a good deal of internal variation with respect to values (Fischer & Schwartz, 2011), such that Schwartz (2014) suggests the existence of a "latent culture" underlying societal institutions (the family, educational systems) shaping individual experience. Thus, culture works "through" those institutions that socialize its members.

Both of these important traditions (Inglehart and Schwartz, see Schwartz 2013 for some extensive theoretical and empirical comparisons) link social structural and cultural patterns with individually experienced values (measured differentially). The key behind these individual priorities, patterned by forces outside of the individuals who hold them, is that there is an emotional force behind the taken-for-granted "rightness" of the various issues in play. When we zoom out, we can see patterns in how national factors structure the feelings and perceptions of their members. To reiterate, we are not claiming uniformity of psychological orientations within countries; we do not think everyone in China is alike, any more than everyone in any large nation could be considered to be identical. However, there are national averages and distributions that tell us how a "typical" member of a society might perceive the world, and these ideal types empirically differ across nations.

CONCEPTIONS OF MORALITY

Scholars have been analyzing potential types of societal moral codes for as long as people have had philosophy and religion. The largely quantitative, empirical study of the range of possible moral patterns within societies traces back for about the last three or four decades, with a newer resurgence in interest in empirically validating the potential forms morality might take at the cultural level. Many of these theories take morality to be a priori important, and fundamental to defining a society, but links to economic and political structures are less developed. We have touched on a couple of the precursors to today's influential models, but for this subsequent overview we present 1, 2, 3, 5+, and 4 mnemonic umbrella (Harkness & Hitlin, 2014) to walk us through what we find to be the most important sets of theories available for linking culture and moral functioning. We will begin with Kohlberg's single notion of morality (1), to Gilligan's response (positing 2 forms), through more recent work highlighting 3 broad moral types, another offering 5+ (building on the 3-fold typology), and then a different tradition suggesting 4 different possible bases for morality. This work traces from different sources; early work is psychological in origin, and some of the most appealing newer work comes from anthropology, while sociology and political science offer relevant insights as well. Fundamentally, the study of morality and society should be an interdisciplinary exercise, and such bridges are starting to develop.

As discussed in Chapter 3, we begin with the early influential, somewhat empirically tested work anchoring morality in a single domain, rationalist notions of universal justice, advanced by Lawrence Kohlberg (1981). He posited a universal pattern of moral development, stages that developing adults necessarily went through to understand the bases for right and wrong. This sequence, he suggested, was part of the development of the human organism. Kohlberg posited six (later streamlined to five) stages, defining morality with an efficient, but simplified understanding of consisting of pro-social behavior (good for others). More complicated, later versions of morality have much "thicker" descriptions

(Abend, 2011); this early work conceptualized morality largely as actions that help others, a standard still used today within research on constructs like the "moral identity" (Acquino & Reed, 2002; Stets & Carter, 2012). According to this view, children internalize moral standards based on not harming others. The initial stage of this learning comes from punishment when such rules are violated, not unlike how we treat pets. Later stages involve children learning to follow moral rules because they are set out by legitimate authorities (parents, police, and government). This is the level that Kohlberg suggested most adults reach, knowing that right and wrong are defined by laws and possibly religious codes. Only a select few in this system obtain knowledge of the universal principle of justice, and understand that some things are just right and wrong regardless of what authorities tell us. For these people, an understanding of morality involves true understanding of the abstract rights and responsibilities human beings have as a result of being members of a society. Justice and fairness are right because they are universal principles, not because the police or a judge tells us they are.

Interestingly, even if one accepts Kohlberg's scheme, there is little evidence that people at the higher stages act with greater morality, even by his own definition. Studies of "moral exemplars," that is to say people who actually did incredibly altruistic things like rescuing victims or dedicating their lives to helping people, suggest that such exemplars do not actually score at the highest levels of Kohlberg's schemes (Hart & Fegley, 1995; Youniss & Yates, 1999). They just did the moral thing largely without abstract philosophical justifications for those actions. The suggestion is that some people at the top of the scale simply have more complicated justification patterns for whatever they wanted to do, not that being at the highest levels caused people to act more morally; somebody high on the scale who wanted to break the law, for example, might simply have more advanced philosophical rationalizations for such behavior. Further, Kohlberg's approach relegates duty, where doing the right thing is one's assigned lot in life, to a lower rationale for morality, thereby relegating many societies' moral codes to being deficient according to this schema (Shweder, Mahapatra, & Miller, 1987). While Kant suggested moral actions could only stem from a sense of duty, Kohlberg seems to suggest that is an inferior motivation.

Kohlberg's work is critiqued on a number of fronts, including its lack of engagement with emotion (Liebert, 1984; Walker & Pitts, 1998), as previously noted. This represents an obvious weakness, though we do want to credit him (and others, see e.g. work by Turiel, 1994) for the positive aspects of a parsimonious theory, limiting moral concerns to issues of justice and harm avoidance. Kohlberg's student, Carol Gilligan (1982), famously engaged this extreme focus on justice by suggesting that it was a masculine conception of morality. According to Kohlberg's measures, women were morally deficient. Gilligan influentially pointed out that women might be using a different approach, thus suggesting two possible moral orientations, rather than the one, and offered a purportedly feminine approach privileging the notions of care and empathy as vital for guiding moral judgment and action.

As mentioned previously, like the harm/justice single-issue moral scheme, this care-based perspective does not fare well in empirical tests (Nunner-Winkler, 1984). Some of the hypothesized gender differences in moral reasoning appear overstated as men and women reach similar moral conclusions when asked to make judgments about moral dilemmas (Jaffee & Hyde, 2000; Walker, 2006). As a social psychologist might suspect, it appears that situational factors influence which of these two styles is employed more than gender itself (Smetana, Killen, & Turiel, 1991). Men would think in "masculine" fashions when presented with situations where that sort of logical, justice-based reasoning is appropriate . . . but so, too, would women. The real world complicates the abstractions underlying these parsimonious one- or two-perspective theories (Haidt, 2001). These potential short-comings were very generational for further research (Sunar 2009), however, and stimulated the field across disciplines.

Anthropological work, prominently by Richard Shweder, directly engaged the limits of the justice/harm approach through a deep engagement with India. These researchers largely accepted Kohlberg's justice framework as a core guiding principle in other cultures, but suggest that it is but one of three frameworks cultures use to establish a collective sense of morality (Shweder et al., 1987; Shweder, Much, Mahapatra, & Park, 1997). They present the CAD model (community, autonomy, and divinity), holding that the Kohlberg approach is a Westernized way of thinking the (ethic of autonomy), suggesting cultures can be organized around two other, distinct ethics of community and/or divinity. Community oriented moral systems highlight the collective's needs over that of the individual, similar to the previously discussed stereotypically "Eastern" end the individualist-collectivist dimension. An emphasis on divinity focuses on local conceptions of the sacred moral order—practices intended to protect the sacred nature of the spiritual realm for individuals and the society as a whole (Sunar, 2009).

This CAD model is more explicitly concerned with emotions than Kohlberg's initial foray, the Big Three dimensions influence emotional expression and experience for members of particular cultures (Shweder & Haidt, 2000; Shweder et al., 1997). The ability to rationally calculate harm and justice concerns, in Kohlberg's scheme, as part of a Kantian tradition almost by definition involves sidelining emotional influences. Giligan's critiques at least highlighted this missing aspect of morality, even if her solution was empirically flawed. For the CAD model, emotions can be the basis for moral functioning within groups; feelings of belonging and awe of sacred forces motivate moral action. One exploration systematically links specific emotions to specific sorts of CAD violations; people feel anger for autonomy violations, contempt for community violations, and disgust for divinity violations (Rozin, Lwery, Imada, & Haidt, 1999). This supports our contention that a person's emotional experience is a result of the ways their culture teach them to perceive and evaluate moral transgressions.

Haidt, previously mentioned as one of the prime movers in recent social scientific work on morality, studied with Shweder and later developed one of the most currently influential theories of possible moral schemes, what he and colleagues term moral foundations theory. This approach originally posited five foundations for morality, and is currently holding six foundations with the possibility for more (Graham et al., 2013; Graham et al., 2011; Haidt & Graham, 2009). Other scholars are haggling over the exact number for a foundations typology. The advantage of this, even as we lose parsimony, is that there is a potential for more nuance than in the aforementioned models.

In brief, Haidt, Graham, and colleagues present two "individualizing" foundations (fairness and care/harm-based moral systems) and three "communal" foundations (in-group loyalty, hierarchy, and purity) that can anchor a culture's moral codes. The same individual-collectivist distinction that we keep seeing—in the early sociological theorists hypothesizing the nature of technological change and growth on society, and in the popular psychological East versus West paradigm—roughly develops here. They argue that these codes are tantamount to taste buds; just as we learn foods we like early in our cultural socialization, narrowing down from a biological set of near-limitless taste possibilities to a culturally delimited selection within those possibilities, so too do we narrow in on internalizing those moral foundations that we encounter as children in a society. Some things that violate a person's or culture's sense of hierarchy (cursing one's parents, for example) might not be seen as a particularly moral violation to a different audience. If a nations' flag is sacred to you (in-group loyalty), then burning it is a moral violation. If you are primarily concerned with harm, then with nobody being physically hurt, flag burning is not something the government should be particularly concerned with.

This model best appears to fit moral judgments in the American context related to non-traditional sexuality (Haidt & Hersh, 2001; see Graham et al., 2011 for an overview). Specifically, conservatives report stronger disgust or repulsion after reading about sexual acts, such as incest or masturbation and descriptions of gay and lesbian sexuality. As discussed with respect to the dual-process model, the emotional reaction takes precedence over any sort of conscious ability to justify the reaction. Participants struggled to come up with logical reasons for these strong moral reactions, a state Haidt and Hersh (2001) evocatively describe as "moral dumbfounding." Yet an inability to justify a reaction did not alter the primacy given to that emotion.

Other possibilities being explored for foundations include liberty, efficiency, ownership, and honesty to address a shortcoming of the original five foundations made salient in the American political context (Graham et al., 2013). As currently constituted, the five foundations model—and some of Haidt's popular work (Haidt, 2012)—suggests that only political conservatives largely subscribe to the "binding" moral foundations of loyalty, hierarchy, and purity, while political liberals place value in care and fairness (Graham et al., 2011; Van Leeuwen & Park, 2009). This trend has been reported in thirteen different countries across the globe, including samples from the United States, Africa, Latin America, Europe, and the Middle East (Graham et al., 2011; Van Leeuen & Park, 2009). Popular opinion leaders have started to gravitate toward this schematic as it purports to explain entrenched political differences between the parties, but this scientific work is currently still early in its development.

One encouraging potential additional foundation comes from Janoff-Bulman and Carnes (2013), who suggest that there may be multiple ways to bind groups. Rather than simply having American conservatives as the only ones holding communal foundations for morality, they suggest that the communal motivation for liberals might be based on a concern with social justice, thus evidencing a *different* binding foundation not found in the original literature. They attempt to rectify this by partially recasting and expanding the five foundations into pre- and proscriptive moral motives that vary along intrapersonal, interpersonal, and intergroup context, including, importantly, two communal orientations: a social order *and* a social justice motivation. While conservatives uphold a social order moral motivation, liberals possess greater social justice motivations. The inclusion and framing of social justice as a binding moral foundation reveals that liberals possess group-oriented moral foundations as well as conservatives. Thus, liberals are not without emotional reactions to issues that violate the moral order, the ways conservatives feel disgust at things that violate perceived societal standards of purity; they just have a different set of triggers for emotions related to injustice and inequity.

Finally, we turn to a distinct approach for anchoring societal morality, this one focusing on the potential array of types of human relationships, offering four basic social bonds that respectively foster certain types of expectations (Fiske 1992; Fiske and Haslam 2005). These Relationship

Regulation (RR) models offer testable hypotheses about what kinds of relationships will trigger specific sorts of moral judgments and evaluations (Rai & Fiske, 2011). Briefly, Fiske and colleagues posit that human relationships take at least one of the following forms: (a) hierarchy (authority ranking), (b) unity (communal sharing), (c) equality (matching), and (d) proportionality (market pricing). People who are oriented toward others in a unity framework, often around peer groups, for example, will expect certain sorts of actions from the other members of the groups, and be morally offended if such expectations are violated in some way (Fiske & Rai, 2015). Actual relationships, as opposed to these ideal types, may in practice be combinations of the four, but for analytical purposes, knowing that people are operating under perhaps a market framework (as in a capitalistic setting), we can better grasp the moral logic that will be in play. Asking for a favor from a child (hierarchy) is different than asking for a favor from a cell phone salesman.

These scholars argue that primitive human societies were oriented around unity and authority ranking, while modern societies tend to prioritize equality and market logics. There is empirical support for this approach (Haslam & Fiske, 1999), though the field is only at its earliest stages linking this all to morality (Sunar, 2009). Emotions play an important role here, as they are understood as reactions to violations of one's cultural moral order (e.g., anger and disgust) or as vital aspects upholding relationships (e.g., love). Fiske (2004) speculates that market pricing relationships garner the strongest emotional reactions linked to a focus on extrinsic consequences of an action (Fiske, 2004), though classic sociological theorizing would suggest that primitive societal forms were based on strong emotional content, more so than modern bureaucratic society.

CULTURE AND MORAL EMOTIONS

Given our general argument that measuring emotion tells us a great deal about a society's organization, we turn now to a brief engagement with the research on moral emotions and culture. Moral emotions, we hope to demonstrate, tell us a good deal not only about how individuals respond to their circumstances and actions, but taken collectively, tell us about the society in which they live. Moral emotions link moral standards to moral behavior and range from positive to negative: from disgust and shame to gratitude and elevation (Haidt, 2003; Tangney et al., 2007; Turner & Stets, 2006). Turner & Stets (2006) and Haidt (2003) divide moral emotions into four general categories: (a) the self-critical emotions of shame, guilt, and embarrassment (we term these *self-sanctioning* in subsequent chapters), (b) the other-critical emotions of contempt, anger, and disgust (we call these *other-sanctioning*), (c) the other-suffering emotions related to empathy, sympathy, and compassion (*compassionate emotions* in our terminology), and (d) the other-praising emotions of gratitude and elevation (we simplify this to *praising emotions*). Moral expressions related to anger and disgust generally have the highest rate of consistent recognition across societies, even coded into our neuroanatomy (Turner & Stets, 2006). There are additional emotions in play, of course; Turner and Stets (2006) suggest things like pride, awe, vengeance, grief (among others) that exist as cross-culturally recognized emotions (Ekman, 1994; Ekman & Friesen, 1971; Haidt & Keltner, 1999).

Although societies appear to largely draw on and use these particular moral emotions, the nuance of these emotional experiences and meanings varies considerably cross-culturally. The East/West distinction, discussed earlier, appears to have some validity as to the types of guilt and shame members report experiencing. Japanese respondents, for instance, label an emotion for a particular form of guilt arising from feeling as though one is not working diligently to achieve daily or long-term goals (De Vos, 1960). Mandarin differentiates between multiple forms of guilt and shame that do not translate easily into English (Bedford, 2004; Li, Wang, & Fischer, 2004). Many Eastern cultures do not distinguish between the sensations of shame, embarrassment, shyness, and modesty as Westerners do (Menon & Shweder, 1994; Shweder et al., 2008).

To exemplify the extent of this cultural variation, let us use the example of shame, which is one of the emotions with pronounced variation in meaning and form (Bedford, 2004; Haidt & Keltner, 1999; Li et al., 2004;

Shaver, Wu, & Schwartz, 1992). Li et al. (2004) report that the Chinese have at least 113 distinct shame concepts that can be categorized in broad strokes as feelings associated with losing face (i.e., concerns with losing personal integrity and others' idea that one is a competent and good person), guilt, disgrace, embarrassment, and condemnation of others' shamelessness. For those in Western cultures, shame is considered to generally be a negative emotional state, similar to anguish, yet for those in Eastern countries, like Japan, shame may take on more constructive state (Romney, Moore, & Rusch 1997). Shame, tied into failing of the entire self (Tugendhat, 1993), is viewed as socially beneficial in certain Eastern cultures (Menon & Shweder's (1994). Shweder (2008) suggests that raw translations lose much of the underlying emotional meaning within a culture, making cross-cultural comparisons particularly difficult.

CONCLUSION

Most of these presented theories were developed in line with empirical measures that tested, refined, and ultimately validated these approaches; hence, they are the current standards for the field. Despite this volume of work about cultural shaping of morality, less work has engaged the sorts of structural approaches we will be advocating. There is some work on social class and moral functioning that we will discuss next chapter, evidence that people higher in a culture's socioeconomic hierarchy have different reactions from those lower (e.g., Haidt et al., 1993; Piff et al., 2012).

   We agree with those who suggest these moral foundations—whether the CAD, moral foundations theory, RR models, the Modernization thesis, or Schwartz's discussion of values—collectively tap into what Vaisey (2009) suggests are deeply internalized, often unconscious moral schema, roughly what Abend (2014) suggests is a society's "moral background." This idea of dual-process modeling links these macro patterns into individual emotional experience, leading people to behave in ways that feel right (or feel negative emotions when they violate cultural standards) without always being consciously aware of the culture's influence, and often being poor at articulating why they behaved the way they did. We turn now toward explicating some ways that this implicit aspect of the self, including our emotional responses, allows us to measure things about the wider society that shapes individual nonconscious experience, the ideals and prohibitions that members of shared communities internalize as "properly" socialized individuals.

5

Morality as a Measure of Society

Studying a society's moral codes is fundamentally important for understanding the nature of that society. All societies have levels of stratification, inequality, and draw distinctions between social groups. But to understand a nation-state, we must also have a grasp of the guiding principles passed from generation to generation, and the values and preferences individuals grapple with in their daily interactions and across the life course. Whether people in any society actually behave in line with these values is a secondary concern; families, organizations, and nations define themselves by those priorities they find sacred and inviolable.

As we have suggested, prioritizing of the moral fabric that exists between and within individuals was once a central concern for social thinkers. Its importance waned alongside the quantification of sociology, criticism of totalizing conceptualizations of social structure, increasing interest in rational decisions and cognitive processes, and, in American sociology at

least, the understandable attempts to comprehend social movements bat-
tling against the entrenched social, political, and economic inequities of
the wider society. The notion that people in a nation shared some fundamental substrate of meaning, emotion, and moral understanding became
passé, even a bit naïve. Such a view seemed to crassly paper over inequalities and inequities that were quite prevalent in American society, if not yet
the focus of social movements and political attention.

JUSTIFICATION FOR OUR CATEGORIZATIONS

The rebirth of scientific interest in morality largely emerged within psychology and neuroscience, perhaps because these person-focused fields
became understandably engaged with the forces that influenced day-to-
day life and interaction. We have no definitive proof of this, but perhaps
the closer one gets to on-the-ground study of human behavior, the more
important dated sociological terms like "norms" and "values" becomes,
shorn of the associations with some idea of a single, unified, widely-
accepted culture. Scholars attempting to study society necessarily must
grapple with the observation that people from different categories—
gender, social class, ethnicity—do not share identical moral outlooks, priorities or life goals. This diversity from a macro perspective contributed
to the shrinking of the study of morality at the macro level, even as those
focusing on micro processes could not escape the evident importance of
these issues.

   As a result, any card-carrying sociologist today would be skeptical of
attempts to totalize groups or societies into any sort of unified, single
entity. Saying "all" members of any group are similar in some basic fashion is bad science, especially when the group is as large as a nation-state.
And yet colloquial understandings of what "Russians" or "Canadians" are
like abound, stereotypes fueling humor and misunderstandings, expectations and interactions. No matter how diverse Americans are, people
know what sort of behaviors are "American" around the world, even if the
majority of Americans do not act precisely in that manner; ditto for other

groupings of people. The same is true for things like gender, where stereotypical conceptions of men and women exist as references for people across the world; the content of those differences are not identical, but the fact of gender difference as an organizing principle of society seems rather widespread (Ridgeway, 2009). "Morality is constructed in and through social interaction, and the analysis of morality has to focus, accordingly, on the intricacies of everyday discourse" (Bergmann, 1998).

STUDYING SOCIETIES THROUGH SOCIAL PSYCHOLOGY

Human beings like to categorize things, especially people (Tajfel & Turner, 1978). This is ubiquitous, and necessary. It helps us predict, organize, and make sense of complicated social worlds. The tricky part, then, for scientists is to find the right balance of grouping social units into meaningful categories that reflect the actual world as it is while not going too far into totalizing or essentializing groups. Although parents in Western nations often teach their children they are unique, we cannot have a science of society if every person if fully unique, like nobody else. Then categories ("plumber", "Hispanic") would have no meaning at all. Yet we self-evidently do not live in a world where people are mindless automatons, blindly following societal rules and norms, with no self-reflection and no change. People are partly distinct while also sharing commonalities with others in their groups (Kluckhohn, Murray, and Schneider, 1953).

The key for handling this is baked into modern social science. We study worlds of probability, not certainty. Variation is at the core of our theoretical and empirical approaches to studying the world. We think probabilistically about the world, not deterministically like much of the natural sciences, where gravity or neutrons or circulatory systems all have constant ways they operate in set environments. That means we rarely make overly broad claims like "Gender causes . . . " or "All rich people do X . . .." Rather, we think that certain factors increase or decrease the probability that any person, group, institution, or nation will act in a certain fashion.

Many members in those categories will be different than the average, but often this variation occurs in predictable ways around some central tendency. So, not all rich people may demonstrate less empathy (Kraus et al., 2010), but on average they exhibit much less empathy than the poor. This may or may not be morally defensible, but as decades of psychological research demonstrates, it is the way the human mind categorizes and processes information (Blair & Banaji, 1996; Brewer & Lui, 1989; Ridgeway, 2011; Ridgeway & Correll, 2004; Stangor, Lynch, Duan, & Glass, 1992).

The rest of the book uses a probabilistic understanding to rectify some of the most obvious critiques of treating whole nations as single entities. We will be discussing countries (specifically the United States, Canada, Japan, China, and Germany) as discrete units, making claims about how our novel measure of moral emotions tells us something about their cultures and social structures. This may read as if we are saying all members of each country are alike in some fundamental way, that all Japanese experience the world in the same way, or that all Germans have the same emotional reactions to the world. This is not our claim, in two important ways that we shall clarify. Instead, our claims are based on the probabilistic understanding of statistical methods that underlies our method, and quantitative social science more broadly.

First, our measurement technique using *Interact*, a database gathered under the auspices of Affect Control theory (discussed in detail Chapter 7), explicitly builds the variation within each country into the algorithms for each nation that organize the raw data we employ. When we start making claims about American or Canadian affective language and meaning, for instance, we are not saying that all people agree on the overall feeling of every word in their culture, but that there are average affective meanings with identifiable patterns in how people vary around these averages. We will not be claiming that all Canadians are the same, but that people who speak Canadian English, on average, have broadly shared understandings of what the vocabulary in their language represents, on quantifiable dimensions that we will spell out later on. And when we say "language" what we mean is the vocabulary of the culture—the words that mark important cultural categories of meaning. While some people in a society see a word like "teacher" as extremely positive while others see it as only mildly positive, we can empirically measure this range of opinion about the words in a language. This does not mean every person fully agrees, but that feelings surrounding words are distributed in measurable ways.

This consensus in what it means to feel empathy, to hug another, to be a mother, and the like, demonstrates the common sources of meaning that we draw on every day to guide our interactions with others and our understandings of our social world. Without this common core of information, we would be left to create every bit of meaning afresh throughout our lives. Instead, these cultural sources of affective meaning serve as the font of collective meaning that help get our social lives up and off the ground. To grease the skids of interaction, as it were. There is a reason why interactions between two people from different cultures can be so tricky, if not rife with misunderstandings: in this instance the actors are not beginning with a shared cultural meaning and must try to predict each other's perspectives without using the cultural short-hand to which we are all accustomed, those things we take for granted. Understanding other people can be difficult enough without being able to intuitively understand the assumptions baked into the language, gestures, and bodily movements you are using to communicate.

Second, our use of *Interact* simulations, which we will explain in greater detail in Chapters 7 and 8, generates the probability that certain feelings will be reported in each society, not that each emotion is necessarily going to occur in each given situation. In the real world, people differ in their responses to their encounters, and even the same person might act or respond differentially over time. A student coming into a professor's office might trigger feelings of empathy, boredom, or annoyance on the part of the faculty member (so we are told); it depends on a variety of factors, and the same student may possess and motivate different feelings at different times. However, we consider there to be a degree of commonality to our social scripts of behavior so that people to have some predictability in response. Similarly, we can measure the ways that people act similarly or differently in distinct situations. If we know a student is coming in to whine about a grade, this is different than a student coming to inquire about the grade. In each culture, presuppositions and affective content contained in the roles (professor, student) and the action (complain, inquire), suggest different—but probabilistically predictable—potential responses. This is the sort of data we will present in Chapter 9. The affective meanings of "teacher" and "student" may diverge between the United States and, say, China. We can measure this through the methods we detail in the second half of the book.

TOWARD A THEORY OF INEQUALITY, CULTURE, AND EMOTION

In this chapter, we build on the macro-to-micro links we have discussed to this point to theorize how being a member of a particular society tells us something about the moral worlds of "typical" people in that society. We will defend the proposition that a national "habitus" (Elias, 1996) or "background" (Abend, 2014) can be measured through our *INTERACT* data as a way of quantifying the collective understanding and sentiments held by members of a society. That is, people in America broadly understand what it means to be a "mother", or how to feel about a variety of behaviors (e.g., "to hit," "to hug." "to work"). We explain how this understanding captures a sense of national identity that we can use to compare countries with one another. To be a member of a society (or any group, but we are focused here on this large grouping of people) is to internalize the meanings, emotions, and expectations of that group. Perhaps you do not agree with our family or workplace or religious organization on each and every point, but you know how a typical member would feel/believe/expect, and how far you personally might be from that ideal type.

We have suggested to this point that individual emotions are a marker of these global cultural processes, that we do not just learn abstract linguistic codes as members of a society, but semantic content that reaches us at an emotional, often unconscious level. Not all emotions are evidence of moral outlooks, but some emotions are more prototypically moral. We will return to the typology of moral emotions that is used in both psychology (Haidt, 2003) and sociology (Stets & Turner, 2006), as a theoretical indicator of how individuals fit themselves into societal moral codes.

To reiterate, at first blush this might seem to be a strictly Durkheimian way of suggesting morality as central to society, an unnecessarily unifying vision of society. Critiques of the Durkheimian vision include John Levi Martin's (2011) suggestion that a Durkheimian vision of society is intrinsically arbitrary, that whatever the organizing principles of a society are, they will apply to individuals from the "top down." In this view, if you accept Durkheim's notion of society being the organizing force behind individual experience, this opens the possibility that any plausible organization of society will filter down to its members. We are making a stronger claim. We are suggesting that the organization of a society is far from irrelevant for individual perception; we suggest that economic inequality is baked into the emotional valences members of a society internalize in the form of language.

For example, as discussed last chapter, there is evidence for differences in the moral systems of East/West cultures (Bedford, 2004), with a Judeo-Christian, Western tradition of drawing boundaries around individual selves permitting freedom and responsibility onto individuals, versus a Confucian tradition focusing on life inherited from ancestors and more anchored within one's family and social groups (Bedford & Hwang, 2003). The conclusion that Easterners and Westerners are fundamentally different appears to be a bit overstated, but these patterns in perception do signal differential worldviews plausibly contributing to the differential development of these cultural traditions even while an overall economic development pattern may exist (e.g., Inglehart & Baker, 2000).

The currently popular term for this sort of embodied commonality in sociology revolves around the notion of habitus, the internalized sets of tastes and dispositions popularized in the work of Bourdieu. In his discussion of the German habitus, for example, Elias (1996) suggests that this "second nature" develops within members of a nation, and how to understand a society you need to go well beyond its laws and official documents. In the German case, he explains how historical developments shaped a national culture that involved striving for perfection, and led to a certain pattern of citizen:

> The anchoring of an autocratic form of rule in the habitus of individual people kept on creating a strong desire for a social structure corresponding to this personality structure: that is, for a stable hierarchy of dominance and subordination, expressed not least in strictly formalized rituals of social distance . . . It drew precise boundaries around the scope for decision-making of each individual, or, in other words, offered the individual person a firm foothold in making his or her own decisions by allocating restricted areas of responsibility." (Elias, 1996, p. 69)

He contrasts this with an English focus on pride and stability, and argues that France's relatively continuous "even" development meant that society did not have to grapple with its essential nature in the same way as Germany:

> The fact that national developments produce not only specific social institutions but also specific national beliefs, doctrines, patterns of conscience and ideals which become part of the personality of individuals contributed considerably to the fact that, in Germany as elsewhere, specific properties of a common tradition of beliefs and behavior could be continued over the generations – so long as the nation as a whole or its ruling groups did not suffer drastic defeats which forced a reorientation of the collective self-image and, with it, of the collective beliefs, moral ideals, and goals. When a nation such as Germany, with a traditional inclination to an autocratic pattern of conscience and a we-ideal which subjected the future to a dream image of a greater past, became caught up, during a national crisis, in a dynamic of escalation in which, first of all, the ruling power elites and later wider social circles drove each other through mutual reinforcement to a radicalization of behavior and beliefs and a progressive blocking of reality-perceptions, then there was an

acute danger that the traditional autocratic traits would intensify into tyrannical harshness and that the fantasy-dominance, although previously moderate, would grow stronger and stronger. (p. 344)

Habitus, then, is one shorthand that can be linked to national culture (Pickel, 2005). While we know there is a lot of variation among members of any group, our statistics largely operate on the same assumption that our schematic mental processes use; finding an average representative of any "type" becomes our cognitive and emotional anchor for making sense of the world and placing things into categories. Ignatow (2009) suggests that the concept of habitus offers a theoretical foundation for a sociological analysis of morality, properly linked to cognition and the body. Our discussion does not hue to a strict engagement with this concept, ubiquitous within the sociology of culture, but the basic notion that an implicit, preconscious set of understandings of the world is communicated to members of a society dovetails well with our eventual treatment of language as a core place to measure this shared set of cognitive and emotional meaning.

There are other social science measures of culture, discussed in the previous chapter (see also Vaisey & Miles, 2014; Miles & Vaisey, 2015 for some suggestions and comparisons). Work employing the Schwartz measure of values, for example, captures a different sense of national priorities that are felt as much as they are consciously chosen (e.g., Longest et al., 2013; Schwartz, 2006). Within the range of possible values, different societies have different relative priorities, and these map onto a variety of societal level behaviors (Hitlin & Piliavin, 2004), including elements of charitable giving, political decisions, and other outcomes that represent the behavior of nation-states. Recent work drawing on Haidt's Moral Foundations theory also has the potential of capturing the implicit understandings (Vaisey, 2009) people develop as members of shared cultures, with different conglomerations of people holding different bases for their moral codes (see the last chapter). These traditions offer other ways of comparing what it means to members of a culture to share understandings, empirically measurable ways of finding out what societal members find important, and even non-negotiable.

LANGUAGE AS A SOCIETAL INDICATOR

Prior to this work on values, moral foundations, and broader cultural codes, lies language. Language, we will now argue, is a prime social object that we can use to study national culture/habitus/shared meaning, this general societal substrate that we are pointing to as existing both outside of its members—a body of implicit knowledge that new members are socialized into, especially if they develop their first language in that society—and as the shaping of the fundamental individual senses of right and wrong, meaning and understanding and expectations for our social worlds. Languages are shared among people, exist long before we are socialized into a community, and instantiate the common understandings, feelings, emotions, and perceptions of a culture. We learn language at a primal level, at least our initial language, and the words and concepts we are provided with fundamentally shape the world as we know it (e.g., Mead, 1934). "These contrasts between the cultures in economy, ecology, and premises about nature have derivatives, three thousand years later, in how language is used to describe humans and their emotions" (Kagan, 2007, p. 131).

Recent evidence suggests that this is fundamentally an emotional process; people make less emotional moral judgments drawing primarily on their cognitive systems when asked to solve moral dilemmas (like those discussed in Chapter 3) in their second language (Costa et al., 2014). When using one's primary language, people make more emotional decisions unwittingly shaped by unconscious – deeply socialized -- mental processes. People are more utilitarian—focused on rational costs and benefits—in their second languages due to the reduced emotional responses triggered by using that less familiar language. These more emotional responses shape moral decision making, suggesting that in learning our primary language we incorporate deep semantic understandings about the world, and thus fill in the content of our automatic mental systems with ways of being-in-the-world anchored in that language.

As we have been building to throughout this manuscript, we suggest that studying a society's most emotionally laden concepts, in this case moral emotions, constitute a novel and productive way to measure the shared implicit assumptions about the social world held by members of a society. Certainly not every member of that country feels exactly the same, but just as we can discuss the average weight of an American being higher than that of a Canadian, we can discuss the average ways that people in a society "feel" about the world. Moral emotions, a particularly influential subset of our emotional experience, are the place that we explore to understand this shared sense of the world.

MORAL EMOTIONS REFLECT THEIR SOCIETY

In Chapter 3, we began our discussion about emotions by focusing on how moral emotions fit into models of individual functioning. This was a precursor to this turn toward the importance of moral emotions for understanding society. Evidence suggests that human groups with more effective emotional interchange were more likely to be evolutionarily successful through building up group solidarities at the collective level (Turner, 2015). People do not simply make rational decisions to band together, effective groups have a sense of cohesion held together by emotional bonds (Durkheim, 1915; Lawler & Thye, 2006; Lawler, Thye, & Yoon, 2008, 2009; Putnam, 2000).

There are vast cultural differences in this general process, some suggest that Western patterns in the development of emotions move away from this sense of relationship with others toward a priority in focusing on one's own experiences (Kagan, 2007). Thus, the possible array of human emotions is selected based on early cultural socialization such that competent adults interpret emotional signals in line with culturally learned scripts that channel how and when such emotional signals operate. If a culture is organized around the primacy of the group, the family, or the self, those understandings will broadly suffuse into its members, and become priorities for socializing future generations.

Broadly, emotions provide information about how people are achieving personal goals (Fiske, 2011). "Through their emotions, people comment, to themselves if not to others, on what the interaction that is occurring says about themselves in a given scene, and they also comment on the overall stories that they are constructing as they shape a path through life" (Katz 1999, p. 324). Emotions signal how we are fitting into situations, and how well our life goals are being reached (Sayer, 2011). This is also the point of view taken by affect control theorists: emotions signal how properly an interaction is unfolding and how well we are able to have others see us, as we would like to be seen (Heise, 2007).

There is a great deal of variation in the expression of emotion around the world, but many have argued there to be a limited number of possible moral emotional systems: "there is a set of emotional states that form the bases for a limited number of universal moral categories that transcend time and locality" (Kagan, 1994 [1984], pp. 118–119). We can have a range of emotions in our daily lives, but moral emotions are refined according to specific cultural frameworks that direct the goals, judgments, and motivations people in a society define as of the utmost importance (Blasi, 1999). Moral judgment relies on emotional socialization (Prinz, 2007) and is tied into societal interests and welfare, or at least the concerns of others (Haidt, 2003b).

Moral emotions help us reveal our values and priorities to ourselves (Eisenberg, 2000), although often in ways that are difficult to articulate (Vaisey, 2009). "When a person is directly asked for his or her moral maxims, the answer will be at a rather abstract level, whereas moral emotions are evaluations of concretely realized, described, or imagined situations" (Montada, 1993, p. 301). Moral emotions help us distinguish "the cultural right from the cultural wrong" (Fiske, 2011, p. 43).

Moral emotions are the "teeth" for societal influence over individual behavior, powerful feelings like guilt, shame, approval, and so on (Turner, 2015). The self-conscious emotions seem to be oriented toward helping people fit into groups without triggering negative judgments from others (Haidt, 2003a). Many scholars (e.g., Turner & Stets, 2006) suggest that the absence of these emotions is linked with sociopathy. The very ability to emotionally clue into societal standards is what it means to be a competent, accepted member of a social group. Television shows and novels

demonstrate how people who are a bit distinct in their emotional processing are fodder for laughter or danger. We possess especially powerful emotional responses when core beliefs or values are threatened (Tetlock et al.,
2000). Moral emotions link moral standards to moral behavior (Tangney
et al., 2007), and range from positive to negative, from disgust (e.g., Haidt
et al., 1993) and shame (e.g., Scheff 1997, 2000) to gratitude and elevation
(Algoe & Haidt, 2009).

Given the large but limited array of potential emotions, moral and
non-moral, we need some organizing framework with which to be able
to explore societal variation. Fortunately, leading psychological and sociological scholars of moral emotions appear to have unwittingly developed largely consonant frameworks for conceptualizing moral emotions.
We categorize moral emotions according to the work of Haidt (2003a)
and Turner and Stets (2006): (a) self-sanctioning (e.g., feeling guilt,
shame, remorseful, humiliated, embarrassment, regret, or mortifica-
tion), (b) other-sanctioning (e.g., feeling outraged, dissatisfied, shocked,
contemptuous, dismayed, or disgusted), (c) compassionate (e.g., feeling
moved by others doings or compassionate), and (d) praising (i.e., feeling thrilled, awe-struck, overjoyed, reverent, ecstatic, or joyful). These
broad categories signal the sorts of self- or other-related feelings we garner
through interaction (real or imagined) that signal how well or poorly we
are living up to valued societal standards. We now discuss each category in
a little bit more detail (see the original papers for an expanded discussion).

SELF-SANCTIONING MORAL EMOTIONS

In the prototypical moral emotions of guilt and shame (Scheff, 1988),
powerful feelings of self-judgment is internalized through cultural understandings of what proper behavior is to be in various situations. Shame is
a result of the threat to social bonds (Scheff, 2000), a rupture in the important, predictable relationships in a person's life. An important aspect of
both shame and guilt is that they are emotions that do not necessarily need
to be actively triggered to have important social effects. The possibility of

feeling guilt or shame can be enough to motivate prosocial (as in, approved by one's society) behavior; this possibility of such emotions is enough of a threat to motivate people to behave in line with community standards (Bothckovar & Tittle, 2008). The anticipation of these painful emotions is a predictor of inhibiting predilections to engage in non-normative, even criminal behavior (e.g., Paternoster & Simpson, 1996). Shame was, perhaps, the key evolutionary emotion—developed at first through punitive groups keeping tribal members in line—that lead to the collective development of an internalized conscience (Boehm, 2012).

In Western models of emotion, guilt, not shame, is seen as reparative to relationships (Wong & Tsai, 2007). Western societies base moral guidance first from the individual, meaning that guilt—and its focus on personal responsibility—is seen as a stronger foundation for a moral system (Bedford & Hwang, 2003). The key to shame is that it arises because people are essentially social beings, and serves as a "moral gyroscope" signaling trouble in relationships and when people have failed to live up to their own or others' standards (Scheff, 2003). Shame is more effective in cultures where the group is paramount (Bedford & Hwang 2003), and the perception of threats of shame can inhibit people in such cultures, like Japan, from violating workplace rules (Kobayashi et al., 2001). In such places, the self is seen as less fixed, and thus feeling bad about the self is normal and expected, since it aids in potential self-improvement (Wong & Tsai, 2007). In some societies, small doses of shame might be triggered even by being in the presence of a social superior (Haidt, 2003a). The closeness of a relationship matters, with closer relationships triggering more intense feelings of shame (Tang et al., 2008).

Eisenberg (2000) suggests that guilt is a more moral emotion than shame, as one can feel shame for all sorts of non-moral transgressions (socially inappropriate behavior). Guilt, in this view, motivates restitution for the violation. Some suggest guilt is internally focused, while shame is focused on others' standards (Ahmed et al., 2001), although some researchers have trouble finding empirical distinctions between the concepts (e.g., Bothckovar & Tittle, 2008).

Significant experiences of shame can lead to a downward spiral or continuing people on maladaptive life paths (Giordano et al., 2007). Some criminologists suggest a distinction between types of shame (e.g., Ahmed et al., 2001; Braithwaite, 1989): stigmatizing vs. reintegrative. The second sort of shame channels the feeling into bringing a violator back into the community. In the right circumstances, shame may motivate later prosocial behavior through building commitment to group values and goals (de Hooge et al., 2008).

Different societies draw different boundaries around these largely universal emotions. A classic study by Menon and Shweder (1994) finds that people from India group happiness and shame together, against anger, a contrast with the American grouping of anger/shame versus happiness. This suggests that shame, in that context, can be socially constructive and thus is seen as a more beneficial emotion. Shweder (2003) argues that a full understanding of shame needs the richness that anthropological engagement with a society can provide. We will not be able to afford such an in-depth analysis here. Instead, in Chapter 8 we will consider how using our affective measure of emotion allows us at least a starting point to be able to empirically compare societies' affective understanding of these moral emotions.

OTHER-SANCTIONING MORAL EMOTIONS

Haidt (2003a) suggests that evolutionary pressures not only channeled human beings toward reciprocal altruism, but necessitated a motivation toward others who pose danger or try to cheat them. The other-sanctioning emotions provide this fuel, directing negative emotions toward others who violate societal or group moral codes (Turner & Stets, 2006). This is discussed as the "hostility triad" (Izard, 2013).

The previously discussed CAD triad (Rozin et al., 1999) suggests that these three types of aversive emotions occur as a result of violations of the three moral codes posited in Shweder's (1990) typology; anger occurs when the principle of autonomy is perceived to have been violated, contempt stems from community violations, and disgust is linked to the notion of divinity and sacredness. These later disgust reactions may draw on a primitive rejection response (Chapman & Anderson, 2013). Disgust serves to increase the severity of moral judgments (Schnall et al., 2008). Early work on this topic grouped disgust and contempt together (Ekman & Friesen, 1975), although they eventually shifted disgust into being a "basic" emotion given its universality and distinction from anger (Ekman & Friesen, 1986). Contempt involves a sense of moral superiority (Izard, 2013). Haidt (2003) quotes Aristotle to link a sense of anger as a moral emotion with a sense of one's honor being violated, and can be triggered on one's own behalf, or on the part of one's friends, community, or society. It can translate into motivation for extreme moral feelings like revenge (Nisbett & Cohen, 1996).

COMPASSIONATE MORAL EMOTIONS

The compassionate emotions (empathy, sympathy) are aspects of role-taking whereby we attempt to determine what others are feeling (Turner & Stets, 2006), a fairly important process for social interaction. We discussed earlier how the human capacity for this was considered central for Adam Smith's theorizing about how the free markets would work and how a capitalist system without this set of emotions would be, in his view, untenable. Lacking in the ability to take this perspective seems to make it hard for individuals with conditions like autism to act in morally appropriate ways (McGeer, 2008).

There is some evidence for empathy being a disposition, that some people carry more empathy within their moral processing (Eisenberg, 2000). Empathy is aroused most strongly by familiar partners (De Waal, 2009), and is quite strongly linked to in-groups (Cikara & Fiske, 2011; Cikara et al., 2011). A line of research (see Batson et al., 2011 for a review) argues that empathy is motivational for altruistic behavior, roughly defined as being elicited by a concern for the perceived welfare of others. It is an umbrella term for feelings like sympathy, compassion, sorrow, concern, and related other-oriented emotions.

PRAISING MORAL EMOTIONS

This set of emotions has not been the focus of nearly as much social science research as the others, though the recent psychological turn toward "positive psychology" (Seligman, & Csikszentmihalyi, 2014) is generating more focus on these apparently beneficial emotions. A wealth of recent studies on happiness has seemingly taken over psychological research, and it has spread into sociology as a major factor to be explored at the cultural level. At a theoretical level, we can parse basic positive feelings (happiness, what animals can feel) from distinct moral emotions that humans develop, things like elevation, gratitude and admiration (Algoe & Haidt, 2009). However, the positive reactions to the world, happiness and these higher order feelings, all represent reactions to events based on cultural presuppositions and expectations that we develop.

These emotions encourage pro-social behavior to broader audiences than the compassionate emotions (Turner & Stets, 2006). A small amount of work on gratitude (summarized in McCullough et al., 2001) suggests that it acts as a signal for recognizing when one has benefitted from another's moral action, it motivates people to be prosocial in return or to others, and it provides encouragement for ongoing prosocial behaviors. Evidence suggests that feeling gratitude is pleasant and distinct from something like feeling indebted (Tangney et al., 2007), often experienced as a negative obligation.

These broad categories of moral emotion will be our indicator of societal moral codes as experienced by individuals. Given their universal nature, at this level of abstraction, we can compare people from different countries as to how and when they experience such emotions. As we will develop in the next chapter, our evidence is consistent with an even stronger claim, namely that the level of economic inequality in a country is "baked in" to its cultural language and the social interactions that people expect, experience, and remember.

The pieces are in place for us to articulate our broader theory linking macro society to individual level experiences of emotion. We develop that next chapter, before turning to our empirical example. To reiterate, we are not able to fully prove that our theory is correct, but we present extensively gathered data that support the contentions we weave together in the next chapter.

6

The Theory of Inequality
and Moral Emotions

nequality may be the central thread of the field of sociology, if there is
a single concept holding our disparate group of scholars together. We
do not share a method, a core theoretical perspective, or even necessarily any presuppositions about how the world works beyond a shared
acceptance that the "social" is important. As we discussed in Chapter 2,
there is a good deal of social science research on inequality, most of which
on the broad topic of stratification within society, what people have what
resources and power, what the stratification hierarchy looks like, and
who holds those positions. While much of this work focuses on where
people are within a system and how that influences social psychological
outcomes, less work has explored variation in the nature of the unequal
systems, themselves.

When we shift focus to our area of expertise, social psychology, we find
an interesting lack of research on the social psychological consequences of
structural inequality. We know a lot about processes whereby individuals

and groups perpetuate stereotypes and understandings about people of different statuses, and we know a good deal about how one's position in the stratification system—their social class—influences thoughts, beliefs, tastes, and behaviors (see Burke, 2006; Delamater & Ward. 2013; and Lawler, Thye, & Yoon, 2015 for overviews of the field). However, there is a missing element whereby the effects of different sorts of inequality, or differing distributions of people within various stratification systems, have not been the focus of social psychological research. We know people in unequal systems experience the world differently, but systems can be unequal in different ways. Some societies have a relatively even distribution with the richest people being relatively close in wealth, income, and resources to the rest of society. Other societies have massive income inequalities whereby the richest few members possess wealth and money more than the entire bottom half of the population. OXFAM International reports that eight men have as much wealth as the poorest half (3.6 billion people) of those in the world. The link between structural position and outcome is well studied; the link between the forms of that structure, itself, is ripe for exploration.

In this chapter, we will bring together the strands of theory and research discussed to this point to introduce our theory on inequality, morality, and justice. The general argument is that in societies that have greater economic inequality, the sanctioning-based moral emotions of anger, contempt, disgust, shame will be more frequent and severe. Societies with lower levels of inequality will conversely normalize and exhibit the more positive and pro-social moral emotions of self-transcendence (compassion, praise, and empathy). Inequality thus begets negative moral emotions, while lesser inequality provides an atmosphere more replete with positive moral emotions.

BACKGROUND

Societally shared meanings, in our case represented by language (but touching on what is more broadly considered "culture") filters down into the emotional reactions held by individuals in that society. These meanings, we argue, affect and are affected by the amount of inequality in social structures present within that society. This is not just an individual-level claim, however. Similarly to how constructs such as values are available for study at both the individual and cultural level, so too is the symbolic material through which people develop a sense of understanding the world around them (as discussed in the previous chapter). This self or habitus or individual cultural predisposition signifies both the societal elements of shared understanding about expectations for self and others, as well as the individual emotional reactions people have when acting within those social frameworks.

In some ways, these frameworks can be instantiated within codified rules, most broadly a society's legal codes. These various emotional reactions to moral events not only guide everyday interaction, but also overlap with the criminal justice systems' reactions to those who offend societies' moral codes. The more negative the moral reaction in a society, the more likely events are to prompt feelings associated with condemning others, the more the criminal justice system will be similarly focused on sanctioning as opposed to rehabilitation. Thus, social inequality and societal attitudes underlying the criminal justice system are inextricably linked by cultural moral codes. However, so much of human interaction happens within boundaries set up by these legal and justice systems that are not subject to formal monitoring or approval. Most of us interact every day with a sense of what is normal and valued in the situations we encounter. That implicit, often uncodified sense, is what we are attempting to capture with the forthcoming analyses.

This chapter walks through the logic of this theory in rather a reverse order, drawing together the ideas set forth in the previous chapters. We will begin with reestablishing the link between culture and moral emotions, a fairly straightforward path trod by many other scholars. The symbolic material that comprises culture involves setting normative expectations for social life, and the violation of those expectations can meet with moral judgment and its accordant emotional reactions. Then we will turn to the slightly harder-to-link culture with societal inequality, tapping into a century and a half of sociological debate about the relative importance of the two prime forces underlying social organization: social structure and culture. For whatever reason, these debates have not filtered fully into social psychology as important explanatory forces shaping the behaviors and social beings we study.

We reiterate that we are establishing an argument that links these previous debates with current understandings of social psychology (largely through the dual-process systems that are in vogue in psychology and slowly gaining purchase in sociology) that is consistent with, not proven by, the data we will turn to in Chapters 7–9. Given the nature of the phenomena, and the difficulty in gathering the data we are exploiting for our purposes, we cannot conclusively demonstrate these concepts are linked in the ways we are advocating—but that is of course the role for subsequent research. The data are consistent with our argument, however, including in cases that provide evidence that our way of conceptualizing these relationships fits better than some other influential approaches. However, we are setting up the argument to motivate other researchers to attend to this issue with different data and methodologies in order to really explore—and likely refine—our way of walking from the form of social structure to individual psychology.

FROM MACRO CULTURE TO MICRO MORAL EMOTION

A great deal of sociological work (see Patterson, 2014 for one review/ critique) has discussed the links between societal culture and individual tastes, beliefs, and actions. Theories of culture have a lack of agreed upon definitions, but scholars tend to share the same general idea that culture involves a set of collectively shaped and maintained meanings that, in turn, become held by individuals. While efforts are being made to bridge the gap between cultural sociology and social psychology (Collett & Lizardo, 2014), we hope to contribute a stronger focus on the nature of the society that is differentially shaping the cultural attitudes and actions of its members via social stratification systems. We know that the rich often like different things (music, entertainment, food) than the poor (e.g., Bourdieu,

1984), and people of different economic classes tend to teach their children different values (Kohn & Schooler, 1983; Kasser et al., 2002). We have a good deal of understanding as to how and when these processes work, such that members of particular social classes end up being shaped in ways that can reproduce the original social structure.

However, while most modern societies are stratified such that some people have more resources, wealth, and power than others, the degree of stratification varies greatly across societies. This is becoming well chronicled in American political debates, with some candidates decrying the "1%", or positing that we are living in "two Americas". While not every politician or voter agrees with this conceptualization, the facts are pretty evident (Congressional Budget Office, 2011, 2016; Saez & Zucman, 2016): a tiny minority of the population has a lot more than the rest of us. This is similar to China, a rapidly expanding nation with a similar spread with a small minority holding a vastly disproportionate aspect of wealth. In Chapter 2, we discussed the Gini coefficient, one of the most prominent measures of this sort of national inequality. What seems to be missing in social psychology is some theorizing and analysis of how this sort of pattern of stratification might filter through society and shape the shared culture that we draw from and become socialized to be a part of.

Why would the greater amount of societal inequality influence this process? We begin with some speculation building off the approach taken by many great sociologists, including Durkheim and his largely erroneous treatment of early aboriginal tribes (Lukes, 1985) as the proper place for understanding the development of modern society. We know much more based on recent evolutionary science, although his insight that interaction channels emotional bonds (see also Collins, 2004) does fit with what we know of early human interaction groups.

EVOLUTION OF SOCIAL GROUPS

In proto-societies, small groups of interactants formed early bands for human social organization and developed the strong emotional ties

discussed by Durkheim and many of the early sociological theorists, tracing into modern work by Jonathan Turner. This highlights the powerful
emotional pulls within groups—a collective effervescence. Early on, moral
concerns in groups were about collective identity and survival of groups
and its members (Abulof, 2015). Given the possibility for face-to-face
interaction with everybody in the group, the lack of contact with other
groups, along with vast physical dangers and shorter lifespans, emotionality was at the center of these groups.

Early groups began with intense social control such that evolutionary
pressures may have favored group members that could control their antisocial impulses (Boehm, 2012). At first, this was due to a fear of punishment, but over time those members of social groups that could best
internalize the group's rules were the most likely to survive, within the
group and as groups competed with each other. Fear led to the development of a social conscience that in turn is a key organizing force for individuals interpreting and evaluating themselves and their social situations
(Hitlin, 2008). Based on evolutionary reasoning, recent neurological studies suggest that groups "inculcate" cultural rules within the brains of its
members (Berns et al., 2012), and such processing means that people do
not weigh costs and benefits of moral issues, but rather focus on "deon-
tic"—absolute—rules (Berns & Atran, 2012).

Durkheim's theorizing posited a societal shift from the sorts of interaction patterns found in small groups (emotional and based on face-to-
face contact and knowledge of other members), to a wider set of social
relations found within bigger groups, towns, cities, and so forth. A variety of early sociological thinkers focused on precisely this historical shift
from small groups to larger forms of social organization. Human history
goes back for quite a long time, and it is only a relatively small percentage of that history whereby humans have lived in cities and nation-states.
The vast majority of our biological capacities for action were most likely
shaped long before we started hanging out in locations whereby things
like laws and governments came into being as meaningful social forces.

In Durkheim's logic, as a group's social structures became more differ-
entiated and complicated, the capacity for more advanced and abstract

thought developed, the need for keeping track of more people than one might plausibly be familiar with necessitated more formal rules, proto-institutions, and other social structures that help organize social life. The idea here, insofar as individual thinking was motivated by external social reality, is that as reality became more complicated, thinking—and moral reasoning—became more complicated as well. But as much of recent psychological and sociological work on non-rational processes demonstrates (see Chapter 3), this advanced capacity for logic and reason did not supersede our species' emotional aspects, it simply evolved—quite literally, in the brain—on top of those core aspects. More recently, McCaffree (2015) suggests a version of this drawing on the idea that increasing societal complexity leads to more social distance between people, making them less likely to interact to form meaningful social bonds across social categories. This causes increased homophily (see McPherson & Smith-Lovin, 2001) contributing to greater dislike of unfamiliar "others."

This process of societal bonding is rooted in emotion. We are emotional beings. We have evolved a remarkable capacity to communicate socially, perceive times and places not directly in front of us, and to record our thoughts and interactions in ways that other animals have not. We have brains allowing us to make plans for the future, communicate instructions and information across vast distances, and be incredibly logical in our approach to science and the natural world. However, these capacities have evolved on top of our "lizard brains," as neurologists might colloquially call them, the emotional systems that have a larger influence on our actions than we believe. Cultural messages shape the very ways we learn to identify and experience emotion (Immordino-Yang et al., 2016).

The socialization of individual children, typically within the family unit, is the proximal area whereby the cultural beliefs, language, and meanings are inculcated into new members of society. This can happen through immigration to new areas, as well, but as we have discussed, our primary language becomes the most deeply rooted anchor for emotional and non-conscious experience of the world. The influential developmental scholar Vygotzky wrote about the internalization of social activity, an active challenge to the widely influential Piaget who argued that private speech plays a very important role for children's development. Piaget began with the child's internal thoughts, Vygotzky (properly, in our view) focused on how children use language—taught initially through family interaction—as a tool for solving problems. This echoes the sociologist (who more likely viewed himself as a philosopher) G. H. Mead, who concentrated on the uses of this external system of meaning for the individual. For both thinkers, the mind is a product of society, not a cause (Tappan, 1997). Minds do not develop on their own; through learning the rules of society and language, they are shaped at the most fundamental levels.

LANGUAGE

Language is a core force binding a community. Not that every single member of a community agrees on the semantic meaning of every single word; chocolate cake might be a treat for some, a health danger for others. But the referent is the same, and both parties of a communication can at a minimum understand what the other person means when he or she uses the term. A collective group or society cannot function without a shared language, and development of such a language can be a core aspect of instituting a new country—as in the case of Israel reviving and altering Hebrew from its use only in sacred texts into a modern way to communicate in daily life.

Another case study is found within Abulof's (2015) recent analysis of the history of French-Canadians within the wider country of Canada. The group of people who held onto French as their primary language did so for increasingly important reasons of self-definition: "Starting in 1867, French had developed from a distinguishing feature into a moral foundation for the community. . . Language became a mainstay of French-Canadian survival, a legitimating force for its identity and political aspirations" (Abulof, 2015, p. 95). In this context, a shared language distinct from the wider societal one became definitional for a people striving for recognition. More so than a flag, a mascot, or some legal document, the notion of having a validated language was a prime force in the enactment of this collective identification.

A less focused upon aspect of language (although a core dimension within affect control theory, the perspective we will discuss in the next chapter), is its evaluative content. Words have strict definitions, found in any dictionary of any language, formal properties and meanings attached to various sounds that we delimit as words. However, embedded into this set of meanings is an entire substrate of moral content, an affective sense of how things *should* be, how a proper member of this society feels, believes, and behaves. Words, ideas, beliefs, and so forth are good or bad, right or wrong ("bad" and "evil" technically are different, dropping a book on your toe is bad, not evil—see Kaminsky, 1984). Embedded in the structure of these words, grammar, and sense of the world around are the expectations and judgments we make for ourselves and others. This evaluation, as we have highlighted many times, is far from emotionally neutral.

> In general, the more evaluative content that filters into the encounter from values, ideologies, symbolic media, and normative systems, the greater is the potential for more intense emotional arousal. Individuals not only evaluate themselves as they role-take with specific others in front of them, but they also compare their and others' actions to the moral yardsticks of culture. As a result, categorization, framing, ritualizing, communicating, sensing justice, and feeling become not just run-of-the-mill expectations but, instead, are super-charged as moral expectations. Categorizing others and the situation correctly, framing the situation accurately, using the proper form of talk and body language, employing the appropriate rituals, calculating justice, and feeling as well as displaying the right emotions all take on greater moral significance when the evaluative content of values, ideologies, symbolic media, and norms is high. (Turner, 2007, p. 176)

The currently fashionable name for this unconscious, internalized sense of knowing how to act in a culture, as mentioned last chapter, is the term *habitus*. Hallett (2007) suggests the habitus is structured for people within the objective conditions they become socialized within. Bourdieu (1990) suggests habitus as a "scheme of perception," deeper than simply a cognitive understanding of the world, but a fully embodied engagement and understanding of how the world operates, and should operate. While social psychologists have a lot more to say about the processes whereby we develop internalized dispositions based on our social location, the main idea of "embodied social learning" (Elias, 1996) is as good a shorthand as any. For Elias, this is the micro-end of what often gets called "national character," those behaviors and feelings that are deeply patterned and associated with a nation-state.

Habitus arises within social systems, and is a property of those systems (Pickel, 2005). Elias explains at length what the German habitus is like, relying on a deep understanding of German history and culture in order to suggest how a particular social structure and history shapes Germans into developing impulses to action that have distinct national patterns as compared to members of other nations. Practitioners who rely on Bourdieu's work may not find our employment of national habitus, here, satisfactory, so we will limit its usage, approaching this issue more as the social psychologists that we are. We simply mirror the aspect of scholarship that holds it possible to consider a country's common culture as linked to individual dispositions; certainly not every (or any) member of a society shares an exactly similar interior life and set of dispositions, but there is a common core around which individual variation occurs. To believe otherwise, to maintain strongly that every person is somehow fully unique, is to render social science impossible.

Developmental psychologists parse this process out with more depth, but agree with the general point that children learn words that represent reality, categories and terms that explain the world and, eventually, motivate them to be "loyal to the moral requirements linked to their social categories: the conviction that the category is a real thing whose properties should be persevered and the sense of enhanced virtue that can accompany membership in the category." (Kagan, 2008, p. 305).

Moral functioning understood, therefore, as a "practical activity"— (what we might call 'moral activity'), is premeditated by a vernacular moral language that fundamentally shapes the ways in which persons think, feel, and act. This vernacular moral language, moreover, is shared by persons who share the same activities, who are engaged in similar social/moral practices. And it is these shared activities that enable persons to understand the predicatized forms of speech by means of which they communicate about moral issues with themselves and with each other B if they did not share these activities they would not share a common moral language. (Tappan, 1997, p. 85)

We draw on these overviews of a complicated and growing field, developmental psychology, to point out the general trend that learning societal competence as a child imbues that person with a host of deeply internalized understandings about the world, and there is a moral dimension to seeing that the world "should" be a certain way. This can be studied at the individual or the situational level. We can focus either on how singular people develop these senses of justice, propriety, and expectations for how others should act. Or, we can move to looking at particular situations, institutions, and types of groups where interaction occurs, studying the collective norms and expectations apart from the idiosyncratic aspects of the people who make up those situations. Both approaches incorporate an understanding of the moral dimension of social life, as understood by those within that context.

SOCIAL ORDER AND ACTION

This points to the alternative possible conception, where we can discuss this common understanding from the point of view of social order, and be less concerned with how it gets internalized so strongly into individuals. Social order involves taken-for-granted understandings that Goffman (1983) and Rawls (1989, 2010) consider as possessing moral force, the collective need for mutual intelligibility and for predictable interactions. Embedded in this are pressures toward reciprocity and cooperation pushing us toward prosocial ends, while at the same time values perpetuating "institutionalized inequalities" maintain the status quo (Rawls 2015). People like to be able to predict their environments, and feel quite distressed when the expected goes awry (e.g., Garfinkel, 1967). At an existential level, as a species we like people to behave in ways that "feel" right, and we get quite bothered when people do not act in line with local or societal norms. We expect people in fast food restaurants to get in line, wait their turn, and otherwise act appropriately for that situation. Violations of this, or with people driving, or in movie theaters, or in classrooms, etcetera, deeply bothers people. Such feelings of violation can be severe, signaling how important predictability can be. This goes for ongoing relationships, workplaces, or other arenas where people develop patterned understandings for each other's actions; violations of these norms can be experienced quite personally and severely, if not directly sanctioned.

Sociological theorists have some long-standing debates about the nature of action that we will largely elide, here. The short version is that most sociological theories are in implicit or explicit dialogue with the stereotypical economic model of the rational actor, the idea that people consciously appraise costs and benefits before they engage in activity. To be fair to modern thinking, even most current rational action theories are far from this simplistic, but the through-line of a great deal of arguments (often couched in pretentious jargon) involves the details around alternative models of action. Sociologists have long held that people are carriers of culture and do not necessarily act conventionally rationally, tracing back to Weber's notions of types of action into today's focus on implicit aspects of human behavior (e.g., Vaisey, 2009; Hitlin, 2008; Srivastava & Banaji, 2011).

We are not the best qualified guides through 60 or so years of these debates (see Joas & Knobl, 2009 for one overview); ultimately as social psychologists we do not find the study of the socially situated individual as problematic as many of our more macro-oriented colleagues. We come from the Meadian tradition within our field arguing individuals are shaped by their environments, and in turn reproduce them with occasional bouts of creativity that may change things. Within theoretical debates, we adopt a version of pragmatism echoing our discussion of Dewey in Chapter 3;

people act habitually to the worlds they have experienced, and when that routine breaks down for some reason, they are more likely to stop and reason and think through alternatives. As Hans Joas (personal communication) puts it, we do not have to spend energy thinking about how to open a door . . . until one day the door is locked. At that point, routine activity has broken down, and we need to explore possible solutions. Perhaps then we become more strictly logical, operating in the costs vs. benefits manner underlying many theories simplifications of human action.

This notion of the habit—linguistically related but conceptually distinct from the previous short discussion of habitus—is yet another term we are linking to this general sociological push toward non-conscious routine behavior channeled through beliefs about the world, personal experience, and embodied understandings of what "works" in daily interaction. This focus on the mechanisms of action (Gross, 2009) is one that social psychology has long been engaged in examining. Our own view is that it is worth understanding what is inside individuals' minds and brains (an important distinction), but for our purposes here, establishing a firm position on this point is a bit of a red herring. Whether you focus more on the interactional strategies people use (Goffman, 1959), the minute details about the behaviors people use to handle an existential need to create predictable order (Garfinkel, 1967), or the ways that situations create "affordances" (Martin, 2011) that are experienced phenomenologically as having a power to impel us toward feeling one behavior is more correct in the situation for another, we can establish our own position in line with these outside-the-person theoretical models of social action.

The messages embedded within language are part of the cultural world that exists before we learn that language, and can be studied apart from the individuals who carry those meanings inside. Our main point is that the cultural meanings embedded within language—empirically able to be studied on its own—is part of whatever the internal habitus/ideology/ implicit beliefs ingrained into its speakers. To be Japanese is, in part, to find the same understandings of nouns, verbs, and adjectives as the others in that society. We can certainly learn the objective meanings of those words, the denotative meaning of language as computers are increasingly able to do, but that is not the same thing as learning the language's connotations, especially if it is the first language one ever learns.

In sum, forces ranging from individual socialization to group expectations serve to impose an invisible social force on interaction to stay within accepted boundaries. This is not a novel observation—it lies at the root of social psychology across sociological and psychological treatments. We are building on the general insight (see Hitlin & Vaisey, 2013 for one overview) that these pressures, internal and external, conscious and implicit, contain within them a moral dimension, an almost primal sense that the world, society, group, and individuals *should* behave in certain ways, and to violate these expectations signals a threat to the achieved social order and a sign that something in the situation is not working correctly. We may not care if somebody chews with his mouth open (unless it is a religious feast, perhaps). We may look the other way if somebody wears an inappropriate outfit (unless it is a funeral or otherwise formal setting with strict moral codes). Minor violations of norms are one thing, but fundamental violations of basic expectations lead to severe reactions and potentially harsh judgment. We want our worlds to proceed as we expect, and feel strong reactions when situations surprise us, for good or for ill.

FROM INEQUALITY TO CULTURE (TO INEQUALITY)

The guiding issue for understanding how societies reproduce themselves through the transmission of language—and the morally embedded beliefs, presuppositions, and feelings embedded within—is the somewhat banal observation that the way a society is today will largely replicate itself (barring some sort of external shock, like a revolution) in the next generation. Certainly societies shift over time, but this process is somewhat predictable (see the discussion of Inglehart's work in Chapter 4) and rarely immediate. "Automatic, habitual, and implicit processes confer a default status on existing patterns of social organization, whether deliberately designed or not" (Marsden, 2015, p. 321). Certainly, things shift over time due to technological, cultural, and political changes; the constant disputes between generations over the years suggests children tend to push back against parental expectations, and the society they encounter is not identical to the one their parents grew up in. But on the whole, the values and priorities delimiting different societies are not reborn whole cloth every 25 years or so. Within a society there are pushes and pulls around various issues of prioritizing potential societal concerns (e.g., should more money be collected by the government, and to what ends?). There is a good amount of inertia, however, motivating some consistency in national character over time.

We are highlighting the ways that language contributes to this consistency across years and generations. Certainly other aspects of the social world aid this consistency, from political systems and norms to economic structures to institutional systems like education and legal structures. We want to dodge (at this stage) the chicken-and-egg question about whether a society's economic structure directly creates the embedded moral assumptions we have been discussing, or whether cultural patterns in thought and action contribute to social actors making choices that produce economic patterns. However it got there, the beliefs that people learn through socialization will shape their values (e.g., Kohn & Schooler, 1983), beliefs, and ideologies (see Hitlin & Pinkston, 2013 for a review). These beliefs, conscious and implicit, channel how people approach their lives and the possibilities provided for them in their societies, neighborhoods, social class location, and so forth. Again, they may not personally agree with the average meaning on every single dictionary term, but to be a competent member of a society means at least knowing the typical uses of terms, even if one rebels against them or tries to appropriate the meanings of those terms, as when members of stigmatized minatory groups usurp the meaning of epithets they encounter. Societies are represented within the languages their members learn, including implicit and emotional facets of the vocabulary contained within those languages. Becoming culturally proficient means developing an internal habitus or background situating one within the expectations transmitted by that larger cultural language.

To this point, our use of language as a vehicle for transmitting culture is far from novel, and we certainly gloss over many of the actual mechanisms of socialization and child development. We are adding to this general approach through focusing not only on the fact that language transmits culture, but that the sort of structural economic inequality in a society itself is a previously unexplored factor in this transmission. If children are brought up in a society with massive economic inequality, we are arguing, they are becoming proficient in a language that is more apt to utilize negative moral emotions when developing judgments and beliefs about how the world works and should be. Understandings of legal and political systems, of "proper" goals for education, marriage, or military use are baked into the very words and syntaxes that people within a culture learn and feel.

Indeed, the very act of navigating a society with a hierarchy involves morality (Sayer 2005). We judge others as superior or inferior through imputing moral essences as underlying their action (Katz, 1975); we see people in the world act in ways and make judgments about their characters as a result. We interpret others' behavior as a result of their character and often not just their position in life, something that happens more in Western societies where action is viewed more as a result of the individual. Kagan (2008) argues that egalitarian societies do not extend credit simply for being a member of a ranked category; a person must enact the actions and earn moral credit by behaving prosaically. Such societies are not supposed to extend credit simply for being a member of a particular ethnic or occupational group: "A priest, physician, and teacher are allowed to feel good at the end of the day because of their benevolent ministrations to others, and not because of their achieved status" (Kagan, 2008, 304).

We also know that the way you perceive the world is based in part on where you are within your social structure. Take, for example, prosocial and antisocial actions. Higher social class membership predicts increased unethical behavior (Piff et al., 2012). Lower class individuals demonstrate more trusting and charitable behaviors (Piff et al., 2010). This appears in part due to a lack of empathy experienced by upper class individuals (Côté, Piff, & Willer, 2013). Alternatively, the subjective belief that you are lower in socioeconomic status contributes to heightened aggressive responses (Greitemeyer & Sagiolglou, 2016).

Lower status people are thought to draw on these moral standards as ways to feel personally empowered within systems that systematically limit their opportunities: "Upholding high moral standards allows individuals in low social status position to gain empowerment by raising their status at the symbolic level, thereby attenuating their low social status (Bourdieu, 1984) . . . . social scientists find that groups in positions of dependency or with limited access to power value solidarity and interpersonal morality" (Lamont et al., 1996, p. 37). A society's moral boundaries maintain the positions of the powerful (Tronto, 1993), and being on the top of an economic system contributes to individuals protecting those resources, in part through drawing moral boundaries against others:

> I have argued that high levels of inequality will lead to processes of social closure, as well. To defend their privileged access to resources, dominant actors will draw a sharp boundary against outsiders while those excluded will depend on each other's solidarity and thus also limit their support networks to group members...inequality (and associated forms of closure) will lead, over time, to cultural differentiation because the privileged will add markers of cultural distinction to differentiate themselves from subordinate actors and to make boundary crossing more difficult." (Wimmer, 2013, p. 210).

Part of keeping those boundaries involves sanctioning others to keep "them" out and sanctioning ourselves to keep "us" in (i.e., to stop us from doing things that may threaten our current position or our ability to move up).

Not only do privileged children develop different orientations than poorer children, but we are arguing that *the amount of disparity between them becomes part and parcel of the shared culture internalized by both*. As a result, the kinds of moral emotions we expect to find within societies with more inequality are different than the amount found in more equal ones; we suspect there are differences both in the internalized experience and the kinds of situations that society sets forth circumscribing how and when its members will interact.

The forms of experience are shaped by structural inequality, captured in cultural products, filter down to the individual. More inequality, we argue, leads to more opportunities for interactions shaped by differences in status, more emotionally loaded categorizations, and thus more negatively-valenced moral content. In societies with a highly diversified stratification hierarchy—where the disparities between the top, middle, and bottom of the ladder are vast—there is the constant threat of losing one's place and falling below. And we know what "below" looks like because it is already there for us to see, even if just in media portrayals. The specter of loss is real. Those at the top fight to keep their place, while many others fight for a higher position and, when mobility is blocked, strive to at least secure their current position. This valorizes those above us while simultaneously raising awareness of threats from all other sides. When this occurs in societies with more perceived possibilities up and down the economic ladder, sanctioning oneself and others may be the more common moral emotional experience because sanctioning maintains hierarchy. Sanctioning oneself keeps you on the righteous path of advancement by noting our faults. Sanctioning others keeps them in-line and below—and in highly unequal societies most people are probably below.

Inequality can be highly divisive. As psychologist Susan Fiske argues (2011), individuals have what seems to be an innate drive to pay automatic attention to the things that divide us hierarchically, with income inequality being a prime example. When this occurs, she argues, we tend to envy those above us and scorn those below. No one is immune to these general processes of social comparison, but with increasing income inequality, these threats to self and others become ever more acute. When we envy others, we may long for their superior place in the hierarchy but feel bitter about it all the same, while scorning others entails either actively or passively denying the legitimacy of those beneath us. Both envy and scorn are associated with sanctioning moral emotions: envy with feelings of anger and shame, and scorn with disgust and disdain. Shame, in particular, becomes more intense when experienced as a result of the judgments of those with more social distance (Tang et al., 2008). Contempt and disdain may arise from breaking community norms, such as disobeying the hierarchical structure of the society (Fiske, 2011; Rozin, Lowery, Imada, & Haidt, 1999).

In more equal societies, people are more similarly arrayed and the divisions between social classes are, by definition, less vast. This allows for less threat and a greater sense of similarity of experience and position along with more understanding, empathy, and compassion. One does not need to worry so much about "falling" or "rising"—there simply is not that far to go and basic, comparable living standards are generally assured. If one does transgress, the ramifications are not nearly so threatening as in a more unequal society, where one's livelihood and future opportunities could very well be at stake. Some of this sense is conscious, discussed openly by politicians and the media, but we suggest that a good deal of this sense of potential threats to one's place—or not—is communicated outside the level of articulation and seeps into the very language people learn as competent members of that society.

Our conception of the relationship between structure, inequality, and culture is "stickier" than that of other theorists tackling the issue of how inequality affects public outcomes. Many inequality researchers assume that inequality directly affects interactions and outcomes by altering factors like trust, social capital, and perceptions of relative deprivation. This means that proximate interventions aimed at increasing trust, social capital, and feelings of deprivation should improve outcomes more effectively in more unequal societies. Going further, distal interventions aimed at reducing inequality would also influence these proximate mechanisms and, in turn, influence other outcomes of concern. We are instead arguing these relationships are not so direct and easy to overcome (if reducing inequality is ever easy). Instead, inequality and culture are enmeshed to the point that to change inequality, one will have to alter a society's deeply rooted culture, including its meanings, norms, and rules of behavior, before a change in outcomes would endure. Inequality involves more than just the distribution of resources or individual senses of trust, social capital, or deprivation. Perhaps this is a reason why structures of inequality are slow to reverse (without something like an enormous external shock, such as a world war)—profoundly embedded cultures must change with them. This position is amenable to that taken by structuration theorists (see Chapter 2) that inequality structures and culture mutually constitute one another (Giddens, 1976, 1984; Sewell, 1992).

Many trees have died in the service of arguing whether structure or culture is paramount in shaping society and its members. We are somewhat agnostic as to which one is more important, ultimately suggesting they are intertwined (see Archer, 2007; Emirbayer & Mische, 1998 for contrasting views). Our focus in this book is on the economic structure as a primary driving force, but given that time is not static, certainly over time the cultural products (media, and in our case, language) it shapes can, in turn, shape the economic structure. We are not hard Marxists, suggesting that everything reduces to economics. Nor can our data allow us to model the interplay of structural and cultural forces in any way so as to test claims about their relative importance. But we are advocating more attention be paid to the level of inequality as an aspect of stratification that has not been previously well-linked to individual experience.

Again, this connection has been made with what we consider a lack of social psychological concreteness within the sociology of culture, a field that seems largely to be oriented toward demonstrating Bourdieu's insights that social class location shapes individual dispositions (tastes). We know, as a field, that one's location within the social stratification system shapes the situations people will encounter, as well as their social psychological beliefs, feelings, and judgments about those situations and the wider world. Inequality, we are suggesting, contributes to shaping the ways people draw moral boundaries, the implicit right-and-wrong understandings that are inculcated into language and transmitted across generations. At that macro level, we know societal inequality predicts a great variety of poor mental and physical health outcomes (see Chapter 2). Our contribution is to offer some suggestive outlines as to how this gets to the micro level.

One might argue that this notion of inequality is instilled into other areas of national life. Much work suggests that authoritarian regimes are harsher with their punishments than liberal democracies (e.g., Huntington, 1991), although some recent work (e.g., Pratt, 2007) argues the opposite. We find interesting parallels here between two very differentially structured polities, China and the United States. Based on international prison data (Walmsley, 2014), China and the United States are the world's two largest penal complexes, each holding 2.3 million prisoners, 43% of the world's prison population (despite representing 24% of the world's population). The United States' rate of incarceration is over four times China's rate. Clearly, if political regime is a key predictive factor, China and the United States should be distinctly different. If punishment regime, such as it is, is important, however, these two distinct countries begin to look much more similar. Additional evidence for unexpected similarities between these two nations comes from a recent study suggesting that, despite cultural differences in parenting styles, parenting practices in both the United States and China have similar effects on children's academic and emotional functioning; parents foster children's functioning when offering "dampened autonomy support" in both societies (Cheung et al., 2016).

In Chapter 9, we will expand on this point by discussing inequality in the five cases that we have data with which to explore this theory. By doing so, we shift the social psychological focus from its typical engagement with differences in stratification toward the *extent* of that stratification, drawing on the Gini coefficient to provide a measure of the level of inequality that, we argue, is captured in the emotional valence of a society's language. What is needed is a way to quantitatively capture the meanings embedded within culture. For that, we turn to Affect Control theory.

7

Affect Control Theory

How Do Cultures Draw Moral Lines?

To empirically test our inequality theory cross-culturally, we draw on the theoretical and methodological insights from affect control theory (ACT; Heise, 1979, 2007; MacKinnon, 1994; Smith-Lovin & Heise, 1988), a research tradition with decades of research and empirical support (see Heise, 2007 for an overview). ACT provides a way of understanding and modeling social interactions making it possible to empirically compare the likely emotions resulting from the same types of interactions in various cultures (Kroska & Harkness, 2011; Osgood, May, & Miron 1975). In this chapter, we will give a broad overview of the theory so that the reader understands why it is useful and provides justification for the empirical analysis used in the book.

Broadly, ACT is a formal, mathematically specified examination of how the various facets of social interaction (such as the identities, behaviors, social setting, and emotions) shape and are reciprocally affected by ongoing social action. ACT distills these various facets to their simplest, most universally recognized dimensions of affective meaning: evaluation (good vs. bad), potency (powerful vs. weak), and activity (fast vs. slow). Put differently, it attempts to quantify the ways people in a society understand their social worlds through how they feel about all of the various aspects of it. Osgood and colleagues' research (Osgood, 1962; Osgood, May, & Miron, 1975; Osgood, Suci, & Tannenbaum, 1957) demonstrated that individuals use these dimensions across societies to make sense of their worlds, and although they are a simplification of the wide variety of cultural understandings, they are a useful, parsimonious, empirically valid way to compare cultures at the level of social meaning and everyday interaction. All concepts, identities, verbs, and various other parts of language can be understood as having values along these three dimensions, and can thus be rated, quantified, and comparatively analyzed within and across cultures.

AFFECT CONTROL THEORY

ACT builds off of Goffman's contention that human interaction is fundamentally about engaging in and maintaining the "expressive order" of our identities (Goffman, 1967)—to understand our social world through the "faces" we present to others (Heise, 2007). Social interaction, at its core, is importantly comprised of the identities people attempt to enact, the behaviors they engage in, the social setting in which the event takes place, and the resulting emotions actors feel during their interaction. Through interaction, people strive to have their identities confirmed by their behavior and the reactions of others to achieve a degree of consistency between their fundamental ideas about their identity and the feedback they receive from others.

As we go through our daily lives, we must interpret the actions and identities of others and our social environments in order to comprehend our world. This involves both the cognitive, intentional side of our brains as we try to directly interpret features of events and the underlying, affective, instantaneous side (Heise, 2007), a core feature of ACT mirroring the dual-process model we outlined earlier. Our affective feelings round out and fill in the gaps that our cognitions leave behind. We use cultural constructs and our language to guide this process because, as Heise (2007) argues, we want to "experience what we already know" (p. 35). Our culture provides us the essential affective meanings allowing us to manage our social experiences, with new cultural constructs being added to our running list as they achieve some degree of social consensus.

The key insight from ACT is that individuals manage social interactions in an effort to maintain their preexisting, fundamental impression of themselves, the people with whom they are interacting, and other elements of the situation. Identities have a reflexive quality as we monitor and compare the feedback we receive from others to the affective standard, otherwise known as the fundamental sentiment, of the identity we are embodying. Through this comparison process, we are able to adjust our behavior to elicit confirmatory responses from others in the social situation. Fundamental sentiments, ACT scholars suggest, represent core societal understandings of situations, actors, and expected actions; they are another way of capturing the elusive constructs of culture and, importantly, morality. It is, fortunately for our purposes, rather consonant with the ways we have discussed linking societal culture to individual functioning.

This approach is also largely complementary to Bourdieu's work, as we have described in previous chapters. Both lines of thought take seriously the idea that language generates and shapes our realities (Bourdieu, 1991; MacKinnon & Heise, 2010). For Bourdieu, symbolic power is generated through our developing language; through interaction, our understandings of the world are made real. ACT and Bourdieu share a common focus on the importance of language and meaning making for drawing out cultural understandings and the construction of reality, as well as the role of perception, cognitive schemas, and classification (Ambrasat et al., 2016; Lizardo, 2004; Pickel, 2005). Bourdieu goes further to focus on examining which groups are privileged enough to create these definitions, and thus have their vision of social reality validated. Thus, over time, the continual production and reproduction of meaning largely advantages those who decide the meanings. In contrast, ACT is largely dedicated to explicating the operations of stable social institutions and systems. But these two approaches and foci are not antithetical. ACT offers a quantifiably measurable and testable set of propositions to engage this basic idea.

As an interaction progresses, we form impressions of that event and generate feelings about our interaction partners that are most likely somewhat different than our initial impressions of who we thought that person to be (termed transient sentiments). We have a mental schema for interacting with somebody, say a student coming into our offices, but of course any individual student is slightly different than that abstract understanding, and as we interact, we take into account how much they diverge from that basic, fundamental feeling. These new impressions refine our initial, vague impression, and guide our behaviors and perceptions as the interaction unfolds.

As an illustration, one of the predominant impression effects identified by ACT researchers is termed, interestingly enough, as the morality effect. Essentially, how good or bad a behavior appears will affect the transient impression of the goodness or badness of the actor who did the behavior. For instance, if an adult lies to a child, the transient impression of the adult after having done so will be far less positive, perhaps being labeled as a scrooge, failure, or hatemonger (result taken from *Interact*, a computerized application of ACT's principles and country-level data). Conversely, if the adult cuddles a child, the adult will then appear exceedingly good. These are simply ways of codifying the vague sense of interaction that we all understand implicitly; our beliefs about people and expectations, based in learned cultural material, shape our interpretation of their activities. Moral judgment is always potentially implicated by people who diverge a great deal—positively or negatively—from what we are taught to expect.

Events that do not go as predicted, seem unlikely or even inconceivable given our working ideas about who is involved in the event generate varying degrees of "deflection," the mismatch between our fundamental and transient sentiments. This deflection produces a state of physiological stress. Even positive deflections can be unsettling; recall from earlier chapters how important sociologists have found it is for people to be able to predict their social worlds no matter the qualities of the anticipated outcomes. All events will generate some degree of deflection, but as events become increasingly unlikely given the going definition of what is happening, deflection will increase correspondingly. In the aforementioned example of an adult cuddling a child, little deflection is created, whereas when an adult lies to the child, a much higher degree of deflection is produced—about ten times higher, according to ACT analyses. Finding out that people are acting outside of our expectations can be unsettling. This stress is uncomfortable and can be allayed by altering our behaviors or even going so far as to re-cast the behaviors or the identities of our interaction partners (Nelson, 2006). Thus, the affective meanings associated with social events shape our behavior and the behavior others direct towards us.

EMOTIONS AND AFFECT CONTROL THEORY

Emotions provide valuable information aiding individuals in their assessments of events. Through interaction, people develop impressions of themselves and other interactants, and emotions allow individuals to feel that impression viscerally. This lets us to figure out just whom we are interacting with and how well the interaction is going (Heise 2007; Smith-Lovin, 1990). But this is not simply some cold, cognitive process. We do not just see people, events, or discuss ideas and code them logically; these objects are deeply imbued with emotional valences, part of the previously discussed automatic mental processing system, and are perhaps the driving forces behind interaction.

As interactions unfold, it may be difficult for each actor to see one another as they would like to be seen. Often we are making a guess as to the identities of the people we are interacting with, albeit probably an educated one based on all the available signals (e.g., clothing, appearance) and histories we have at our disposal. Often these guesses may need to be refined, occasionally they are completely off-base. If a professor is interacting with a graduate student and wants to be heard as a "mentor" but the student sees her more as a "friend," that can throw the interaction off kilter. Rarely do we sit down and consciously decide the roles we want to play and those we want from others. Rather, we have impressions based on expectations and histories that intertwine with our short-term and longer-term goals. The key to all of this, as discussed by Goffman and Garfinkel and at the root of ACT, is that we want interactions to run smoothly and with few surprises.

Emotions serve as a signal for how well these impressions are being attuned to and maintained—an interactional bellwether, if you will. In this example, this there is an important mismatch between the identity the professor is enacting and the one she is understood to be by the other person. This may produce frustration and even anger on the part of the professor, who is getting feedback contradicting her interactional goals. Sensing this, the graduate student may note that he has misstepped, reevaluate the identity enactment of his professor, and re-identifying her correctly (hopefully, if the interaction is to smooth back out; Heise, 1989).

Let us take another example, one more directly related to moral emotional reactions, that we will translate into ACT-speak. We might consider an adult haranguing a child without cause. A parent feeling annoyed at their child is a common thing, but if the parent snaps and is scolding the child for no reason, the adult may feel very bad, impotent, and inactive (the ACT dimensions mentioned earlier), consequently experiencing a pang of being ashamed. In this case, the child would feel unpleasant but very active and experience anger or contempt as a result (taken from *Interact*). Conversely, if a child does something that causes a display of shock in others, the child would feel embarrassed that her behavior caused such a response.

These in-the-moment transient emotions allow interactants to sense how well the interaction is proceeding and guide the determination of who our interaction partners are and how we are to proceed. Emotions become trustworthy signals that guide our impressions of others and ourselves and, as such, they are "vital for social organization" (Heise, 2007, p. 57). This neatly aligns with social intuitionist psychology (Haidt, 2001; Haidt & Bjorklund, 2008; Vaisey, 2009), as described in Chapter 3. For both groups, emotions are near instantaneous, visceral impressions of events, providing important information helping us to make sense of our social world. When events either go against or uphold our culturally-held moral codes, moral emotional reactions will occur. The ideas in this section so far are not novel to our argument, they are simply a refinement of the ideas discussed so far in to a more formal way of thinking about linking culture and the individual within concrete situations.

EVALUATION, POTENCY, AND ACTIVITY

We now turn to the important discussion of how these sentiments are measured. Just as there are multiple ways to group countries and multiple facets to morality, social psychologists have long argued for various ways to understand identities and interactions. Popular formats for capturing identities involve asking people to rank order their valued roles and group memberships, open-ended interviews, or collecting survey information about the content of what being in a particular position (e.g., parent, teacher, Wizards fan) means to the respondent. There is quite a large literature across psychology and sociology about the nature of these identities, where they come from, and how they influence social interaction.

While there are many aspects of meaning we may strive to match (like the stereotypical descriptive connotations of identities and behaviors), ACT focuses on the affective meaning of identities, behaviors, emotions, and the like, arguing that, at our core, people strive to maintain these affective meaning standards (called fundamental sentiments). For our purposes, the same ideas we have walked through in the previous chapters dovetail nicely with the presuppositions of ACT; these standards (or sentiments) are largely culturally determined and learned through socialization. Consequently, there is a great degree of cultural consensus about their exact meaning (Heise 2007, 2010; see also MacKinnon & Robinson, 2014 for an overview), a point to which we will later return.

As mentioned earlier, these affective dimensions of meaning have been parsimoniously whittled down to the most universal sentiments: evaluation, potency, and activity (EPA). These are the three universal dimensions of meaning Osgood and colleagues identified in their cross-cultural research (Osgood, 1962; Osgood, May, & Miron, 1975; Osgood, Suci, & Tannenbaum. 1957). Studies across more than 20 cultures have shown that assessments of social concepts universally involve responses across these three dimensions (Osgood et al., 1975). There may be additional dimensions within any specific culture, but these three are found universally and vastly subsume various other categories of meaning. Even though just these three dimensions of affective meaning account for a huge variety of meaning making –evaluation, potency, and activity are able to differentiate thousands of concepts. As stated by Osgood, Suci, and Tannenbaum (1957) about the dimensions:

> In every instance in which a widely varied sample of concepts has been used . . . the same three factors have emerged in roughly the same order of magnitude. A pervasive *evaluative factor* in human judgment regularly appears first and accounts for approximately half to three-quarters of the extractable variance. Thus the *attitudinal* variable in human thinking, based as it is on the bedrock of rewards and punishments both achieved and anticipated, appears to be primary. . . .The second dimension of the semantic space to appear is usually the *potency factor*, and this typically accounts for approximately half as much variance as the first factor – this is concerned with power and the things associated with it, size, weight, toughness, and the like. The third dimension, usually about equal to or a little smaller in magnitude than the second, is the *activity factor*—concerned with quickness, excitement, warmth, agitation, and the like. (pp. 72–73)

The evaluation dimension assesses feelings about goodness and closely aligns with self-esteem assessments when pertaining to identities and morality more broadly (Heise, 2007; MacKinnon, 1994). This dimension ranges from feelings like good, nice, sweet, heavenly, and happy to bad, awful, sour, hellish, and sad (terms and those following as listed in

Heise, 2007). The potency dimension gauges perceptions of strength, size and force and is similar to the social psychological understanding of self-efficacy, the perceived capacity to exert influence on the world. Additional adjectives used to describe this dimension include big, powerful, strong, and full, as contrasted with little, powerless, weak, and empty. Finally, the activity dimension pertains to considerations of stimulation, speed, age, and keenness with fast, noisy, young, active to slow, quiet, old, and inactive as further adjectives anchoring this dimension.

Together, these three dimensions provide an EPA profile for how individuals in a particular culture affectively experience and understand each concept. Every concept within a language can theoretically be rated by its speakers along these three quantifiable dimensions. These EPA dimensions are affective because they mark how you feel about the goodness, potency, and activity of important features of our social world. For example, feeling humiliated in the United States is quite bad, impotent, and slightly inactive, whereas it is fairly neutral across EPA space in Japan (we used the EPA dictionaries freely available at http://www.indiana.edu/~socpsy/ACT/interact.htm to generate these and all other EPA results).

To construct these dictionaries of affective meanings, respondents are asked to rate a concept, like embarrassment, according to its evaluation, potency, and activity using what are termed *semantic differential scales* anchored by some of the adjectives listed previously for each of the evaluation, potency, and activity scales. The scale points between these anchors are labeled as infinitely, extremely, quite, somewhat, and neutral—from, say, infinitely good to infinitely bad (more modern iterations of these semantic differential scales use a slide rule instead of discrete points along the scale to gain even finer indicators of respondents affective assessments, but the slide rulers are still labeled with these descriptors; Heise, 2010). These points are then translated to numerical values ranging from infinitely (±4.3), extremely (±3), quite (±2), somewhat (±1), and neutral (0). This provides a numerical EPA profile for all facets of an event, but please keep in mind that the numbers in an EPA profile merely stand in for this infinitely-to-infinitely continuum.

Due to the universality of EPA affective understandings, ACT research-ers have spent decades amassing EPA dictionaries containing thousands of concepts from multiple cultures. These dictionaries are contained within *Interact*, and we encourage readers to explore them. We will describe these dictionaries in greater detail, but for now just note that using these cultural EPA dictionaries we can empirically compare affective meaning cross-culturally. This is done, again, using dimensions of meaning that are universal and universally understood. What ACT researchers theorize and measure are not the after-the-fact rationalizations or accounts of what happened but rather the theory is about the "in-the-moment" understand-ings of how the event is unfolding. As we have suggested, this may be an alternative way to measure a national habitus, the sociologically salient concept attempting to gauge the embodiment of culture. This may also be a measure of the moral background (Abend, 2014), presuppositions that we bring to the table. This is an empirically valid method for capturing implicit affective reality and making its processing explicit for researchers.

CULTURAL CONSENSUS: VARIATION WITHIN

Even though the EPA dimensions are universally recognized, the opera-tive question for our purposes becomes just how much variation within a culture there is regarding the terms we use and those found in the EPA dictionaries. Is there a vast amount of individual variation? Do people, in fact, interpret roles/objects/behaviors the same way? ACT researchers would argue that while there is certainly individual variation, there is con-siderably more similarity in affective meaning leading to a high degree of consensus within a culture and variation between cultures.

To understand this, first consider the interactions you have had throughout your life. These interactions are important fonts for meaning-making and refinement. As we talk to others, we must begin with similar ideas about the world in order for the encounter to go smoothly. Children, for example, do not know the cultural meanings in the world and spend much of their time asking questions about the way the world works and how they should see it. Adults also talk with one another about people, places, behaviors, and emotions, in the process learning how others view the world. Children, as well as adults, also spend much of their time watching how various people are treated, discussing past encounters, and consuming media. Throughout all of these daily activities, we come to develop a shared sense of all the known aspects of our social world. These understandings flow through our own personal social networks, which are linked in some way to the social networks of everyone else, creating a vast web of cultural meaning. We learn from others throughout our lives and normative understandings are created, as we are social beings. We are not all identical, but this sense of shared understanding is the basis for making society function. Those who do not follow these normative strictures are labeled iconoclastic or as members of a sub- or counter-culture.

Undoubtedly, your own EPA rating of a concept is influenced not just by these normative understandings, but also by your unique worldview and experiences. The word "dog" has different valences for different people, but just how much individual variation is there? Empirically, individualized meanings account for upwards of just 20% of the variation in the evaluation dimension, and up to 40% of variation in the potency and activity dimensions (Heise, 2007). In more homogenous groups, this individual-level variation is even lower. Thus, at any period in time, our affective sentiments are predominantly shared with others in our culture, especially ideas about how good and bad something is, which are, again, largely moralistic sentiments.

Importantly, there also is empirical consensus within a society over time. When comparing EPA ratings within a culture between various time points (and some dictionaries, like those from the United States, Germany, and Canada are 20 to 25 years apart on entirely different cohorts of respondents), evaluation ratings are at least 90% similar, potency ratings are between 80 to 90% similar, and activity ratings are 60-90% similar (Heise, 2007). This is of course not perfect agreement but neither are these dramatic shifts. Instead, we see stability across all three dimensions, particularly concepts' evaluation (the dimension most closely associated with moral assessments), even in the face of the myriad widespread changes each of these countries experienced in this timeframe. Cultures may shift a bit over time, but changing agreed upon understandings of language is generally a gradual process, as we argued in Chapter 6.

Heise (2007) has a particularly illustrative way of describing this phenomenon, as we are sure many of our readers probably instead feel as though our culture changes quickly and is much more dynamic:

> A carousel with its bright colors, flashing lights, loud music, bobbing ponies, and circular motion is fascinating and challenging to a four-year-old. Yet basically nothing is happening, so the same carousel is boring and insultingly simplistic to an eight-year-old. We are like the four-year-old in confronting our contemporary culture. With hundreds of thousands of concepts and sentiments in the culture, a change of just one-tenth of a percent per year confronts us with hundreds of points of flux—a fascinating and challenging torrent of change. Yet the overall culture is nearly static! (pp. 15-16)

We are not suggesting there to be a complete lack of cultural variation or that cultural shifts never happen, however. Mackinnon and Luke (2002), for instance, examined changes in the Canadian EPA dictionaries between 1981 and 1995, finding some important changes did occur to affective meanings during this time period. In particular, identities related to the social institutions of religion, sexuality, and politics were most altered. Religious identities declined in evaluation and potency, perhaps reflecting lower adherence rates to organized religion. Gay and lesbian identities experienced an increase in evaluation, suggesting a reduction in stigmatization and increasing public tolerance of these identities. Political identities saw a decrease in evaluation and activity, which they suggest demonstrates Canadian's general loss of faith in their political establishment.

Structural and cultural change does indeed occur, and this predominantly affects the cultural sentiments about the concepts most closely associated with institutional change. Periods of widespread social tumult resulting from disasters, wars, political upheaval, and the like may produce more rapid and concordantly widespread affective change; however, whether any alteration in affective meaning would become entrenched, rebound back to pre-event levels, or persist in only certain subcultures remains an empirical question. The affective meanings of the wider language, however, remain largely intact to ensure people maintain a common understanding to communicate effectively and comprehend their worlds. Particularly, the meaning of core concepts, like moral concepts, should be largely unchanged.

ACT researchers have also spent much time examining the cultural meanings found in sub-cultures. Sub-cultures are groups of people within a society with particular subsets of affective meanings, usually surrounding the elements of their culture distinguishing them from the mainstream, like music sub-cultures. Some of this research includes examinations of the white separatist subculture in the United States (Berbrier, 1998), gay and non-gay Christians (Smith-Lovin & Douglass, 1992), occupational subcultures (Heise, 1979; MacKinnon & Langford, 1994), Alcoholics Anonymous participants (Thomassen, 2002), and the Jamband scene (Hunt 2008, 2010, 2013). Shared meanings among members of these groups are, in fact, what distinguish them from the wider society.

CULTURAL CONSENSUS: VARIATION ACROSS

Affective meanings do differ cross-culturally. Sentiments tend to be fairly similar in their general form (e.g., mothers are typically perceived to be "good"), but the degree of meaning differs (e.g., mothers are rated as quite good in the United States [evaluation = 2.48] and extremely good in China [evaluation = 3.44]). In a large-scale examination of affective meanings across 17 cultures in the Atlas dataset (Osgood et al., 1975; Heise, 2014), Heise found a high degree of similarity in meaning across these cultures, with some of the largest differences occurring between German affective meanings and those from Iran, Malaysia, and Brazil. When differences were found, they were largely based on degrees of secularism and histories of colonialism and slavery. "Cultures largely agree regarding the affective meanings of most concepts, at least in the sense that cultural differences

132   UNEQUAL FOUNDATIONS

for any specific concept are relatively small compared to average cross-cultural feelings about different concepts" (Heise, 2014, p. 10).

Although the Atlas data are more than 50 years old, Heise's (2007) analysis of more contemporaneous EPA data also finds similar levels of agreement. Heise used a correlational analysis to see how distinct the Japanese, German, Irish, and Canadian EPA dictionaries are from that of the United States, finding that generally the Canadian ratings are the most similar across EPA space to the US ratings. The potency of behaviors is where most of the differences appear to be, with correlations between .38 and .60. Interestingly, the evaluation ratings of both identities and behaviors are highly correlated (meaning they are quite similar) between these various countries (identity correlation of .81 and behavioral correlation of .88), showing there is a fair degree of consensus across these societies on what people and actions are moral and immoral. Though, as we shall see, even with this degree of general moral consensus, there are still important differences in the types of moral reactions found among these cultures.

With the fundamentals of ACT covered, we hope the reader is better equipped to understand the principles undergirding the ensuing research study. A few points to keep in mind before we turn to a discussion of our analysis strategy in Chapter 8: ACT's guiding principle is that people act in ways to confirm their fundamental affective meanings, as parsimoniously represented by the evaluation, potency, and activity ratings of any and all event elements, like identities and behaviors. EPA dimensions are universally understood and subsume a great deal of affective meaning, yet are able to distinguish between thousands of cultural concepts. Further, there is a great deal of consensus both between and especially within cultures in EPA meaning, and stability in these meanings over time. This is particularly true of the evaluation dimension (the moralistic dimension of good and bad and moral versus immoral acts), yet as we shall see and have already argued, this similarity does not mean that cultures react to events in the same moral fashion nor do they have identical feelings about the meanings of various moral emotions. But before we put the cart before the horse, we turn now to a discussion of how we came to these conclusions.

8

Methodology and a Description of the Data

Our empirical analyses investigate how key moral emotions are viscerally experienced across five countries: the United States, China, Germany, Japan, and Canada. Recall that we are using moral emotions as an indicator of wider social patterns, having argued that these sorts of reactions suggest intrinsic moments within a culture. Those actions garnering strong emotions tell us something about the internalized, implicit expectations of a society. Moral emotions, as we have discussed in detail, are particularly important manifestations of these reactions highlighting events that illuminate the collective priorities, values, expectations, and taboos of a particular society.

To get to the root of our empirical analysis of these moral emotional reactions, this chapter proceeds as follows: First, we discuss our *Interact* data sources before proceeding to how moral emotions are differentially felt across our five cultures using these data. Then, we will walk through our analysis strategy for generating likely moral emotional reactions across these cultures before delving deeper into this cross-cultural variation to statistically tease apart the general trends in these reactions.

EVALUATION, POTENCY, AND ACTIVITY
DICTIONARIES

Interact is home to numerous EPA dictionaries from various cultures and across time, with more dictionaries being continually collected. Currently, these data represent the only source of culturally comparable emotions of which we are aware. These data tell us not only how an emotion is normatively experienced within certain cultures, but we are also able to ascertain the expected frequency with which these emotions may be felt in various scenarios. Cultural meanings currently represented in *Interact* include US dictionaries taken from Indiana, North Carolina, and Texas; Ontario, Canada; Northern Ireland; Germany; Japan; and China. For this project we use the following dictionaries:

   United States, 2002–2004: Ratings of over 1000 behaviors, identities,
      and event modifiers were collected at Indiana University; 1027
      respondents; roughly equal numbers of male and female students
      participated (Francis & Heise, 2006)
   Mainland China, 1991: Ratings of over 1000 event elements were col-
      lected at Fudan University in Shanghai, Peoples Republic of China
      from about 380 undergraduate students (Smith & Yi Cai, 2006)
   Germany, 1989: Ratings of over 800 event elements were col-
      lected at Manheim University and at two German Studenten des
      Grundstudiums and Gymnasiasten (to proportionately match the
      age distributions of the US 1978 EPA dictionary sample); roughly
      520 students participated (Schneider, 1989)
   Japan, 1989–2002: Ratings of almost 2,000 event elements from
      over 700 students at Tohoku University (1989); Kyoritsu Women's
      University, Japan Women's University, Rikkyo University, and

Teikyo Universities (1995–1996); and Rikkyo University and Tokyo
University (2002) (Smith, Matsuno, Ike, & Umino, 2002)

Canada, 2001: Ratings of over 2000 event elements taken from undergraduate students from Guelph, Ontario (MacKinnon, 2003)

Generating these dictionaries is quite time, labor, and monetarily expensive. As such, we are lucky to be able to analyze five dictionaries for this
project, although in the future we hope to bring additional cultures into
the analysis. We would first like to acknowledge that although there is
broad consensus in EPA ratings over time, as noted in Chapter 7, some
of these datasets were gathered around periods of social unrest in these
countries. For example, the US data were collected a few years after the
9/11 terrorist attacks, the Chinese data a few years after the Tiananmen
Square Protests, and the German data the same year as the fall of the
Berlin Wall. This may have generated some period effects in our analyses
that longitudinal data would help to verify and disentangle. With the longitudinal data we do have for the United States and Germany (collected
in 1978 and 2007 respectively), however, a statistical comparison of the
average goodness of moral emotions related to sanctioning or compassion
and praise (for a list of these emotions, see Table 9.6) reveals there to be no
significant differences within these countries over time.

Also, all of the dictionaries are derived from convenience samples of
undergraduate students, meaning that statistically these samples do not
represent the overall population. Recent research by Ambrasat et al.
(2014) assessed the extent to which there is cultural consensus in affective
meanings from a much larger, stratified sample of Germans. They again
find broad similarity in EPA ratings, with small differences arising due to
socioeconomic status.

Furthermore, these are cultural surveys, wherein the goal is to gather
normative understandings held by a population. More traditional survey
methods have a different goal: to seek out variability so we can find statistically significant differences in outcomes or groups. In the case of cultural
surveys, the purpose is to measure concepts with cultural consensus (i.e., a
lack of variation) to reveal norms. Here, the responses from one person are

strongly associated with the responses from the remainder of the sample because the survey is tapping into shared cultural meaning (Heise, 2010), as we have seen in the arguably small amount of variation in EPA profiles over time noted earlier. Variation occurs, but this variation tends to be smaller than that garnered in traditional statistical surveys. A caveat, though, occurs when the sample for the cultural survey is strongly affiliated with aspects of their possible subculture, like the use of college students to measure attributes of youth or education. In this event, the sample will most likely not provide widespread knowledge of these particular dimensions of the culture. Apart from this, small, intentional samples are sufficient, if not preferred, for ascertaining cultural meaning and norms if they represent the wider culture (Heise, 2010), as our cross-cultural examination of moral emotions aims to do.

MORAL EMOTIONS BY COUNTRY: EPA VARIATION

Moral emotions range from negative to positive, from shame and disgust to empathy and reverence. As previously discussed, we categorize moral emotions along the lines posited by Haidt (2003) within psychology and by Turner and Stets (2006) within sociology. Two of these broad categories of moral emotions we typify as being more affectively negative, as they involve sanctioning either oneself or others. We call the former *self-sanctioning* and the latter *other-sanctioning* moral emotions. These categories map onto Turner and Stets's and Haidt's self-critical and other-critical terminology, although we have chosen to highlight the predominantly sanctioning nature of these emotions with our terminology. Self-sanctioning emotions include feeling shame, guilt, and embarrassment toward oneself. Other-sanctioning directs those emotions toward other people or groups, including disgust, anger, and contempt for others' behavior or ways of being. These reactions largely show that individuals have morally transgressed and are being pressured to fall back in line either by one's conscience or the judgments of other people.

The remaining two categories are more positive, as they emphasize understanding, kindness, and uplifting others. The first we term *compassionate* moral emotions (Turner and Stets generally term these other-suffering moral emotions) and the latter *praising* moral emotions (other-praising in Turner and Stets's terminology). These more positive moral emotional reactions highlight emotions that connote understanding and bind people together through affective elevation and transcendence. Compassionate moral emotions include feeling moved by others' actions, as well as feelings of sympathy and empathy. Praising moral emotions are largely uplifting, encompassing the expression of gratitude, joy, and being pleased and thankful. It is important to note that both negative and positive moral emotions serve to point out the normative moral order of a society, but these reactions do so through different means: one through punishment and the other through understanding and positive reinforcement.

Although societies appear to draw on all of these various moral emotions, there is considerable cross-cultural variation in the affective experience and meaning of these emotions. We have discussed the moral emotions to some extent, but let us explore a particular moral emotion, shame, that Scheff (2000) considers the quintessential moral emotion, as it is most deeply keyed into social expectations and their potential violation. Shame takes different forms (Bedford, 2004; Haidt & Keltner, 1999; Li et al., 2004; Shaver, Wu, & Schwartz, 1992; see also the work of Smith & MiowLin, 2006). Mandarin Chinese, for example, contains distinct variations of shame (also guilt, a related but conceptually distinct emotion) that are hard to translate (Bedford 2004). Perhaps as many as 113 distinct forms of shame exist (Li et al., 2004), including concerns about personal integrity, losing perceived competence in the eyes of others, or being disgraced. These are distinct concepts from condemning others' shameful behavior. As discussed, shame is largely considered negative within Western cultures, while in Eastern nations shame can take on some reparative elements, rendering it a more positive, socially helpful emotion (Romney, Moore, & Rusch, 1997).

Menon and Shweder (1994) trace shame's potentially positive aspects back to a Hindu parable about the goddess Kali, whose feelings of shame prevented her from destroying the world. According to the parable, the goddess becomes enraged when feeling deceived by other gods, and as a result decides to get revenge by demolishing the world. In her fevered state, Kali accidentally steps on her husband Siva's chest, an exceptionally disrespectful action. Kali is forced to face the consequences of this act and experiences a state of *lajja*, a feeling of violating an important social bond that supplants her rage. *Lajja* is often translated as "shame" but has different connotations in Hindu culture, where there is a strong state-supported focus on respecting the social hierarchy through civility and personal restraint (Menon & Shweder, 1994; Shweder et al., 2008). Thus it becomes important, almost constitutive, of members of this society to develop and cultivate a sense of *lajja*, as it allows societal members to keep their impulses in check and maintains social order.

BENEFITS OF EVALUATION, POTENCY, AND ACTIVITY MEASURES OF MORAL EMOTIONS

In this sense, Shweder (2003, 2008) argues that deep understandings of these sorts of moral emotions are a large obstacle to facile cross-cultural comparisons. While our approach would perhaps not satisfy his important focus on deep understanding, we can empirically observe this variation by examining the EPA profiles of these various emotions cross-culturally. Using EPA dictionaries allows us to capture some of the nuance that would be lost with a simple translation between, say, general survey questions asked in multiple countries. Our goal is to capture the underlying affective schema triggered by descriptions of emotions in each society. EPA questions allow this because respondents are merely giving a sense of how they feel about a particular word, however they interpret it, and whatever it means to them. In so doing, they are reporting learned cultural knowledge they employ every day.

As a reminder, affect control theorists measure affective meaning through assessing its evaluation (good vs. bad), potency (powerful vs. powerless), and activity (active vs. inactive). These are a parsimonious yet universal means by which individuals affectively "feel" their social worlds, including their emotional experiences (Osgood, May, & Miron, 1975). Affect control theorists have amassed datasets from various cultures asking individuals to rate concepts, such as "guilt," according to its evaluation, potency, and activity using semantic differential scales. These ratings range from infinitely good to infinitely bad (numerically represented by ±4.3), with points connoting extremely (±3), quite (±2), somewhat (±1), and neutral (0) marked along the continuum. Please see Figure 8.1 for an example of an EPA survey, which was used for data collection by Kroska et al. (2014, 2015). These datasets may be found and examined in *Interact* (http://www.indiana.edu/~socpsy/ACT/interact.htm), the computerized version of affect control theory.

Looking at these terms through the lens of ACT, we can start to get a handle on what it means to quantify these emotions. Please remember that these numbers merely correspond to where respondents rated each term on this scale. When we say that, for instance, embarrassment rates at a −1.12 in evaluation (good vs. bad), we merely mean that −1.12 is the average response given by respondents in a particular country and that indicates embarrassment is generally felt as somewhat bad. By associating a numerical value to our affective sentiments, we gain the opportunity to submit these affective assessments to comparative and statistical analysis while still honoring the visceral feelings we have for these cultural concepts.

Let us examine a single emotion from each moral emotion category in each of the countries we investigate here (see Figure 8.2, Figure 8.3, and Figure 8.4). When examining the moral emotions contained in the United States', China's, Germany's, Japan's, and Canada's EPA dictionaries, we can see a large amount of affective variation in these emotional meanings, although the ratings for each term are generally all in the same direction. Beginning with the *sanctioning* moral emotions, feelings of remorse (self-sanctioning) are fairly neutral in the goodness-badness dimension

In this section of the survey, you are asked to report your understanding of different types of cultural identities.

Each row of circles is like a ruler for measuring how you feel. Select a circle that indicates how close something is to the description at one end of the ruler or the other. If something is not close to either description, select the middle circle. For example, if you were rating "a grandfather," you might rate it like this:

A grandfather is

	infinitely	extremely	quite	slightly	neutral	slightly	quite	extremely	infinitely	
Bad, Awful	○	○	○	○	○	○	○	⊙	○	Good, Nice
Powerless, Little	○	○	○	○	○	○	⊙	○	○	Powerful, Big
Slow, Quiet, Inactive	○	○	○	○	⊙	○	○	○	○	Fast, Noisy, Active

In this example, a grandfather is rated as extremely good and nice, quite powerful and big, and neutral in activity.

Figure 8.1 Instructions for an Affect Control Theory Survey

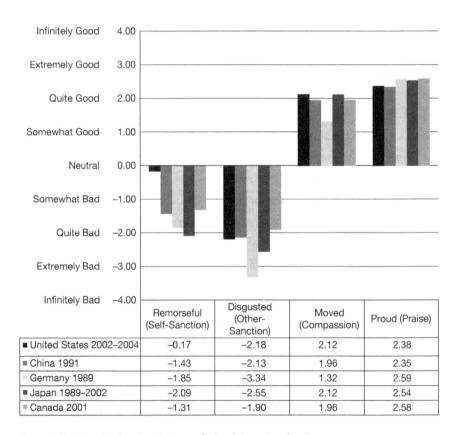

	Remorseful (Self-Sanction)	Disgusted (Other-Sanction)	Moved (Compassion)	Proud (Praise)
■ United States 2002–2004	−0.17	−2.18	2.12	2.38
■ China 1991	−1.43	−2.13	1.96	2.35
▨ Germany 1989	−1.85	−3.34	1.32	2.59
■ Japan 1989–2002	−2.09	−2.55	2.12	2.54
▨ Canada 2001	−1.31	−1.90	1.96	2.58

Figure 8.2 Mean Evaluation Ratings of Moral Emotions by Country

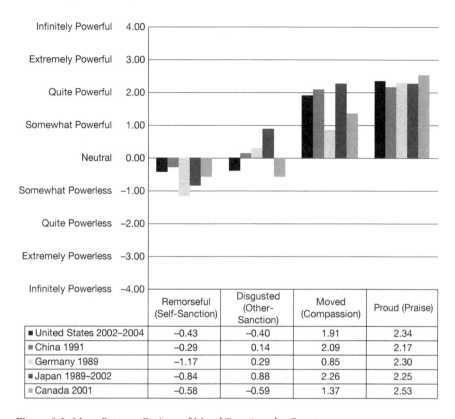

	Remorseful (Self-Sanction)	Disgusted (Other-Sanction)	Moved (Compassion)	Proud (Praise)
■ United States 2002–2004	−0.43	−0.40	1.91	2.34
■ China 1991	−0.29	0.14	2.09	2.17
▢ Germany 1989	−1.17	0.29	0.85	2.30
■ Japan 1989–2002	−0.84	0.88	2.26	2.25
▨ Canada 2001	−0.58	−0.59	1.37	2.53

Figure 8.3 Mean Potency Ratings of Moral Emotions by Country

in the United States (−0.17) but are quite bad in Canada (−1.31), China (−1.43), Germany (−1.85), and Japan (−2.09). Disgust, a distinctly important other-sanctioning moral emotion, is also extremely bad in Germany (−3.34) but is about one order less negative in the remaining countries (evaluation ratings: United States = −2.18; Canada = −1.90; Japan = −2.55; China = −2.13). From this, we can say with some precision that disgust is judged to be not a nice emotion overall, but especially in Germany. Thus, we can begin to make some comparisons about what it means to have these emotions within the contexts present in each society.

A second dimension for comparison involves the powerfulness ratings of these moral emotions, which also differs across these cultures. Being remorseful is judged to be neutral in power, although in Canada, Japan, and especially Germany the emotion becomes progressively less powerful

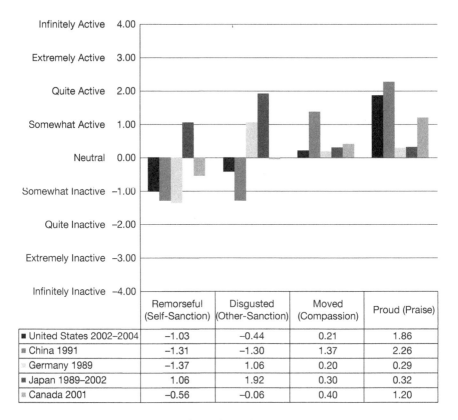

Figure 8.4 Mean Activity Ratings of Moral Emotions by Country

	Remorseful (Self-Sanction)	Disgusted (Other-Sanction)	Moved (Compassion)	Proud (Praise)
■ United States 2002–2004	−1.03	−0.44	0.21	1.86
▥ China 1991	−1.31	−1.30	1.37	2.26
▦ Germany 1989	−1.37	1.06	0.20	0.29
■ Japan 1989–2002	1.06	1.92	0.30	0.32
▥ Canada 2001	−0.56	−0.06	0.40	1.20

(in order: China = −0.29; United States = −0.43; Canada = −0.58; Japan = −0.84; Germany = −1.17). Disgust also stimulates conflicting potency ratings: those in North America report it to be neutral to somewhat impotent (potency ratings: United States = −0.40; Canada = −0.59), while the China data shows it to be neutral in potency (0.14). Conversely those in Germany and Japan experience this emotion to be somewhat potent (potency ratings: Germany = 1.21; Japan = 0.88).

The most complex and divergent affective meanings we see for these emotions are related to the third affective dimension: how the activity, or liveliness, of these emotions is experienced. The Japanese data indicate that those in this culture tend to experience the sanctioning emotions as somewhat to quite active (activity ratings: remorseful = 1.06; disgusted = 1.92), whereas those in the remaining cultures generally report that these emotions are neutral to quite inactive, especially in the American and Chinese data (American activity ratings: remorseful = –1.03; disgusted = –0.44; Chinese activity ratings: remorseful = –1.31; disgusted = –1.30). The other standout here is Germany, whose activity rating for remorse is somewhat to quite inactive or reserved (–1.37), while the activity rating for disgust is somewhat potent (1.06), demonstrating that these two sanctioning emotions differ markedly in their affective liveliness.

Thus, in the societies we are studying, we can develop a locally valid profile for each emotion along these three dimensions that tells us a good deal about how that feeling is experienced within that society. Being disgusted, for instance, stands out differently in different nations, and these ratings tell us a bit about how good, powerful, and active this emotion "feels" in each society. Recall from last chapter that all of the words in each language's dictionary have these ratings. The global nature of these three dimensions allows us purchase on cross-cultural, quantitative comparison that can advance understanding of links between social structure and individual emotion.

Turning to the positive moral emotions, we see that across the five countries there is greater consistency in the affective assessment of these emotions. Feeling moved (a compassionate moral emotion) or praise is affectively quite good, with praise being felt as slightly more positive than being moved. The only difference in these trends pertains to German evaluations of feeling moved in that it is slightly less positive than the trend (1.32 compared to other countries evaluations of about 2.00). The tendencies in the evaluation ratings are also evident in the potency ratings. Respondents in all five countries see these two emotions as being somewhat to quite potent, with Germany having the lowest potency rating of .85.

There is much greater variation in the ratings of activity (as we saw with the sanctioning moral emotions). All countries except China experience feeling moved as neutral to somewhat active (United States = 0.21; Germany = 0.20; Japan = 0.30; Canada = 0.40), whereas in China, this emotion is much more active (1.37). Experiencing praise is also an active moral emotion, although for Germany and Japan, it is only neutral to somewhat active (Germany = 0.29; Japan = 0.32) and for the remaining countries, it is much more active (in order: Canada = 1.20; United States = 1.86; China = 2.26).

These reported differences are suggestive of cross-cultural disparities in how emotions are typically experienced. Although there are some consistent trends, the strength and depth of feeling for many of these moral emotions varies cross-culturally even though the labels for these emotions may be the same. No one country particularly stands out, with each having higher or lower and highest and lowest ratings across EPA dimensions and emotions. Nevertheless, as Kagan (2007) notes, "Both the culture and its unique vocabulary influence the features of a feeling or emotion that will be the prototype." (p. 124).

For our investigation of which moral emotions are more likely in a given society, we let this variation come through in our subsequent analyses. This is an important feature of this work because we are allowing for the unique visceral experiences of these emotions to be expressed in the analyses by utilizing country-specific EPA dictionaries to produce the simulation results consisting of the bulk of our analyses.

We hope this provides a sense of the degree of cross-cultural variation there is in these EPA dictionaries from just these four emotions. When we later explain how often our simulations triggered various moral emotions, you can refer to these charts to understand how the people in that society understand that emotion. We also encourage you to delve into the dictionaries contained in *Interact* to explore the EPA profiles of these various moral emotions yourselves. You can also play around with your own simple analyses to see how different societies are represented. To gain a further understanding of *Interact* and our exact analysis strategy, we now turn to a discussion of our method.

ANALYSIS STRATEGY AND *INTERACT*

Research can be hard. In a perfect world (for a sociologist), we would be able to magically compare the exact same kinds of people in different societies to see how they feel and behave. Short of telepathy, there is no perfect way to understand how people really feel about events or to perfectly observe their behavior in all settings. If you watch people in the real world, you cannot know all of the factors that are present in their actions; if you bring them into an experimental laboratory where you can control those factors, you necessarily lose much of this complexity. There are always trade-offs. These typical issues are compounded when trying to understand people across cultures, for all of the reasons we have outlined so far. *Interact* allows us some purchase on this problem, however, through its ability to compare the constituent factors underlying each culture with the same format—evaluation, potency, and activity sentiments.

With these analyses we want to compare whether and how the same types of interactions in our five societies produce moral emotional reactions and of what type (i.e., self-sanctioning, other-sanctioning, compassionate, or praising). In many ways this is a difficult feat for cross-cultural research because we need to allow for the distinct cultures of these societies to shine through while controlling for the exact contours of the interaction. Affect control theory's principles allow for this to occur because the affective meaning of the interaction is paramount to understanding any interaction between individuals. This, again, is represented by the EPA profiles of the identities of the interactants, their behaviors, and their emotional reactions. By using the same event EPA profiles to run our analyses, we are effectively "controlling for" the interaction, meaning we can simulate affectively the exact same interactions within each society in *Interact*. Because EPA space is universally used to construct meaning and understandable, we gain leverage on the seemingly intractable problem of being able to compare interactions cross-culturally.

There is no existing data of which we are aware providing a remotely comparable way to examine the emotional reactions to the exact same scenarios cross-culturally, especially with such detailed interactional information. We would like to stress, however, that our data are based in simulations of events. While the equations used within *Interact* to run these simulations and the data informing them are based in the empirical reality of each culture, it is up to future research to assess how strongly our results match those resulting from real-life interactions. Nevertheless, affect control theory researchers have already put many of these simulation results to the test, finding a strong correspondence between the predicted results from the simulations and actual behavioral data (e.g., Schröder & Scholl, 2009; Wiggins & Heise, 1987), although these studies have largely been limited to the United States.

INTERACT SIMULATIONS AND IMPRESSION FORMATION EQUATIONS

Martin suggests that objects in a society have "intersubjectively valid qualities" (2011, p. 265), and as we learn what various people and objects mean in a society, we also internalize a social logic that impels us to act and feel certain ways when certain combinations of these people and objects exist within a situation. What *Interact* offers, we are suggesting, is a way to render these valences empirical, and thus test our broader theory of inequality. For Martin, this meaning is not a property of the people or objects, but the relationships between them as taught within a particular society or social group. Our modeling is, perhaps, not a perfect rendering of this approach, but we argue that it is a valuable treatment.

Researchers can use *Interact* to simulate various aspects of social interaction to discover the way an interaction is likely to unfold, how people might recast or reevaluate one another, what resulting emotions interactants are likely to experience, as well as various other features of events. Importantly, *Interact* is programmed with country-specific, empirically derived simulation rules, termed impression formation equations, which generate these predictions (Heise, 2007; Smith-Lovin, 1987a; 1987b). These impression-formation equations are based on ordinary OLS regression equations predicting how people respond to events. Here, events are very simple interactions wherein someone does a behavior toward another (actor-behavior-object).

To generate the equations, ACT researchers begin by analyzing each of these events. First, researchers asked respondents to rate the evaluation, potency, and activity of various features of these simple interactions in context. So they might have asked respondents to rate, say, "a neighbor" in the event "a neighbor expresses remorse to a friend" or "admonishing" in the event "a mother admonishes a child." Next, researchers collect EPA ratings of all of these concepts in isolation (e.g., "a friend" "express remorse to," "a child," etc.). Impression formation equations are developed by regressing the EPA ratings of the event elements on the isolated, out-of-context event elements. With A = actor, B = behavior and O = object-recipients (i.e., the person the actor does something to), the initial, main effects equation for predicting the evaluation of the actor in an particular event would be:

$$A_e' = a + b_1 A_e + b_2 A_p + b_3 A_a + b_4 B_e + b_5 B_p + b_6 B_a + b_7 O_e + b_8 O_p + b_9 O_a.$$

The dependent variable in this equation includes all in-context evaluation ratings of actors, while the independent variables are the out-of-context evaluation, potency and activity ratings of actors, behaviors and objects.

This same basic initial equation is also used for predicting other portions of the event, like the activity of the actor or the evaluation of the behavior. Interaction terms are then added to all the main effects equations to maximize how fully each equation explains the remaining variation in the data. These full equations include numerous significant interaction terms. One popular example is of the $B_e O_e$ effect showing that actors are evaluated more positively when their behavior and the identity of the objects are similar in evaluation (both good or both bad). For example, doing a good deed to a good person creates a greater increase in the actor's evaluation after having done so than doing a good deed to a bad person.

In addition to being continually refined, this process has been done for all of the countries we investigate, so that each country has its own set of impression formation equations underlying the event simulations. Thus, individuals from each country are not only asked to rate each of these concepts using scales that are universally understandable and meaningful, but also these culture-specific ratings are used to develop the culture-specific equations underlying the simulations we are about to present. These are not your typical computer simulations, such as those used in agent-based modeling. Instead this method of investigating social reality is fundamentally designed to allow culture to shine through.

Recall from Chapter 6 that we argue, along with structuration theorists (Giddens, 1976, 1984; Sewell, 1992), that structure and culture are intertwined and that structures of inequality fundamentally affect and are affected by culture. This makes the impacts of inequality "stickier" such that inequality and cultural norms and schemas for action mutually constitute one another. These culture-specific impression formation equations are a representation of these cultural rules. They characterize the normative courses of action and assessment found in a culture. Thus, our empirical investigation permits the lived, cultural experience of these emotions to come through, as well as the culturally-specific interaction rules that govern their expression. Cultural-specificity and variation is thus central to our work.

But how are emotions generated by these equations? Once an event has been simulated and a working impression of the actor and object in the event has been generated from the equations (termed a transient impression), *Interact* then combs through the appropriate dictionary to find the emotion that most closely matches that transient identity for the actor and the object. *Interact* then presents the emotions that most closely approximate what a typical member of that society would feel if she or he were either doing the action or the recipient of that action. Again, short of telepathy, this is about as good a way to systematically and accurately represent a culture and the emotions its members are normatively socialized to experience that currently exists. These reported emotions for each person are the emotions we then investigate empirically.

GENERATING OUR SIMULATIONS

To create a dataset of these simulations, we first began by generating EPA profiles for the actor, behavior, and object-recipient (i.e., the person the actor does something to). We could have used identities already included in the various cultural dictionaries, but this would have made comparing the events tricky as not all terms are included in each dictionary (although there is a large degree of overlap): Some identities and behaviors are culture-specific. Some are terms that particular researchers wanted EPA profiles for at the time of data collection for their own particular project, which was never repeated. Some dictionaries are just smaller than others as collecting these data are quite resource intensive. And etcetera.

More important, had we simulated events using the same labels (like "a neighbor expressing remorse to a friend"), this would have made comparability across countries much more difficult. What "expresses remorse to" connotes and affectively means in one culture may be truly different than in another, as our past discussions of moral emotion variation can attest. As we have already seen, even one simple moral emotion may spark vastly different affective ratings between two cultures. Furthermore, how we would have gone about selecting identities and behaviors and creating the events would have been biased by our own American understandings of these words. This is precisely the issue that Shweder (2003) and others have cautioned cross-cultural researchers about: incommensurate translations and definitions of words.

This is, again, where the utility of *Interact* comes in. Instead of forcing equivalent terms across nations, we chose to use the affective meaning inherently captured by the EPA scale (infinitely –4.3 to infinitely +4.3) to simulate events that have the *exact same* affective feeling in each of our five countries. Take, for example, an event where the actor has a profile of (1.00, 1.17, .13), the behavior the actor does has a profile of (2.73, .01, 1.29), and the object-recipient has a profile of (–1.32, –.75, .67). Running this event in Interact using the American, Chinese, Germany, Japanese, and Canadian impression formation equations would generate culture-specific outcomes from an event that is affectively understood to be essentially the same in each country. Instead of using, say, the term "mother" in each dictionary with its different ratings across countries, we are able to choose mathematically *and* affectively equivalent terms in each culture, rather than being forced to artificially make words equivalent.

Because *Interact* allows researchers to import their own EPA profiles for the actor, behavior, and object-recipient to simulate events, we can make *Interact* simulate event profiles that affectively "feel" the same in different cultures, regardless of what that linguistic term actually is. We do not need to translate the strict words, we can use the mathematical values to test equivalently good, active, and potent (or not) concepts across nations. This is a novel use of the instrument (see also Kroska & Harkness, 2011), and a novel approach (to our knowledge) for cross-cultural social psychological research.

To generate our EPA profiles, we used a random number generator to compile EPA profiles for a total of 200 events. For each event, a random number was generated for the evaluation, potency, and activity of the actor, behavior, and object-recipient. We restricted the numbers generated in two ways: First, the numbers had to be between the normal EPA bounds of ±4.3. Second, most EPA profiles cluster around the middle, neutral point of the scale. To account for this, the generator selected from a normal distribution of numbers with an average of 0.00. This ensured that we would receive more numerical profiles that would also be around the mid-point of the scale and few at the extremes like most EPA terms. In other words, rather than just randomly selecting words (which, again, would lead to all sorts of translation problems), this approach, while random, means that our profile selections are more likely to represent commonly felt and understood affective states in each language culture. The odds of picking extreme profiles are small, but present, suggesting that the simulated samples we develop are a good representation—not merely a random one—of the most typical affective states within each culture.

We then submitted these 200 events to *Interact* to generate the resulting simulated emotions that the actor and object-recipient would likely experience once the action was committed, according to the impression formation equations that represent each nation's cultural processing. We did this using each of the five countries' EPA dictionaries: United States (2002–2004), China (1991), Germany (1989), Japan (1989–2002), and Canada (2001).

Interact is zlxo constructed with a male and female version of each dictionary and impression formation equations. One must select at the start of a simulation whether the actor is male or female and, having done so, *Interact* then uses the "gender appropriate" version of that culture's dictionary and equations. We therefore ran a total of 400 simulations for each of the five countries: 200 simulations for women actors and 200 simulations for male actors. This generated a total of 2000 simulated events. Because we opted to use a random number generator to develop the EPA profiles for our events, some events were effectively unintelligible and yielded no reported emotions felt by either the actor or object-recipient (an emotion result labeled as "no words in range" to use *Interact* parlance). This means that our randomly generated mathematical value did not, in these cases, closely represent any "actual" words that were collected within that nation's dictionary. Simulations yielding this null result are coded as missing in our dataset so as not to bias the overall number of emotions reported. Doing so would have affected our analysis of whether any particular countries are more likely to react to an event morally.

Having run the 2000 simulations, we then coded the reported emotions that the interactants would have likely felt according to whether the emotion falls into our previously defined, four category moral emotion schema: self-sanctioning, other-sanctioning, compassion, or praise. Here are the emotions that comprise each category:

Self-sanctioning—humble, sorry, remorseful, self-pitying, repentant, contrite, embarrassed, humiliated, regretful, ashamed, mortified, crushed (if experienced by the actor)

Other-sanctioning—shocked, resentful, agitated, exasperated, contemptuous, irate, aggravated, displeased, outraged, irritated, smug, furious, dissatisfied, angry, mad, fed-up, disgusted, crushed (if experienced by the object-recipient)

Compassion—moved, compassionate

Praise—reverent, touched, proud, awe-struck, charmed, appreciative, glad, ecstatic, thrilled, overjoyed, happily surprised, pleased, joyful, thankful

In the following chapter, we turn to a more in-depth analysis of these moral emotions and we will show that even though there is this remarkable similarity in event profiles, there are several important and consistent differences in the likelihood of particular moral emotions—differences that are arrayed by the structural features of these societies themselves.

9

Empirical Analysis

With our empirical analysis, we investigate the following questions: Do moral emotion reactions vary cross-culturally, and if so, are there consistent patterns to these differences? Namely, do these reactions differ according to the structural conditions of these societies, such as their levels of inequality (as we have thus far argued), or by some other means, such as the classic East-West distinction? As a refresher, we argue that societal levels of inequality fundamentally shift the type of moral emotion reactions its members experience and use. Members of more equal cultures tend to be more pro-social and communal, resulting in a greater use of compassionate and praising moral emotions. Conversely, members of more inequitable cultures, where the hierarchical environment is an everyday presence, will be more likely to sanction both themselves and others for moral acts. Order must be maintained and people kept in their appropriate place, while the threat of falling lower in the hierarchy and the pressure to advance is omnipresent.

The countries we investigate offer a strong test of this theory because they differ in a number of theoretically important ways. There are two Eastern countries (China and Japan) and three Western countries (the United States, Germany, and Canada), allowing us to test the classic cultural psychology argument that this distinction should produce divisions in moral reactions. This is perhaps the key distinction in cross-cultural psychology, one holding that fundamental psychological processing is different for people raised within these two traditions. Supposedly, people from Eastern backgrounds have a more interdependent, collective way of perceiving and experiencing the world, while people in the West are more individualistic, with America being perhaps the epitome of a self-focused society. The primary alternative hypothesis to our focus on structural inequality would certainly involve this distinction.

While we are limited to societies that have extensive, pre-collected EPA dictionaries, we end up with a fortuitous additional test of our basic assertion. If the East-West hypothesis were to be supported, we would expect a rather similar pattern of results for two of the countries, the United States and Canada, which share a native language, a boarder, as well as a continent. In fact, on many the possible ways one might array nations, the United States and Canada should be fairly equivalent, leading to expectations that their cultures might be more similar than the remaining countries that do not share these linguistic or geographic factors (although Japan is an island nation, it is generally viewed as part of the Asian continent). As we shall see, however, one factor distinguishing the United States from its Canadian neighbors is its level of economic inequality. This provides us with quite an interesting comparison case for our analyses.

Immigration levels are yet another distinguishing feature. The United States has historically had some of the highest levels of immigration according to United Nations data (2015). This is seconded by Germany, Canada, and then Japan. China, meanwhile, has had a negative net migration rate for at least the past 60 years (see data visualizations here: http://www.migrationpolicy.org/programs/data-hub/international-migration-statistics). Immigration rate is an interesting dimension to consider, as many researchers have proposed that increasing immigration leads to more fracturing of a society's citizenry. Fiske (2011) notes that countries with lower immigration rates—China being the prime example in our study—tend to have a more cohesive and enveloping sense of "us," the citizenry, versus "them," everyone else. This potentially leads to a greater sense of cohesion and equality. Countries with high levels of immigration, like the United States, instead see more multiplex "us" versus "them" distinctions drawn even for subgroupings of its own people. This leads to greater uncertainty when interacting with others, greater status competition, and therefore a higher prevalence of envy and scorn and their associated sanctioning moral reactions. This alternative explanation would therefore predict the United States and China to be the most distinct in their moral emotional reactions.

Another way to distinguish these countries involves their differing levels of human development. Table 9.1 presents data related to each country's human development index score (HDI), which is a measure created by the United Nations indexing life expectancy at birth, education (mean and expected years of schooling for adults and children respectively), and standard of living (as measured by logged gross national income per capita). Higher scores represent higher levels of human development across these three domains. For the countries we investigate, the United States has the highest HDI scores, followed by Canada, Germany, and then Japan. The UN notes that these four countries have a "very high" level of human development. China, however, has comparatively much lower human development during the same time frames. China's HDI has steadily increased since 2000, although still ranks much lower than these other countries even today. Thus, we have another potentially important way to distinguish these five countries as another alternative hypothesis. This one would also predict, along with immigration, that the United States and China would be the most distinct in their cultural patterns of moral emotion.

These countries also importantly differ in their level of inequality, and while it should not be a surprise to people who have stayed with us throughout this book, we argue that inequality is going to be the organizing factor for our individual-level emotional results. Here we see similarities

TABLE 9.1.   DESCRIPTIVE STATISTICS OF EACH COUNTRY

	United States	China	Germany	Japan	Canada
Gini Coefficient[a,b]	37.7 (1987); 40.5 (2000); 41.8 (2007)	29.9 (1987); 32.4 (1990); 42.6 (2008)	24.5 (West Germany 1989); 28.3 (2007)	26.0 (1989); 24.9 (1993); 26.8 (2002)	31.1 (1990); 31.8 (1997); 33.6 (2000)
Human Development Index[c]	.825 (1980); .858 (1990); .883 (2000)	.423 (1980); .502 (1990); .591 (2000)	.739 (1980); .782 (1990); .854 (2000)	.772 (1980); .817 (1990); .858 (2000)	.809 (2000); .848 (1990); .867 (2000)

NOTE: These particular years are selected to match the time periods of *Interact* data from the United States (2002–2004), China (1991), Germany (1989), Japan (1989–2002), and Canada (2001).

[a] Statistics come from the World Bank.

[b] Statistics come from gini-research.org.

[c] Statistics come from the United Nations; composite index measuring health, longevity, education, and standard of living.

between the United States and China that are not drawn when looking at human development levels, East/West theories of perception, or other measures such as geopolitical location or Gross Domestic Product (GDP). Table 9.1 also presents a basic inequality measure for our countries. As the reader may recall from Chapter 2, the Gini coefficient is a measure of the distribution of income for a nation's people with 0 representing perfect equality wherein everyone makes the same income and 100 representing perfect inequality (one person in the population makes all of the income and everyone else makes none). Higher Gini coefficients indicate greater levels of inequality. Across the various years we see some consistent trends: Germany and Japan have lower levels of inequality, Canada has low to moderate inequality, and the United States and China have higher levels of inequality.

In fact, the U.S and China have little in common other than this level of inequality and, interestingly, the trajectories of inequality within their nations. Both the United States' and China's inequality sharply increased throughout the 1990s, especially for China. According to a recent trend analysis by Xie and Zhou (2014), cross-national comparisons of Gini coefficients show that most countries' inequality decreases as they become more economically developed (as measured by their gross domestic product per capita), but for both the United States and China, inequality is significantly higher than in countries with similar levels of development, with China much higher than the United States. In recent years China's increasing inequality has vastly exceeded the level that would be expected by similarly developed countries, reaching as high as 53-55 in 2005 and 61 in 2010 (Hu, 2012; Xie and Zhou, 2014).

Interestingly, China's National Bureau of Statistics stopped reporting official data after 2000 when their Gini coefficient reached 41.2 because their income data was "incomplete" (Hu, 2012). The country only again began to release official statistics again in 2012 after the Chinese Household Finance Survey Center of Chengdu's Southwestern University released a report stating that their Gini coefficient had risen to an alarming 61 in 2010 (Hu, 2012). China's official statistics retroactively state that their Gini coefficient peaked at 49.1 in 2008; these data have been met with skepticism even though they are still quite high and essentially matches the United States' current Gini (Rabinovitch, 2013). According to a report from China's National Economic Research Institute (as reported in Rabinovitch, 2013), there are vast quantities of hidden wealth in China that are not accounted for in the official statistics.

China's and the United States' inequality has sharply increased through the 1990s and 2000s and are quite similar to one another, although China's inequality is arguably higher than that of the United States. China's GDP also increased during this time significantly (although it is still far lower than that of the other countries we examine), suggesting that while the living standards for some segments of the population increased, it did little to stem the increasing amounts of money going to the top portions of China. The United States did not experience this jump in overall GDP during this time (nor did Germany, Japan, or Canada), even as inequality increased. At the same time, the inequality level of our remaining countries is much lower, with Germany and Japan's slightly lower than

Canada's. In sum, given this range of potential national-level factors, the factor that the United States and China share is their heightened inequality. Only using this perspective would scholars expect patterns in emotional functioning to be similar between these nations, more than other countries with equivalent GDP, human development levels, or even shared languages.

RESULTS

Now that we have walked you through some general aspects of *Interact*, its EPA dictionaries, and how we generated our simulation data in Chapter 8, we turn to our results. We begin by examining the categories of moral emotions produced by the simulations for all the countries put together. One of the easiest ways to see the relative frequency with which these emotions are reported is with word clouds, as the relative size of the words designates their frequency with larger fonts signifying higher occurrence. Figure 9.1, Figure 9.2, Figure 9.3, and Figure 9.4 present word clouds for each category of moral emotion.

Figure 9.1 Self-Sanctioning Moral Emotions Wordcloud

shocked
displeased crushed
exasperated
angry · dissatisfied
agitated
furious ᗺ smug fed-up
resentful
contemptuous
aggravated mad   disgusted
irritated irate
outraged

Figure 9.2 Other-Sanctioning Moral Emotions Wordcloud

The most common self-sanctioning moral emotions we found across our five countries are feelings of being humble, sorry, and remorseful. Being shocked is the most common other-sanctioning moral emotion, followed by being resentful, agitated, and exasperated. Being moved is the most common compassionate moral emotion, although there are only two emotions in this category, the other being "compassionate." Finally, feeling reverent and touched are the most common praising moral emotions from our simulation results, followed by feeling proud and awe-struck.

compassionate
moved

Figure 9.3 Compassion Moral Emotions Wordcloud

Figure 9.4 Praising Moral Emotions Wordcloud

Recall that, given the machinery used in compiling *Interact* dictionaries and impression formation equations for these languages, what we are presenting are those terms most likely to be experienced in these nations. These resulting moral emotions are representations of these various cultures and their affective ways of life.

SIMULATION DETAILS

To give a sense of the type of events that were likely to produce these emotions, we took the average EPA profile that produced each type of moral emotion in each country. We then imputed these event profiles to *Interact* to find the identities and behaviors that most closely matched these profiles for both women and men. Table 9.2, Table 9.3, Table 9.4, and Table 9.5 present these EPA profiles and events. Please recall that these are very simple events without any frills and some license may be taken with their interpretation. *Interact* is programmed to automatically provide concepts that are within 1 Euclidean distance from the designated profile. This often results in multiple options of the action and identities from which we can select. These tables present the concepts making the most intuitive sense, but there were many other possible events we could have included. We offer this to provide some context to the simulated interactions.

There are two main conclusions we draw from these events: First, across societies and moral emotional reactions, the average EPA event profiles are not very extreme in their ratings, with most being only neutral-to-somewhat good/bad, potent/impotent, and active/inactive. Profiles are rarely more extreme than ±1.00. Considering that EPA profiles generally fall in this range, this suggests just how commonly events may spark moral emotions across the cultures we are investigating. If moral emotions are the normative glue holding societies together, it follows that they should be regularly experienced, regardless of culture. This also shows our randomization technique of sampling from a normal distribution centered on 0.00 did not work against us: moral emotional reactions frequently occur in this affective space. Extreme events are not a necessary condition for generating a moral event.

Second, and perhaps more interestingly, even though the EPA profiles we simulated were randomly generated, the resulting events are intelligible across our five countries. Regardless of culture, the events generally make intuitive sense as to why an event might likely result in a particular moral emotion. When a schoolteacher doubts an expert in Germany, the expert understandably feels a sense of self-sanctioning. As does when a Canadian critic exalting a neophyte feels a sense of praise or a Japanese junior high school teacher expressing remorse to a staff member feels compassion. Admittedly, there was some picking and choosing when we compiled these identities and behaviors, but we feel it is still remarkable

TABLE 9.2. AVERAGE ACTOR-BEHAVIOR-OBJECT EVENTS PRODUCING SELF-SANCTIONING MORAL EMOTION BY COUNTRY

	Actor: Self-Sanction			Object: Self-Sanction		
	Actor	Behavior	Object	Actor	Behavior	Object
United States:	EPA: 0.37, -0.21, 1.13	0.25, -0.72, -0.48	0.46, 0.46, -0.26	EPA: 0.39, -0.04, -0.47	0.10, -0.12, 0.22	-0.06, -0.31, 0.39
Female Dictionary	Stepsister	Kowtows to/ Borrows money from	Stepparent	Stranger	Curries favor from/Dotes on	Lesbian/ Defendant
Male Dictionary	Adolescent	Clings to	Stepfather	Stranger	Upbraid/ Gawks at	Nut
China:	EPA: 0.11, 0.24, 0.06	0.22, -0.12, 0.29	-0.42, -0.22, -0.12	EPA: -0.02, 0.17, -0.16	0.16, -0.14, 0.10	-0.37, -0.07, -0.02
Female Dictionary	Tax Collector	Apes	Debtor	Tax Collector/ Jeweler	Apes	Debtor/ Divorcee
Male Dictionary	Local Elected Official	Apes	Political Prisoner	Wholesaler	Overrates/ Imitates	Cashier

Germany:	EPA: 0.51, 0.59, 0.43	-0.84, -0.89, -0.68	0.09, -0.17, -0.23	EPA: -0.10, 0.58, 0.03	-0.86, 0.24, 0.20	1.03, 0.65, -0.49
Female Dictionary	Stepbrother	Submits to	In-Law	Plainclothesman	Questions	Specialist
Male Dictionary	Teacher	Eludes	Bystander	Schoolteacher	Doubts	Expert
Japan:	EPA: 0.52, 0.65, -0.47	-0.07, -1.22, -0.24	0.14, -0.13, 0.31	EPA: -0.12, 0.10, 0.12	-0.11, 0.98, -0.07	0.17, 0.01, -0.01
Female Dictionary	Close relative	Compromises with	Cousin	Plaintiff	Disciplines/ Physically examines	Third party
Male Dictionary	University lecturer	Seeks advice from	Junior high teacher	Steelworker	Reprimands	Section Chief
Canada:	EPA: 0.24, -0.40, 0.14	-0.63, 0.08, 0.13	0.33, 0.06, -0.04	EPA: -0.25, 0.54, -0.63	0.32, 0.34, 0.85	-0.19, -0.82, -0.27
Female Dictionary	Agnostic	Subjugates	Ethnic Minority	Progressive Conservative	Jests/Cajoles	Spendthrift
Male Dictionary	Egghead	Doubts/Detests	Ethnic Minority	Evangelist	Dares	Outsider

NOTE: *Interact* dictionaries used: United States 2002–2004, China 1991, Germany 1989, Japan 1989–2002, Canada 2001.

TABLE 9.3. AVERAGE ACTOR-BEHAVIOR-OBJECT EVENTS PRODUCING OTHER-SANCTIONING MORAL EMOTION BY COUNTRY

	Actor: Other-Sanction			Object: Other-Sanction		
	Actor	Behavior	Object	Actor	Behavior	Object
United States:	EPA: 0.72, 0.01, 0.50	-0.62, -0.46, 0.58	-0.10, 0.01, 0.07	EPA: 0.09, -0.21, -0.35	-0.16, 0.14, 0.22	0.20, -0.12, -0.23
Female Dictionary	Evangelist	Joggles	Spinster/Lesbian	Blind date	Harangue	Spendthrift
Male Dictionary	Saleslady	Quibbles/Dickers with	Spendthrift	Sponger	Fondles	Convalescent
China:	EPA: -0.12, -0.52, 0.05	0.16, -0.15, 0.87	-0.06, 0.07, -0.03	EPA: 0.35, -0.04, 0.25	-0.15, 0.33, 0.85	0.17, -0.25, 0.18
Female Dictionary	Stepchild	Imitates	Stranger	Immigrant	Imitates	Hick
Male Dictionary	Office clerk	Rattles	Cashier	Customer	Deprecates/Teases	Sales clerk
Germany:	EPA: 0.67, -0.15, 0.33	-1.13, 0.19, 0.66	-0.01, 0.42, -0.34	*No Other-Sanctioning Emotions Reported*		
Female Dictionary	Co-worker	Deflates/Upsets	Professor			
Male Dictionary	Customer	Overrates	Electrician			

Japan:	EPA: 0.69, 0.18, -0.04	-0.99, -0.20, 0.26	0.30, -0.11, -0.15	EPA: 0.21, 0.20, -0.10	-0.77, 0.79, 0.74	0.87, -0.58, -0.13
Female Dictionary	Close acquaintance	Intimidates/Frowns at	Bachelor	Remarried person	Brushes off	Do gooder
Male Dictionary	Junior High Teacher	Grouses to	Aunt/Granny	Bachelor	Shocks	Bride
Canada:	EPA: -0.08, 0.45, 0.04	-1.04, 0.62, 0.60	0.08, -0.34, -0.38	EPA: -0.24, 0.02, -0.12	-0.57, -0.22, 0.00	-1.02, 0.53, 0.06
Female Dictionary	Stepmother	Berates/Rebuffs	Salesman	Pencil pusher	Stalls	Used car salesman
Male Dictionary	Critic	Discredits	Neophyte	Neophyte	Doubts	Henchman

NOTE: *Interact* dictionaries used: United States 2002–4, China 1991, Germany 1989, Japan 1989–2002, Canada 2001.

TABLE 9.4. AVERAGE ACTOR-BEHAVIOR-OBJECT EVENTS PRODUCING COMPASSIONATE MORAL EMOTION BY COUNTRY

	Actor: Compassion			Object: Compassion		
	Actor	Behavior	Object	Actor	Behavior	Object
United States:	EPA: −0.53, −0.78, 0.18	0.62, 0.31, 0.34	−0.09, −0.04, 0.14	*No Compassionate Emotions Reported*		
Female Dictionary	Yes-Man	Serves/Lauds	Defendant			
Male Dictionary	Divorcee	Sexually Propositions/Extols	Spinster			
China:	EPA: −1.03, −0.46, −0.39	0.29, −0.45, 0.20	−0.19, −0.01, −0.19	*No Compassionate Emotions Reported*		
Female Dictionary	Fortune teller	Oversees/Coaches	Cynic/Divorcee			
Male Dictionary	Defendant	Begs	Political Prisoner			
Germany:	EPA: 0.04, −0.11, 0.08	0.55, 0.25, 0.23	0.34, 0.68, −0.30	EPA: 0.26, 0.87, −0.16	−1.11, 0.33, −0.16	−0.67, −1.11, −1.46
Female Dictionary	Informant	Talks to	Witness	Veterinarian/Lawyer	Questions	Patient/Defendant
Male Dictionary	In-Law	Talks to	Stepbrother	Grownup	Pays something for	Crippled Person

Japan:	EPA: -0.13, 0.08, 0.28	0.40, -0.05, 0.37	-0.47, 0.17, -0.85	EPA: 0.47, -0.03, 0.16	-0.03, -0.01, 0.26	0.20, 0.20, -0.26
Female Dictionary	Neighbor	Bestow something to/Receive something from (normal or honorific)	Middle aged male	Colleague	Entrusts decision to	Close acquaintance
Male Dictionary	Bachelor	Makes courtesy call on	Middle aged male	Junior high teacher	Expresses remorse to	Educational staffer
Canada:	EPA: 0.41, -0.23, -0.12	0.25, 1.35, 0.38	-0.38, -0.45, 0.34	EPA: -0.12, -0.21, 0.38	0.39, -0.91, 0.18	0.14, 0.24, -0.36
Female Dictionary	Roomer	Reforms	Gambler	Agnostic	Needs	Pagan
Male Dictionary	Bystander	Restrains	Suspect	Defendant	Obeys	Police Officer (Flatfoot)

NOTE: *Interact* dictionaries used: United States 2002–4, China 1991, Germany 1989, Japan 1989–2002, Canada 2001.

TABLE 9.5.   AVERAGE ACTOR-BEHAVIOR-OBJECT EVENTS PRODUCING PRAISING MORAL EMOTION BY COUNTRY

	Actor: Praising			Object: Praising		
	Actor	Behavior	Object	Actor	Behavior	Object
United States:	EPA: −0.32, −0.45, −0.04	0.52. 0.21, 0.07	0.29, 0.14, 0.13	EPA: 0.51, 0.38, 0.07	0.63, 0.68, −0.01	0.01, −0.78, 0.04
Female Dictionary	Stranger	Yields to	Blind date	Blind date	Lauds	Yes-man
Male Dictionary	Agnostic	Turns to	Catholic	Sponger	Pays something for	Temporary worker
China:	EPA: 0.44, −0.41, 0.79	0.52: 0.49, −0.21	0.73, 0.00, 0.07	EPA: −0.05, −0.64, −0.22	0.10, 0.98, 0.06	−0.01, −0.60, −0.12
Female Dictionary	Employee	Educates/Coaches	Bank customer	Runaway	Confides in	Stepchild
Male Dictionary	Trainee	Reveres	Accountant	Cashier/Bookkeeper	Indoctrinate	Temporary worker
Germany:	EPA: −0.72, −0.26, −0.47	0.62, 0.09, 0.13	−0.11, −0.10, 0.04	EPA: −0.04, 0.14, −0.09	−0.07, 0.41, 0.15	−0.26, 0.09, −0.35
Female Dictionary	Divorcee	Asks about/Talks to	Blind date	Witness	Instructs	Plainclothesman
Male Dictionary	Skeptic	Talks to	Schoolteacher	In-law	Exalts	Stepson

Japan:	EPA: -0.23, 0.29, 0.07	0.22, 0.07, 0.25	0.03, 0.16, -0.07	EPA: -0.17, 0.08, 0.02	0.02, 0.09, 0.36	-0.26, 0.10, -0.35
Female Dictionary	Neighbor	Receives something from	Neighbor	Neighbor	Expresses remorse to	Alter
Male Dictionary	Steelworker	Makes business report to	Wholesaler	Steelworker	Places order with	Metal forger
Canada:	EPA: -0.07, -0.12, 0.01	0.69, -0.16, 0.30	-0.04, 0.12, -0.09	EPA: -0.05, -0.08, 0.19	0.21, -0.21, 0.33	0.25, -0.09, -0.21
Female Dictionary	Spendthrift	Approaches/Implores	Salesman	Agnostic	Placates	Pagan
Male Dictionary	Critic	Considers/Exalts	Neophyte	Plainclothesman	Serves	Bystander

NOTE: *Interact* dictionaries used: United States 2002–4, China 1991, Germany 1989, Japan 1989–2002, Canada 2001.

just how legible these events are, especially across all of these cultures and given the random sampling method developed to garner these simulations. These events also span many different institutional spheres from school, work, religion, and family, to chance meetings between strangers. Multiple life domains are represented in these simulations, and these are only the average, more commonplace events.

PREDICTED MORAL EMOTIONS BY COUNTRY

Now we turn to what our simulations say about the book's central question: Given the important differences in the level of inequality between our five chosen countries, do they differ in their moral reactions to events? First, as displayed in Figure 9.5, more moral emotions were reported in the simulations using the German, Japanese, and Canadian *Interact* dictionaries, than in the United States' and China's. The Canadian simulations, for example, resulted in over 100 more moral emotions than in the United States and China, providing our first indication that moral reactions may be different in the United States and China than in the remaining countries.

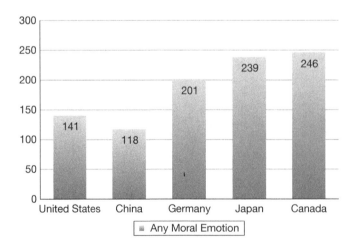

Figure 9.5 Number of Moral Emotions by Country

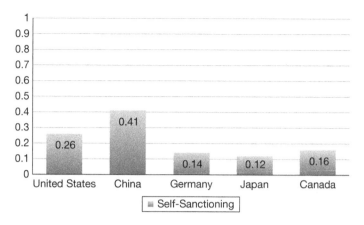

Figure 9.6 Proportion of Self-Sanctioning Moral Emotions to Total Moral Emotions by Country

We then use this number to determine the underlying proportion of the various classes of moral emotion reactions in each country. This allows us to ask the question: Regardless of the frequency of moral emotion reactions, does the composition of these reactions differ by country? Figure 9.6, Figure 9.7, Figure 9.8, and Figure 9.9 display the proportion of each class of moral emotions in each country. Rather than just reporting the

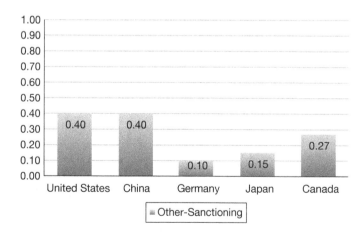

Figure 9.7 Proportion of Other-Sanctioning Moral Emotions to Total Moral Emotions by Country

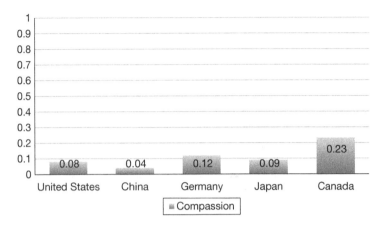

Figure 9.8 Proportion of Compassionate Moral Emotions to Total Moral Emotions by Country

raw counts of the moral emotions produced by the simulations, this proportion is methodologically important. Recall that *Interact* lets the user know what sorts of feelings would be considered typical within that country after each event; not all emotions are moral, and we have been making the case that moral emotions represent a special class of emotional experience offering a greater window into a culture. Additionally, some of the simulations were so random—because we are doing this stochastically

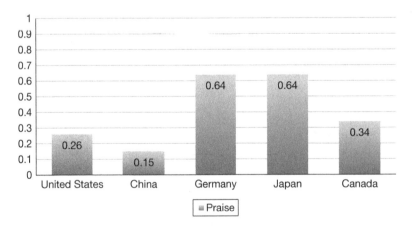

Figure 9.9 Proportion of Praising Moral Emotions to Total Moral Emotions by Country

and not based on words already in each EPA dictionary—that the "events" were not meaningful in that society or, more likely, produced an affective state without pre-collected matches in the dictionaries. We ignore those non-results by instead focusing on the relative prevalence of the four main categories of moral emotions compared to the overall number of moral emotions. Mathematically, this represents the proportion of the number of reported moral emotions in each category divided by the total number of moral emotions produced in each country. We largely avoid the question of just how moral a society is relative to another and instead ask that when an event compels a moral reaction, what type of reaction is it? Sanctioning or self-transcendent?

Beginning with the self-sanctioning moral emotions (Figure 9.6), we see their prevalence in United States and China is different than in Germany, Japan, and Canada, with more self-sanctioning emotions being experienced in the United States (26% of moral reactions) and particularly in China (41% of moral reactions). The same pattern exists for other-sanctioning emotions (Figure 9.7) with 40% of the moral emotion reactions in both the United States and China being of this type. Other-sanctioning reactions occur in only 10% of the German simulations, 15% of the Japanese simulations, and 27% of the Canadian simulations, providing a clear contrast. Thus, the overall trend in these data are for the sanctioning moral emotions to be most often experienced in the countries with the highest levels of inequality, as our theory would predict, and something that most theories of national cultures might miss.

Turning to the more self-transcendent moral reaction of being compassionate toward others, we begin to see the opposite trend. These emotions occur in only 4% of the simulations producing a moral event in China, 8% of the time in the United States, as well as 9% of the time in Japan and a slightly higher 12% of the time in Germany. Interestingly, in Canada, a country presumably most like the United States at least in terms of its geopolitical location, compassionate moral emotions are experienced almost three times as often: 23% of the time. Praising moral emotions show an even stronger distinction. Praising is experienced 64% of the time in both Germany and Japan, seconded by in 34% of the simulations in Canada. In the United States, however, it is expected to be experienced only 26% of the time and only 15% of the time in China. Once again, few factors would predict the United States and Canada being less similar than the United States and China, and both being so distinct from Germany and Japan.

We again see indications that the structural level of inequality appears to predict these divergent moral reactions, especially for praising moral emotions (although compassion is the least experienced moral emotional category in these data). Overall, in the United States, people are antici-pated to more likely experience the sanctioning moral emotions a com-bined 66% of the time and the self-transcendent emotions only 34%. In China, a country with arguably even greater inequality than in the United States, 81% of the moral emotions produced related to sanctioning either oneself or others. However, in more equal countries, the positive, pro-social moral emotions were instead more likely to occur in the simula-tions. In Germany, self-transcendent emotions arose 76% of the time, compared to 73% in Japan, and 57% in Canada. Figure 9.10 presents pie charts of this information. For readers interested in the particular break-downs of exactly which moral emotions were produced in each country and how frequently, please see Table 9.6.

To this point, our book's argument has very striking face validity. We can look at the word clouds, figures, and the numbers to argue that our perspective fits with these data. We are social scientists, however, mean-ing we have to ask the question: Are these trends statistically significant? To answer this we submitted our data to logistic regression analysis. Regression analysis is the primary way social scientists test for the pres-ence of strong relationships between a variety of variables. We use logistic regression because the dependent variable consists of whether a sanction-ing or self-transcendent moral emotion was present (coded as 1) or not (coded as 0) for the actor, the object-recipient, or both. In these regres-sions we also control for the gender of the interactants (coded as 1 for female and 0 for male) and the EPA profiles of the actor, behavior, and object recipient in order to account for any effects due to the features of the event itself (although the results do not differ by whether these are included in the models). For readability, we present the reduced table that does not report the effects of these controls (Table 9.7).

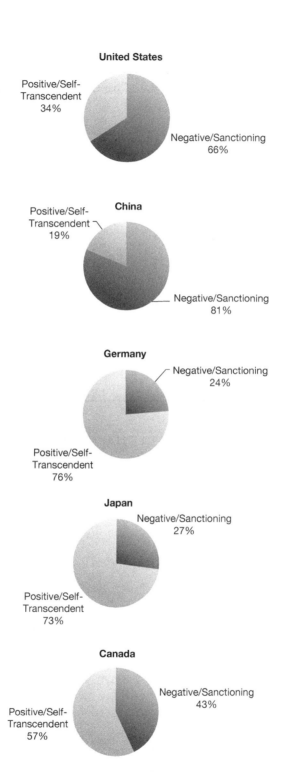

Figure 9.10 Overall Negative and Positive Moral Emotion Reactions by Country

TABLE 9.6. TOTAL REPORTED MORAL EMOTIONS BY COUNTRY

	All	United States	China	Germany	Japan	Canada
Self-Sanction						
humble	50	6	17	0	12	15
sorry	35	4	5	0	6	20
remorseful	27	4	5	15	0	3
self-pitying	18	0	13	5	0	0
repentant	11	11	0	0	0	0
contrite	10	10	0	0	0	0
embarrassed	8	2	1	3	2	0
humiliated	6	0	2	0	3	1
regretful	6	0	0	3	3	0
ashamed	5	0	3	2	0	0
crushed	2	0	2	0	0	0
mortified	2	0	0	0	2	0
Sum	180	37	48	28	28	39
Total Reported Moral Emotions	945	141	118	201	239	246
Proportion	0.19	0.26	0.41	0.14	0.12	0.16
Other-Sanction						
shocked	51	7	0	0	5	39
resentful	27	0	3	19	5	0
agitated	25	10	9	0	4	2
exasperated	21	20	0	0	1	0
contemptuous	15	10	0	0	0	5
irate	11	2	6	0	0	3
aggravated	11	0	3	0	7	1
displeased	10	2	6	0	2	0
outraged	10	0	4	0	1	5
irritated	9	0	4	0	4	1
smug	8	1	1	0	1	5
furious	7	1	3	0	2	1

TABLE 9.6. CONTINUED

	All	United States	China	Germany	Japan	Canada
dissatisfied	6	0	5	1	0	0
angry	6	3	2	0	0	1
mad	4	1	0	0	1	2
crushed	2	0	1	0	1	0
fed-up	2	0	0	0	0	2
disgusted	2	0	0	0	2	0
Sum	227	57	47	20	36	67
Total Reported Moral Emotions	945	141	118	201	239	246
Proportion	0.24	0.40	0.40	0.10	0.15	0.27
Compassion						
moved	92	4	2	24	10	52
compassionate	26	7	3	0	12	4
Sum	118	11	5	24	22	56
Total Reported Moral Emotions	945	141	118	201	239	246
Proportion	0.12	0.08	0.04	0.12	0.09	0.23
Praise						
reverent	161	7	0	70	9	75
touched	75	3	3	28	41	0
proud	33	4	0	12	17	0
awe-struck	31	11	12	0	7	1
charmed	27	4	0	0	22	1
appreciative	17	0	0	0	17	0
glad	15	1	0	1	12	1
ecstatic	14	0	0	2	12	0
thrilled	12	0	3	9	0	0
overjoyed	11	2	0	7	2	0
happily surprised	10	0	0	0	10	0

(*continued*)

TABLE 9.6. CONTINUED

	All	United States	China	Germany	Japan	Canada
pleased	8	2	0	0	0	6
joyful	5	1	0	0	4	0
thankful	1	1	0	0	0	0
Sum	420	36	18	129	153	84
Total Reported Moral Emotions	945	141	118	201	239	246
Proportion	0.44	0.26	0.15	0.64	0.64	0.34

NOTE: Simulation results from United States 2002–4, China 1991, Germany 1989, Japan 1989–2002, Canada 2001 *Interact* dictionaries.

To interpret these results, please know that the coefficients are presented as log odds, meaning that a positive coefficient shows that country to evidence greater levels of a particular moral emotion than the comparison country, the United States. A negative coefficient designates that country to have fewer of a particular moral reaction than in the United States. Additionally, some regression analyses require a great deal of attention to the specific values tied to the independent variables submitted to the regression analysis (i.e., their coefficients): a person's years of schooling may more or less shift the size of the outcome as compared to, say, their gender. For our purposes, the coefficients' direction and significance is our key concern. To interpret a coefficient's statistical significance, look to the presence of asterisks next to it: more asterisks means, essentially, a lesser chance that the relationship was found coincidentally, with no asterisks indicating the relationship is not strong enough to eliminate the possibility its association with the dependent variable (prevalence of a moral reaction in our case) is due to chance. Further, all country-level differences, including those discussed earlier and those presented in Table 9.1, are subsumed into the variable for each country. We would then expect the direction and significance of the country variables to behave in certain ways if, say, the level of human development was the stronger predictor of moral reactions than inequality.

TABLE 9.7. LOGISTIC REGRESSION OF MORAL EMOTIONS
ON COUNTRY AND SIMULATION CHARACTERISTICS

	Sanctioning		Self-Transcendent	
Country (USA Omitted)				
China	0.88	*	−1.01	**
	(0.35)		(0.33)	
Germany	−2.36	***	2.48	***
	(0.31)		(0.32)	
Japan	−2.16	***	2.19	***
	(0.29)		(0.29)	
Canada	−1.19	***	1.20	***
	(0.28)		(0.27)	
Constant	1.09	***	−0.82	***
	(0.23)		(0.23)	
Model Fit				
Chi²	318.08		316.06	
Degrees of Freedom	14		14	
N	816		816	

NOTE: Coefficients reported as log odds; standard errors in parentheses; $+p<.10$, $*p <$ .05, $**p < .01$, $***p < .001$ (two-tailed tests); Models control for the gender of the actor and the EPA profiles of the actor, behavior, and object. Simulation results from United States 2002–4, China 1991, Germany 1989, Japan 1989–2002, Canada 2001 *Interact* dictionaries.

Overall, these more formal tests provide statistical support of our conclusions: Sanctioning occurs even more often in the Chinese simulations than in the United States ($b = .88$, $p = .012$). Given that China was experiencing a rapid rise in their level of inequality at this time, we argue that this result is in line with our predictions. Sanctioning also occurs less often in the more equal countries of Germany ($b = -2.35$, $p < .001$), Japan ($b = -2.16$, $p < .001$), and Canada ($b = -1.19$, $p < .001$). We see a similar pattern of results for the more self-transcendent, pro-social moral emotions: Compassion and praise occurs even less often in China as compared to the United States ($b = -1.01$, $p = .003$) and more often in Germany, Japan, and Canada ($b = 2.48$, $p < .001$; $b = 2.19$, $p < .001$, $b = 1.20$, $p < .001$ respectively).

Overall, these results suggest that China and the United States have similar moral emotional cultures—although China's is perhaps the most extreme—and these two societies' moral cultures are set apart from that of Germany, Japan, and Canada, which are each more similar to each other. This is a counterintuitive finding for most theories, but one that a focus on the importance of economic inequality would predict.

CONCLUSIONS

We began this chapter with a discussion of the various ways in which these countries differ from each other and touched on some of the most likely options available for predicting how different societies' moral experiences may differ. Two of the nations in our sample are from the East and three are from the West. Two, Canada and the United States, share a border, a continent, and a common native language. They all have varying degrees of immigration, with the United States and China being at separate ends of the spectrum. And all but one, China, have some of the highest levels of human development according to the United Nations. We can carve up the global map in a variety of ways.

The data, however, support our contention that the factor consistently linked with this set of outcomes maps onto these countries' structural levels of inequality. Germany, Japan, and Canada have consistently lower levels of inequality than the United States. The United States and China, in contrast, have far higher levels of inequality, with China experiencing an even greater escalation in their inequality throughout the turn of the last century. Consistently we find when events prompt a moral reaction, we find that sanctioning is predicted to be more likely in the United States and China, while feelings of compassion and especially praise are more likely in the less hierarchical countries of Germany, Japan, and Canada. The counterintuitive nature of these findings is noteworthy, and while it cannot prove our contention—as we stated at the beginning of the book—it is highly suggestive that inequality patterns moral cultures.

Our goal of linking perhaps the greatest macro-organizing factor for a society with individual emotional experience required a number of theoretical steps and a fairly thorough understanding of what *Interact* provides. But if you can accept that Affect Control Theory's primary method has validity, as a multitude of academic papers have contended and arguably established, then our data are clearly consistent with our focus on the impact of inequality. A society's moral culture represented in the affective meanings and feeling rules internalized by its members, is fundamentally based in economic inequality.

10

Conclusion

I n 2013, President Obama delivered an economic speech highlighting growing economic inequality as the "defining challenge of our time." Interestingly for our project, he continued on to quote Adam Smith to say that working a full-time job should be enough to let you live "tolerably." Our project draws on a different element of Smith's work, namely the concern that extreme inequality distorts human senses of sympathy too greatly toward the rich. "Smith argues emphatically that our tendency to sympathize more fully and readily with the rich than the poor tends to undermine morality" (Rasmussen, 2016, p. 7). One possible negative result of increasing inequality, our work supports, is a general increase in the lack of sympathy toward most people in your society; Smith worried that this would be due to an increasing global sense of envy and crediting the winners of an inequality spread with some sort of false virtue.

Our data support this linkage between unequal social structures and moral emotions. Not necessarily because people are envious of the rich, but we find striking support for our contention that living in a vastly economically unequal society leads to a general negative sense of moral emotionality suffusing that society. The issue goes well beyond the traditional sociological focus on stratification, on how people at the top or bottom of economic structures are socialized to think, feel, and behave. We are arguing that sociologists should attend more to the links between structural inequality and social psychological functioning. We see this as building beyond the important contributions from the Social Structure and Personality paradigm linking structure and individual psychological functioning. Their basic contention has been so successful that it has emigrated into most sociological subfields. People who study families, or organizations, or mental health, or education largely agree that advantage/ disadvantage and individual functioning are linked in important ways. Rather than an exclusive focus on a person's location in a stratified system, we want to expand to look at the nature of the system itself. Our project calls attention to the nature of that structure, itself, as disseminating into individual outlooks, beliefs, and social interactions.

The trend in social science books about human behavior is to have a section in their conclusion that explains What Authors Think You Should Do, prescriptions for improving whatever social ill has been under discussion. We are expressly *not* going to give societal advice. We certainly advocate the position that less inequality in a society is preferable to more inequality, something agreed on by most Americans, regardless of political party (Norton & Ariely, 2011). Interestingly, most Americans in Norton and Ariely's (2011) study were unaware of the facts underlying inequality in their own society, expressing opinions that the level of inequality in Sweden was even too much when presented the data without context and country identifier. Sweden's inequality is dwarfed by America's, suggesting that more information might change the policy preferences of the American public.

But we do not claim any special policy expertise on how best to achieve this goal, or what level of inequality rewards citizens and motivates economic behavior without punishing those at the bottom of the ladder, whether through misfortune, neglect, or poor decisions. Indeed, a key aspect of the psychological orientations perpetuating inequality involve the belief that there is freedom of opportunity such that people in a society believe they have a chance to move up the economic ladder. Such beliefs are linked to acceptance of inequality, both in surveys around the world and in experimental explorations (Shariff et al., 2016). We do suggest, however, for interested readers pursue more policy-oriented scholarship from people with more expertise in how to positively influence macro-level political and economic structures (e.g., Wilkinson and Pickett 2011).

What we are advocating is a more social science oriented perspective, tying together literatures that have not fully been brought into a single framework alongside novel treatment of cross-cultural data. Many scholars have connected aspects of macro and micro social analysis, we are synthesizing the range of that work all the way from the most abstract, macro perspective—the level of economic inequality in societies—all the way down to the most micro emotional system. Studying emotions allows us to bridge work on culture and the individual, as they exist as the most personal aspects of our lives, yet they are shaped by and attached to the collective understandings internalized by competent members of a society. For our purposes, we employ tools motivated by Affect Control theory (ACT), a well-established sociological treatment of language and cultural meaning.

Previous work in ACT has not been especially focused on comparing the different language dictionaries, and certainly not as related to the general macro characteristics of the nations that have gathered this extensive data. Within other parts of the field, the work linking social structural position to a range of individual values and behaviors has not, itself, focused on comparing aspects of those structures across nations. Morality, fundamental ways of understanding how relationships should work, the obligations that institutions and others are expected to fulfill, and how a "proper" person behaves, is the pivot for this link. Moral concerns suffuse all aspects of collective life, and if most daily interactions are not expressly moral, this is because people tend to be proficient at keeping their behaviors within the bright lines (Hitlin, 2008) that society dictates are appropriate.

For example, Fiske and Rai (2015) suggest that violence stems, in part, from damage to a social relationship that is perceived as wrong, thus immoral behavior contributes to violence (as opposed to, say, only selfish desires). They suggest that reducing societal violence can be done through defining it as immoral. According to our research, rectifying extreme inequality would be a step toward the same goal. Moving toward equality may not be a goal for all people or societies, and may be at odds with other virtues, like individual liberty, however. This is how many current American political debates end up being framed:

> Both liberty and equality are among the primary goals pursued by human beings through many centuries; but total liberty for wolves is death to the lambs, total liberty of the powerful, the gifted, is not compatible with the rights to a decent existence of the weak and less gifted . . . both attitudes embody values which for some men or women are ultimate, and which are intelligible to us all if we have any sympathy or imagination or understanding of human beings. Equality may demand the restraint of the liberty of those who wish to dominate; liberty . . . may have to be curtailed in order to make room for social welfare . . . to allow justice or fairness to be exercised." (Berlin 1990, pp.12–13)

BROAD CONTRIBUTIONS

We offer two main contributions to the research literature. First, we link a variety of topics under a broad umbrella, showing ways that national cultures, intertwined with levels of societal inequality, shape individual experience. There is a good deal of work on how people in different levels of the social structure are socialized differently, and end up with divergent attitudes, values, preferences, and can make different choices about personal and professional life. We are building on this by focusing not only on one's place in the social structure, but on the nature of that social structure, itself.

Living in a society with vast differences in income inequality creates multitudes of divisions between people. Interactions occur more often between people of unequal status or between status rivals rather than between equals (Kemper 2015). There are stronger, divisive sentiments of "us versus them," which can tear away at the collective fabric of trust and community binding a populous together. Unequal societies are more personally economically precarious as well—the threat of losing one's place in the hierarchy is real and ever-present. Keeping oneself from losing position and being surpassed by others further enhances sanctioning to maintain the hierarchy. Fellow members of your culture are perceived—perhaps justly—more as competitors than comrades.

These divisions, threats, deprivations, and status distinctions—or lack thereof in more equal societies—become baked into the culture's language and rules for action. Inequality thus becomes a more intractable problem to contend with because, over many, many decades, it has affected the cultural knowledge and normative rules of behavior that we, as members of our cultures, take to be right, proper, true, and natural. It is no wonder that attempts to lessen inequality tend to be met with resistance—this threatens one of the pillars defining a culture.

Our second contribution is to offer a new use of an established tool, suggesting that the data built into *Interact* can actually tell us a lot about the fabric of a society, based on the semantic information gathered—and resultant inductively derived impression formation equations—measuring cultural meaning. As we explain theoretically, and then model in chapter 9, *Interact* allows us to treat language as a tool tantamount to a thermometer, measuring the inequality in a culture as embedded in the emotional experiences of its practitioners. A moral sensation is a personal interpretation of an event based on general cultural assumptions (Tappan, 1997).

In more accessible terms, we are offering a social scientific way to explore colloquial understandings that we have of our own, and other, societies. In the Netherlands, apparently, there are terms that translate roughly as "American conditions" (*Amerikaanse toestanden* in Dutch), a warning against acting in ways that would exacerbate gaps between the rich and poor, or provide poorer access to medical treatment or education. This folk understanding of America captures the actual social arrangements in the United States along with a bit of a judgment comparing that society to this one. These are stereotypes, of course, but they capture a sense of lived reality that, we are suggesting, tells us something about the moral expectations members of a society have for their own worlds, and how they interpret and understand other societies' social arrangements.

These typifications are cognitive shorthand for what people share as members of a culture, for the sorts of mannerisms, beliefs, priorities, and values that strike people as feeling natural and typical for that group. Again, this is not to say that everyone in any country or group exemplifies these stereotypes. Yet as a species well-served by our ability to categorize and find patterns, these intuitive shortcuts help us know what to expect, and to judge any single person we are interacting with as being more or less like the stereotypes we associated with people in that category. In some societies this process can contribute to institutional discrimination against people in categories that are culturally or contextually devalued.

Another version of our argument dovetails with a recent book (Abend, 2014) positing the "moral background" as a separate level of analysis for the fledgling sociology of morality. Abend suggests that most of the scientific exploration of morality occurs at the level of behavior and then at the level of judgments/beliefs/social norms. He suggests that the moral background of a society sets the terms for what arguments are even considered moral, and what objects are subject to moral judgment and scrutiny. Members of a community, he argues, generally agree on what the world is like, "they share an inventory or repertoire of concepts that is at their disposal—that is, the set of concepts they may choose to use" (p. 29). As an example, he contends in American society it would be plain crazy to morally evaluate a pig's behavior; that falls outside the shared understandings of what is allowed to be morally evaluated.

It is plausible that *Interact* serves as an instrument for discerning parts of this moral background. Studying emotions using the method we advocate does more than simply measure things at the level of thoughts/norms; we are making the strong claim that this is a window into the cultural substrate that a society shares. The affective meanings contained in the EPA dictionaries and the impression formation equations built into *Interact* are representations of the normative schemas for thought, action, and emotional reaction deeply embedded in each and every member of a culture. This may not be a perfect representation of Abend's concept, but his focus on "structurally ingrained patterns" (p. 316) echoes our own measure. As he puts it, much of the moral background is not up to the people who instantiate it, presuppositions about reality that are fundamentally social and shape individual reactions to the world. Regardless of approach, national language and the beliefs, judgments, and emotions that get translated to its members, is a core aspect of human life. And while Durkheim and Marx felt that nationalism would disappear as modern times advanced; they appear to have been quite incorrect (Guibernau, 2007).

We argue that greater levels of inequality magnify the presence of sanctioning while reducing the use of compassion, and therefore possibly empathy. This inequality may contribute to social distance among all members of a society, not just between the "haves" and the "have nots." Our argument might also be consonant with McCaffree's (2015) recent exploration of the nature of morality. He focuses broadly on how societal changes in social distance, not unlike those from our discussion in Chapters 3 and 4, have shifted the ways that dyads interact. His focus on "perceptual overlap" is potentially applicable here, offering a mechanism for how social systems become deeply internalized. For McCaffree, the distance—physical, social, and eventually perceptual—between people in modernizing societies contributes to a lack of empathy: "Proximity, status, and exchange contexts partition perceptions between people and the partitioning of perceptions produces immorality" (p. 105).

SPECIFIC FINDINGS

Moral sanctioning maintains hierarchy, and will occur more often when people feel under threat, which happens—explicitly and implicitly—in societies with more inequality. This suggests that societal economic organization is a driving factor underlying individual emotional experience, even more (we suggest) than more commonly credited national factors such as how individualistic a culture is, the ubiquitous East/West distinction highlighted so often within cross-cultural psychology. The key is that the more individualistic cultures in the world—the United States (Woodard, 2016), and one of the least—China—operate similarly in our data. Thus, the long-standing East/West cultural divide (e.g., Hofstede, 2001; Markus and Kitayama, 1991; Triandis, 1995) dominating cultural psychology for a long time is not in evidence here with our novel approach to capturing cross-cultural interaction and emotional reaction.

Beyond this East/West distinction, we also investigated differences between two countries that, geopolitically, should be quite similar: Canada and the United States. These countries share a border, a continent, and a common language. Yet Canada's moral emotional system operates more like Germany's and Japan's. The countries also experience differential levels of immigration, with American immigration rates being the highest and China's the lowest. Immigration, however, also does not explain the patterns we see, as American and Chinese moral emotional reactions are quite comparable. This partially contradicts the work of Susan Fiske (2011) and colleagues who suggest that countries with high levels of immigration would be rife with scorn for the outsiders (and therefore, we would argue, high levels of sanctioning and reduced sympathy). This theory may be accurate for the American case, but at the very least, it does not explain moral emotions in China. And although China has the lowest level of human development according to the United Nations of any country we investigate, again, its moral emotional system is more like that of the United States, which has one of the highest levels of human development.

The factor differentiating these countries that does predict the observed empirical differences in moral emotional reactions is the societal level of inequality. Germany, Japan, and Canada have consistently lower levels of inequality than the United States. The United States, in contrast, has arguably either the same or slightly less inequality than China, even in the time periods during which the EPA dictionaries were collected. And in these more unequal countries, the self-and other-sanctioning moral emotions are far more prevalent than the positive, pro-social, self-transcendent emotions of compassion and praise. These emotions are experienced mostly in more equal countries. We are certainly not claiming that sanctioning never happens in more equal societies, or that Americans and the Chinese do not feel compassion or praise toward others. We are talking about relative frequencies here, with sanctioning expected to be more often felt in unequal societies than self-transcendent emotions.

FUTURE ITERATIONS

We hope this project is generative of future research. We are taking the strong position linking economic inequality all the way down to the individual in part to motivate other scholars to examine these wide-ranging links with different tools. There are a number of types of potential inequality in a society, we have focused on the broadest and most commonly measured economic type. But societies differ by race, religion, gender composition, urbanicity, and other factors that stratify power and resources. These sorts of organizations have not been extensively linked with the social psychological orientations and behaviors that are of interest to many sociologists. We know that people can be shaped differentially based on whether they have more or less power, status, or resources in a society, we know less about how each particular social structure influences us.

Gathering the data within a country to assess these interactional moral processes is almost prohibitively expensive, so it is difficult to replicate our ideas within a wider array of countries and methodological techniques. However, if our theory has merit, we hope others will pick up on the broad links between macro and micro (to employ common, if slightly tired terminology) to refine, or argue with, our thesis.

There certainly are myriad differences among subgroups in terms of their views of morality; while our measure necessarily homogenizes culture, or at least takes the variation of a culture into account while discerning central tendencies, we are open to the fact that other important social variables predict moral experience. In the American context, for example, gender, religious affiliation, and birth cohort are important predictors of moral beliefs, with education and marital status being important but less so (Miles, 2014).

Despite the diversity within any society or group, there are also ideal typifications that become captured in stereotypes about those people. No stereotype is strictly true, but at the same time, using ideal types to describe kinds of people (doctors, criminals, Yankees fans) is part of everyday life. We need standards to allow us to have expectations for interaction; we cannot start from scratch with every situation that we enter. Emotions signal when interactions deviate from these expectations, and the expectations come from societal forms instantiated within language. These ideas operate at the collective level, through the semantic meanings attached to linguistically defined words, and at the individual level, as people internalize and use culture in their everyday lives.

We attempt to bring some coherence to a variety of social science approaches along the route from macro-structure to micro-functioning. The level of economic inequality in a society shapes institutions, organizations, and interactions in some potentially surprising ways. We suggest this spread of incomes suffuses into everyday life, potentially creating an environment of threat given the stakes of everyday choices. This leads to greater proportions of negative moral emotions, signaling more opportunities to feel viscerally endangered—even at non-conscious levels—by the risks inherent in dealing with other people. We cannot adjudicate what causes what, but greater amounts of negative emotion serve to erode social trust and cohesion. We know this happens in small groups, we are suggesting that it is related to the wider structure of society.

In societies with more equality, likely perpetuated through stronger economic safety nets and social programs, we find in our simulations a greater number of positive, pro-social emotions, the sorts of things that bind societies and people together. Perhaps the risks of any particular choice are not as extreme, when basic living wages and medical support are closer to being guaranteed, when the "winners" of society are not able to accumulate the sheer percentage of economic (and likely political) capital as in the most unequal societies. This is more speculative for us, given the data at hand, but we attempt to model a theory walking from inequality through moral systems to individual emotions, and our data fit with this approach. Relevant work suggests that issues of trust and status are possible mechanisms linking inequality to individual psychology (see Buttrick & Oishi, 2017 for a review). These two constructs are core sociological processes that deserve further study within our framework.

In conclusion, we simply want to reiterate that there are a number of ways to group the five nations we study: China, Japan, German, Canada, and the United States. We suggest that very few academic or lay approaches would put the United States and China in one box, apart from the other three. Our theory of inequality and culture does, however, and is strongly supported through our data simulations. Future work needs to engage our thesis in multiple ways, with different tools and better explorations of potential mechanisms linking the micro and macro. We hope this project is but a first step in an ongoing conversation, certainly not the final word on this topic. While sociology has done great work linking individual functioning with social stratification, there is much to be done with respect to the kinds of stratification across societies. The societal foundations for our behavior are quite unequal across the world.

REFERENCES

Abend, Gabriel. 2011. "Thick Concepts and the Moral Brain." *European Journal of Sociology* 52(1):143–72.

Abend, Gabriel. 2014. *The Moral Background: An Inquiry into the History of Business Ethics*. Princeton, NJ: Princeton University Press.

Abulof, Uriel. 2015. *The Mortality and Morality of Nations*. New York: Cambridge University Press.

Ahmed, Eliza, Nathan Harris, John Braithwaite, and Valerie Braithwaite. 2001. *Shame Management Through Reintegration*. Cambridge, England: Cambridge University Press.

Alesina, Alberto, Rafael Di Tella, and Robert MacCullouch. 2004. "Inequality and Happiness: Are Europeans and Americans Different?" *Journal of Public Economics* 88:2009–42.

Algoe, Sara B., and Jonathan Haidt. 2009. "Witnessing Excellence in Action: The 'Other-Praising'emotions of elevation, gratitude, and admiration." *The Journal of Positive Psychology* 4(2):105–27.

Alwin, Duane F., Ronald L. Cohen, and Theodore M. Newcomb. 1991. *Political Attitudes over the Life Span: the Bennington Women After Fifty Years*. Madison, WI: University of Wisconsin Press.

Ambrasat, Jens, Christian von Scheve, Markus Conrad, Gesche Schauenburg, and Tobias Schröder. 2014. "Consensus and Stratification in the Affective Meaning of Human Sociality." *Proceedings of the National Academy of Sciences* 111:8001–06.

Ambrasat, Jens, Christian von Scheve, Gesche Schauenburg, Markus Conrad, and Tobias Schröder. 2016. "Unpacking the Habitus: Meaning Making across Lifestyles." *Sociological Forum* 31. doi: 10.1111/socf.12293.

Anderson, Steven W., Antoine Bechara, Hanna Damasio, Daniel Tranel, and Antonio R. Damasio. 1999. "Impairment of Social and Moral Behavior Related to Early Damage in Human Prefrontal Cortex." *Nature Neuroscience* 2(11):1032–37.

Anderson, Steven W., Hanna Damasio, Daniel Tranel, and Antonio R Damasio. 2000. "Long-Term Sequelae of Prefrontal Cortex Damage Acquired in Early Childhood." *Developmental Neuropsychology* 18(3):281–96.

Aquino, Karl, and Americus Reed II. 2002. "The self-importance of moral identity." *Journal of Personality and Social Psychology* 83(6):1423.

Archer, Margaret S. 2007. *Making Our Way Through the World: Human Reflexivity and Social Mobility*. Cambridge, UK: Cambridge University Press.

Atkinson, Anthony B., and Andrea Brandolini. 2008. "On Analyzing the World Distribution of Income." *Society for the Study of Economic Inequality Working Paper Series*. Available at http://www.ecineq.org/milano/wp/ecineq2008-97.pdf

Atkinson, Aanthony B., and S. Morelli. 2014. "The Chartbook of Economic Inequality." www.chartbookofeconomicinequality.com

Babcock, Mary K., and John Sabini. 1990. "On Differentiating Embarrassment from Shame." *European Journal of Social Psychology* 20(2):151–69.

Bader, Christopher D., and Roger Finke. 2010. "What Does God Require? Understanding Religious Context and Morality." In *Handbook of the Sociology of Morality*, edited by Steven Hitlin and Stephen Vaisey (pp. 241–54). New York: Springer.

Babones, Salvatore J. 2008. "Income Inequality and Population Health: Correlation and Causality." *Social Science and Medicine* 66:1614–26.

Baker, Wayne. 2005. *America's Crisis of Values: Reality and Perception*. Princeton, NJ: Princeton University Press.

Bandura, Albert. 1991. "Social Cognitive Theory of Moral Thought and Action." In *Handbook of Moral Behavior and Development*, edited by William M. Kurtines and Jacob L. Gewirtz (pp. 45–103). Hillsdale, NJ: Lawrence Erlbaum.

Bandura, Albert. 1999. "Moral Disengagement in the Perpetration of Inhumanities." *Personality and Social Psychology Review* 3(3):193–209.

Bargh, John A., and Tanya L. Chartrand. 1999. "The Unbearable Automaticity of Being." *American Psychologist* 54(7):462–79.

Batson, C. Daniel, Nadia Ahmad, and David A Lishner. 2011. "Empathy and Altruism." In *The Oxford Handbook of Positive Psychology,* edited by C. R. Snyder and S. J. Lopez (2nd ed., pp. 417–26). New York: Oxford University Press.

Bechara, Antoine, Antonio R Damasio, Hanna Damasio, and Steven W Anderson. 1994. "Insensitivity to Future Consequences Following Damage to Human Prefrontal Cortex." *Cognition* 50(1):7–15.

Bedford A. Olwen. 2004. "The Individual Experience of Guilt and Shame in Chinese Culture." 10(1):29–52. Issue published: March 1, 2004.

Bedford, Olwen, and Kwang-Kuo Hwang. 2003. "Guilt and Shame in Chinese Culture: A Cross-cultural Framework from the Perspective of Morality and Identity." *Journal for the Theory of Social Behaviour* 33(2):127–44.

Beckfield, Jason. 2004. "Does Income Inequality Harm Health? New Cross-National Evidence." *Journal of Health and Social Behavior* 45:231–48.

Bellah, Robert, Richard Madsen, William M. Sullivan, Ann Swidler, and Steven M. Tipton (Eds.). 1985. *Habits of the heart individualism and commitment in American life*. Berkeley: University of California Press.

Berbrier, Mitch. 1998. "Half the Battle: Cultural Resonance, Framing Processes, and Ethnic Affectations in Contemporary White Separatist Rhetoric." *Social Problems* 45:431–50.

Berger, Joseph, and M. Hamit Fisek. 2008. "Immigrant Groups and the Emergence of Status Inequality: An Application of Spread of Status Value Theory." Presented at the ISA World Forum of Sociology in Barcelona, September 5–9.

Bergmann, Jorg R. 1998. "Introduction: Morality in Discourse." *Research on Language and Social Interaction* 31(3&4):279–94.

Berlin, Isaiah. 1990. *The Crooked Timber of Humanity*. Princeton, NJ: Princeton University Press.

Berns, Gregory S., and Scott Atran. 2012. "The Biology of Cultural Conflict." *Philosophical Transactions of the Royal Society, Ser. B* 367(1589):633–39.

Berns, Gregory S., Emily Bell, C. Monica Capra, Michael J. Prietula, Sara Moore, Brittany Anderson, Jeremy Ginges, and Scott Atran. 2012. "The Price of Your Soul: Neural Evidence for the Non-Utilitarian Representation of Sacred Values." *Philosophical Transactions of the Royal Society, Ser. B* 367:754–62.

Berreby, David. 2005. *Us and Them: Understanding Your Tribal Mind*. New York: Little, Brown, and Co.

Black, Donald. 2011. *Moral Time*. New York: Oxford University Press.

Blair, Irene V., and Mahzarin R. Banaji. 1996. "Automatic and Controlled Processes in Stereotype Priming." *Journal of Personality and Social Psychology* 70:1142–63.

Blair-Loy, Mary. 2010. "Moral Dimensions of the Work-Family Nexus." In *Handbook of the Sociology of Morality*, edited by Steven Hitlin and Stephen Vaisey (pp. 439–53). New York: Springer.

Blair, Robert Jr., and Lisa Cipolotti. 2000. "Impaired Social Response Reversal." *Brain* 123(6):1122–41.

Blasi, Augusto. 1999. "Emotions and Moral Motivation." *Journal for the Theory of Social Behaviour* 29(1):1–19.

Bloom, Paul. 2013. *Just Babies: The Origins of Good and Evil*. New York: Random House.

Boehm, Christopher. 2012. *Moral Origins: The Evolution of Virtue, Altruism, and Shame*. New York: Basic Books.

Boltanski, Luc, and Laurent Thévenot. 1999. "The Sociology of Critical Capacity." *European Journal of Social Theory* 2(3):359–77.

Botchkovar, Ekaterina, and Charles R. Tittle. 2008. "Delineating the Scope of Reintegrative Shaming Theory: An Explanation of Contingencies using Russian Data." *Social Science Research* 37(3):703–20.

Boudon, Raymond. 2008. "Which Theory of Moral Evolution Should Social Scientists Choose." *International Review of Sociology* 18(2):183–96.

Bourdieu, Pierre (Ed.). 1977. *Outline of a Theory of Practice*. Cambridge, England: Cambridge University Press.

Bourdieu, Pierre. 1990. *The Logic of Practice*. Palo Alto, CA: Stanford University Press.

Bourdieu, Pierre. 1991. *Language and Symbolic Power*. Harvard University Press.

Braithwaite, John. 1989. *Crime, Shame and Reintegration*. Cambridge, England: Cambridge University Press.

Brandolini, Andrea, and Timothy M. Smeeding. 2009. "Income Inequality in Richer and OECD Countries." In *The Oxford Handbook of Economic Inequality*, edited by B. Nolan, W. Salverda, and T. M. Smeeding. New York: Oxford University Press.

Brewer, Marilynn B. 1991. "The Social Self: On Being the Same and Different at the Same Time." *Personality and Social Psychology Bulletin* 17:475–82.

Brewer, Marilynn, and Layton Lui. 1989. "The Primacy of Age and Sex in the Structure of Person Categories." *Social Cognition* 7:262–74.

Brown, Donald E. 1991. *Human Universals*. Philadelphia: Temple University Press.

Brown, Donald E. 2004. "Human Universals, Human Nature, and Human Culture." *Daedelus* 133(4):47–54.

Burke, Peter James. 2006. *Contemporary Social Psychological Theories.* Palo Alto, CA: Stanford University Press.

Burkhauser, Richard V., Jan-Emmanuel De Neve, and Nattavudh Powdthavee. 2016. "Top Incomes and Human Well-Being around the World." Center for Economic Performance Discussion Paper No 1400.

Buttrick, Nicholas R., and Shigehiro Oishi. 2017. "The Psychological Consequences of Income Inequality." *Social and Personality Psychology Compass* 11(3):1–12.

Camille, Nathalie, Giorgio Coricelli, Jerome Sallet, Pascale Pradat-Diehl, Jean-René Duhamel, and Angela Sirigu. 2004. "The involvement of the Orbitofrontal Cortex in the Experience of Regret." *Science* 304(5674):1167–70.

Chaiken, Shelly, and Yaacov Trope. 1999. *Dual-Process Theories in Social Psychology.* New York: Guilford Press.

Chapman, Hanah A., and Adam K. Anderson. 2013. "Things rank and gross in nature: a review and synthesis of moral disgust." *Psychological Bulletin* 139(2):300.

Charlesworth, Simon J., Paul Gilfillan, and Richard Wilkinson. 2004. "Living Inferiority." *British Medical Bulletin* 69:49–60.

Cheon, Byung You, Jiyeun Hwang Chang, Gyu Seong Shin, Jin Wook Kang, Shin Wook Lee, Byung Hee Kim, and Hyun Joo. 2013. "Growing Inequality and Its Impacts in Korea." http://gini-research.org/system/uploads/439/original/Korea.pdf?1370077269

Cheung, Cecilia S., Eva M. Pomerantz, Meifang Wang, and Yang Qu. 2016. "Controlling and Autonomy-Supportive Parenting in the United States and China: Beyond Children's Reports." *Child Development* 87(6):1992–2007.

Churchland, Patricia S. 2011. *Braintrust: What Neuroscience Tells Us about Morality.* Princeton, NJ.: Princeton University Press.

Colby, Anne, and William Damon. 1992. *Some Do Care: Contemporary Lives of Moral Commitment*. New York: The Free Press (Simon & Schuster).

Collett, Jessica L., and Omar Lizardo. 2014. "Localizing Cultural Phenomena by Specifying Social Psychological Mechanisms: Introduction to the Special Issue." *Social Psychology Quarterly* 77(2):95–99.

Collins, Randall. 2004. *Interaction Ritual Chains*. Princeton, NJ: Princeton University Press.

Congressional Budget Office. 2011. "Trends in the Distribution of Household Income between 1979 to 2007." http://www.cbo.gov/sites/default/files/112th-congress-2011-2012/reports/10-25-HouseholdIncome_0.pdf

Congressional Budget Office. 2016. "The Distribution of Household Income and Federal Taxes, 2013." https://www.cbo.gov/publication/51361

Cook, Karen S. 2014. "Social Capital and Inequality: The Importance of Social Connections." In *Handbook of the Social Psychology of Inequality*, edited by J. McLeod, E. J. Lawler, and M. Schwalbe (pp. 207–27). New York: Springer.

Costa, Albert, Alice Foucart, Sayuri Hayakawa, Melina Aparici, Jose Apesteguia, Joy Heafner, and Boaz Keysar. 2014. "Your Morals Depend on Language." *PloS One* 9(4):e94842.

Côté, Stéphane, Paul K. Piff, and Robb Willer. 2013. "For Whom Do the Ends Justify the Means? Social Class and Utilitarian Moral Judgment." *Journal of Personality and Social Psychology* 104(3):490–503.

Cuddy, Amy J. C., Susan T. Fiske, and Peter Glick. 2007. "The BIAS Map: Behaviors from Intergroup Affect and Stereotypes." *Journal of Personality and Social Psychology* 92:631–48.

d'Andrade, Roy G. 1995. *The Development of Cognitive Anthropology.* Cambridge, England: Cambridge University Press.

Damasio, Antonio. 1999. *The Feeling of What Happens*. San Diego: Harcourt.

Damasio, Antonio. 2003. *Looking for Spinoza: Joy, Sorrow, and the Feeling Brain*. Orlando: Harcourt.

Damasio, Antonio. 2005a. "The Neurobiological Grounding of Human Values." In *Neurobiology of Human Values*, edited by Jean-Pierre Changeux, Wolf Singer, Antonio R. Damasio, and Yves Christen (pp. 47–56). Berlin, Germany: Springer-Verlag.

Damasio, Hanna. 2005b. "Disorders of Social Conduct Following Damage to Prefrontal Cortices." In *Neurobiology of Human Values*, edited by Jean-Pierre Changeux, Wolf Singer, Antonio R. Damasio, and Yves Christen (pp. 37–46). Berlin, Germany: Springer-Verlag.

Damasio, Antonio R., Daniel Tranel, and Hanna C. Damasio. 1991. "Behavior: theory and preliminary testing." *Frontal Lobe Function and Dysfunction* 217.

Damon, William. 1984. "Self-understanding and moral development from childhood to adolescence." In *Morality, Moral Behavior, and Moral Development*, edited by Kurtiness, William M., and Jacob L. Gewirtz (pp. 109–127). New York: Wiley.

de Hooge, Ilone E., Seger M. Breugelmans, and Marcel Zeelenberg. 2008. "Not So Ugly After All: When Shame Acts as a Commitment Device." *Journal of Personality and Social Psychology* 95(4):933–43.

De Vos, George. 1960. "The relation of guilt toward parents to achievement and arranged marriage among the Japanese." *Psychiatry* 23(3):287–301.

de Waal, Frans. 2009. *The Age of Empathy: Nature's Lessons for a Kinder Society*. New York: Crown Publishing Group.

DeLamater, John D., and Amanda Ward. 2013. *Handbook of Social Psychology*. New York: Springer.

Delhey, Jan, and Ulrich Kohler. 2011. "Is Happiness Inequality Immune to Income Inequality? New Evidence through Instrument-Effect-Corrected Standard Deviations." *Social Science Research* 40:742–56.

Dickerson, Sally S., and Margaret E. Kemeny. 2004. "Acute Stressors and Cortisol Responses: A Theoretical Integration and Synthesis of Laboratory Research." *Psychology Bulletin* 130: 355–91.

DiMaggio, Paul. 1997. "Culture and Cognition." *Annual Review of Sociology* 23:263–87.

DiMaggio, Paul. 2002. "Why Cognitive (and Cultural) Sociology Needs Cognitive Psychology." In *Culture in Mind: Toward a Sociology of Culture and Cognition*, edited by Karen Cerulo (pp. 274–81). New York: Routlege.

DiMaggio, Paul, and Filiz Garip. 2012. "Network Effects and Social Inequality." *Annual Review of Sociology* 38:93–118.

DiMaggio, Paul, and Hazel Rose Markus. 2010. "Culture and Social Psychology Converging Perspectives." *Social Psychology Quarterly* 73(4):347–52.

Dinh, Jessica E., and Robert G. Lord. 2013. "Current Trends in Moral Research: What We Know and Where to Go from Here." *Current Directions in Psychological Science* 22(5):380–85.

Durkheim, Émile. 1965. *The Elementary Forms of Religious Life* (1912). New York: Free Press.

Eckersley, Richard. 2015. "Beyond Inequality: Acknowledging the Complexity of Social Determinants of Health." *Social Science and Medicine* 147:121–25.

Eisenberg, Nancy. 2000. "Emotion, Regulation, and Moral Development." *Annual Review of Psychology* 51:665–97.

Ekman, Paul. 1994. "All Emotions Are Basic." In *The Nature of Emotion: Fundamental Questions*, edited by P. Ekman and R. Davidson (pp. 15–19). New York: Oxford University Press.

Ekman, Paul, and Wallace V. Friesen. (1986). "A new pan-cultural facial expression of emotion." *Motivation and Emotion* 10(2):159–168.

Ekman, Paul, and W. V. Friesen. 1971. "Constants Across Cultures in the Face and Emotion." *Journal of Personality and Social Psychology* 17(2):124–29.

Ekman, Paul, and Wallace V. Friesen. 1975. *Pictures of facial affect.* Consulting Psychologists Press.

Elder, Glen H., Michael J Shanahan, and Julia A. Jennings. 2015. "Human Development in Time and Place." In *Handbook of Child Psychology and Developmental Science*, Vol. 4: *Ecological Settings and Processes in Developmental Systems*,edited by Marc Bornstein and Tama Leventhal (ch. 2). Hoboken, NJ: Wiley.

Elias, Norbert. 1996. *The Germans: Power Struggles and the Development of Habitus in the Nineteenth and Twentieth Centuries*. New York: Columbia University Press.

Emirbayer, Mustafa, and Ann Mische. 1998. "What is agency?." *American Journal of Sociology* 103(4):962–1023.

Evans, Jonathan St. B. T. 2008. "Dual-Processing Accounts of Reasoning, Judgment, and Social Cognition." *Annual Review of Psychology* 59:255–78.

Evans, William, Michael Hout, and Susan E. Mayer. 2004. "Assessing the Effect of Economic Inequality." In *Social Inequality*, edited by K. Neckerman (Pp. 933–68). New York: Russell Sage Foundation Press.

Fernandez-Kelly, Patricia. 2008. "The Back Pocket Map: Social Class and Cultural Capital as Transferable Assets in the Advancement of Second-Generation Immigrants." *Annals of the American Academy of Political and Social Science* 620:116–37.

Fesmire, Steven. 2014. *Dewey.* New York: Routledge.

Festinger, Leon. 1954. "A theory of social comparison processes." *Human relations* 7.2 117–140.

Firat, Rengin, and Steven Hitlin. 2012. "Morally Bonded and Bounded: A Sociological Introduction to Neurology." *Advances in Group Processes* 29:165–99.

Firebaugh, Glenn. 2000. "The Trend in Between-Nation Income Inequality." *Annual Review of Sociology* 26:323–39.

Fischer, Ronald, and Shalom H. Schwartz. 2011. "Whence Differences in Value Priorities? Individual, Cultural, or Artifactual Sources." *Journal of Cross-Cultural Psychology* 42(7):1127–44.

Fiske, Alan Page. 1992. "The Four Elementary Forms of Sociality: Framework for a Unified Theory of Social Relations." *Psychological Review* 99(4):689.

Fiske, Alan Page, and Nick Haslam. 2005. "The Four Basic Social Bonds: Structures for Coordinating Interaction." In *Interpersonal Cognition*, edited by Mark W. Baldwin (pp. 267–98). New York: Guilford Press.

Fiske, Alan Page, and Tage Shakti Rai. 2014. *Virtuous Violence: Hurting and Killing to Create, Sustain, End, and Honor Social Relationships.* Cambridge, England: Cambridge University Press.

Fiske, Susan T. 1998. "Stereotyping, Prejudice, and Discrimination." In *The Handbook of Social Psychology*, edited by D. T. Gilbert, S. T. Fiske, and G. Lindzey (pp. 357–411). Boston, MA: McGraw-Hill.

Fiske, Susan T. 2004. "What's in a Category? Responsibility, Intent, and the Avoidability of Bias Against Outgroups." In *The Social Psychology of Good and Evil*, edited by Arthur G. Miller (pp. 127–40). New York: Guilford.

Fiske, Susan T. 2011. *Envy Up, Scorn Down: How Status Divides Us.* New York: Russel Sage Foundation.

Fourcade, Marion, and Kieran Healy. 2007. "Moral views of market society." *Annual Review of Sociology* 33: 285–311.

Fournier, Marcel, and David Macey. 2013. *Emile Durkheim: A Biography.* Cambridge, England: Polity Press.

Foy, Steven, Robert Freeland, Andrew Miles, Kimberly B. Rogers, and Lynn Smith-Lovin. 2014. "Emotions and Affect as Source, Outcome and Resistance to Inequality." In *Handbook of the Social Psychology of Inequality*, edited by J. McLeod, E. J. Lawler, and M. Schwalbe (pp. 295–324). New York: Springer.

Francis, Clare, and David R. Heise. 2006. Mean Affective Ratings of 1,500 Concepts by Indiana University Undergraduates in 2002–3 [Computer file]. Distributed at http://www.indiana.edu/~socpsy/ACT/interact/JavaInteract.html

Frankfurt, Harry G. 1971. "Freedom of the Will and the Concept of a Person." *The Journal of Philosophy* 68(1):5–20.

Franks, David D. 2010. *Neurosociology: The Nexus between Neuroscience and Social Psychology.* New York: Springer.

Garfinkel, Howard. 1967. *Studies in Ethnomethodology.* Upper Saddle River, NJ: Prentice Hall.

Garland, David. 2013. "Penality and The Penal State." *Criminology* 51(3):475–517.

Gelfand, Michele J., Jana L. Raver, Lisa Nishii, Lisa M. Leslie, Janetta Lun, Beng Chong Lim, Lili Duan, Assaf Almaliach, Soon Ang, and Jakobina Arnadottir. 2011. "Differences between tight and loose cultures: A 33-nation study." *Science* 332(6033):1100–1104.

Gibbs, John C. 2003. *Moral Development & Reality: Beyond the Theories of Kohlberg and Hoffman.* San Diego, CA: Sage.

Giddens, Anthony. 1976. *New Rules of Sociological Method: A Positive Critique of Interpretive Sociologies.* London: Hutchinson.

Giddens, Anthony. 1984. *The Constitution of Society: Outline of the Theory of Structuration*. Berkeley, CA: University of California Press.

Gilligan, Carol (Ed.). 1982. *In a Different Voice: Psychological Theory and Women's Development*. Cambridge, MA: Harvard University Press.

Giordano, Peggy C., Ryan D. Schroeder, and Stephen A. Cernkovich. 2007. "Emotions and Crime over the Life Course: A Neo-Median Perspective on Criminal Continuity and Change." *American Journal of Sociology* 112(6):1603–61.

Goffman, Erving (Ed.). 1959. *The presentation of self in everyday life*. Garden City, NY: Doubleday.

Goffman, Erving (Ed.). 1967. *Interaction ritual: Essays in Face-to-Face Behavior*. Chicago: Aldine Publishing Co.

Goffman, Erving. 1983. "The Interaction Order: American Sociological Association, 1982 Presidential Address." *American Sociological Review* 48(1):1–17.

Graham, Jesse, Jonathan Haidt, Spassena Koleva, Matt Motyl, Ravi Iyer, Sean Wojcik, and Peter Ditto. 2013. "Moral Foundations Theory: The Pragmatic Validity of Moral Pluralism." *Advances in Experimental Social Psychology,* 47:55–130.

Graham, Jesse, Brian A. Nosek, Jonathan Haidt, Ravi Iyer, Spassena Koleva, and Peter H. Ditto. 2011. "Mapping the Moral Domain." *Journal of Personality and Social Psychology* 366–385.

Greene, Joshua. 2013. *Moral Tribes: Emotion, Reason, and the Gap Between Us and Them*. New York: Penguin.

Greene, Joshua D., Leigh E. Nystrom, Andrew D. Engell, John M. Darley, and Jonathan D. Cohen. 2004. "The Neural Bases of Cognitive Conflict and Control in Moral Judgement." *Neuron* 44:389–400.

Greitemeyer, Tobias, and Christina Sagioglou. 2016. "Subjective Socioeconomic Status Causes Aggression: A Test of the Theory of Social Deprivation." *Journal of Personality and Social Psychology* 111:178-194.

Grimm, Stephanie D., A. Timothy Church, Marcia S. Katigbak, and Jose Alberto S. Reyes. 1999. "Self-Described Traits, Values, and Moods Associated with Individualism and Collectivism: Testing Theory in an Individualistic (U.S.) and a Collectivistic (Phillipine) Culture." *Journal of Cross-Cultural Psychology* 30(4):466–500.

Gross, Neil. 2009. "A Pragmatist Theory of Social Mechanisms." *American Sociological Review* 74(3):358–79.

Guibernau, Montserrat. 2007. *The Identity of Nations*. Cambridge, England: Polity Press.

Haidt, Jonathan. 2001. "The Emotional Dog and Its Rational Tail: A Social Intuitionist Approach to Moral Judgement." *Psychological Review* 108(4):814–34.

Haidt, Jonathan. 2003. "The Moral Emotions." In *Handbook of Affective Sciences*, edited by R. J. Davidson, K. R. Scherer, and H. H. Goldsmith (pp. 852–70). New York: Oxford University Press.

Haidt, Jonathan. 2006. *The Happiness Hypothesis: Finding Modern Truth in Ancient Wisdom*. New York: Basic Books.

Haidt, Jonathan. 2008. "Morality." *Perspectives on Psychological Science* 3(1):65–72.

Haidt, Jonathan. 2012. *The Righteous Mind: Why Good People are Divided by Politics and Religion*. New York: Pantheon Books.

Haidt, Jonathan, and Fredrik Bjorklund. 2008. "Social Intuitionists Answer Six Questions about Moral Psychology." In *Moral Psychology*, edited by Walter Sinnott-Armstrong (Pp. 181–217). Cambridge, MA: MIT Press.

Haidt, Jonathan, and Jesse Graham. 2009. "Planet of the Durkheimians, Where Community, Authority, and Sacredness Are Foundations of Morality." In *Social and Psychological Bases of Ideology and System Justification*, edited by J. Jost, A. C. Kay, and H. Thorisdottir (pp. 371–401). New York: Oxford University Press.

Haidt, Jonathan, and Matthew A. Hersh. 2001. "Sexual Morality: The Cultures and Emotions of Conservatives and Liberals." *Journal of Applied Social Psychology* 31(1):191–221.

Haidt, Jonathan, and Dacher Keltner. 1999. "Culture And Facial Expression: Open-Ended Methods Find More Expressions and a Gradient Of Recognition." *Cognition & Emotion* 13(3):225–66.

Haidt, Jonathan, Silvia Helena Koller, and Maria G. Dias. 1993. "Affect, Culture, and Morality, or Is It Wrong to Eat Your Dog?" *Journal of Personality and Social Psychology* 65(4):613–28.

Haidt, Jonathan, Evan Rosenberg, and Holly Hom. 2003. "Differentiating Diversities: Moral Diversity Is Not Like Other Kinds." *Journal of Applied Social Psychology* 33(1):1–36.

Hallett, Tim. 2007. "Between Deference and Distinction: Interaction Ritual Through Symbolic Power in an Educational Institution." *Social Psychology Quarterly* 70(2):148–71.

Halteman, James, and Edd Noell. 2012. *Reckoning with Markets: Moral Reflection in Economics*. Oxford, England: Oxford University Press.

Harkness, Sarah K. 2017. "Spread of Status Value: Rewards and the Creation of Status Characteristics." *Social Science Research* 61:98–111.

Harkness, Sarah K., and Steven Hitlin. 2014. "Morality and emotions." In *Handbook of the Sociology of Emotions: Volume II* (pp. 451–471). Springer Netherlands.

Hart, Daniel, and Suzanne Fegley. 1995. "Prosocial Behavior and Caring in Adolescence: Relations to Self-Understanding and Social Judgement." *Child Development* 66:1346–59.

Haslam, Nick, and Alan Page Fiske. 1999. "Relational Models Theory: A Confirmatory Factor Analysis." *Personal Relationships* 6(2):241–50.

Heise, David R. 1977. "Social Action as the Control of Affect." *Behavioral Science* 22:163–77.

Heise, David R. 1979. *Understanding Events: Affect and the Construction of Social Action*. New York: Cambridge University Press.

Heise, David R. 1989. "Effects of Emotion Displays on Social Identification." *Social Psychology Quarterly* 52:10–21.

Heise, David R. 2007. *Expressive Order: Confirming Sentiments in Social Actions*. New York,: Springer.

Heise, David R. 2010. *Surveying Cultures: Discovering Shared Conceptions and Sentiments*. Hoboken, NJ: Wiley.

Heise, David R. 2014. "Cultural Variations in Sentiments." *SpringerPlus* 3:1–11.

Hewitt, John P. 1989. *Dilemmas of the American Self*. Philadelphia: Temple University Press.

Higgins, E. T. 1996. Knowledge activation: Accessibility, applicability, and salience. In E. T. Higgins & A. W. Kruglanski (Eds.), *Social Psychology: Handbook of Basic Principles* (pp. 133–168). New York: Guilford Press.

Hipp, John R. 2007. "Income Inequality, Race, and Place: Does the Distribution of Race and Class within Neighborhoods Affect Crime Rates?" *Criminology* 45:665–97.

Hipp, John R. 2011. "Spreading the Wealth: The Effect of the Distribution of Income and Race/Ethnicity across Households and Neighborhoods on City Crime Trajectories." *Criminology* 49:631–65.

Hitlin, Steven. 2008. *Moral Selves, Evil Selves: The Social Psychology of Conscience.* New York: Palgrave Macmillan.

Hitlin, Steven, and Jane Allyn Piliavin. 2004. "Values: A Review of Recent Research and Theory." *Annual Review of Sociology* 30:359–93.

Hitlin, Steven, and Kevin Pinkston. 2013. "Values, Attitudes, and Ideologies: Explicit and Implicit Constructs Shaping Perception and Action." In *Handbook of Social Psychology*, edited by John Delamater and Amanda Ward (pp. 319–39). New York: Springer.

Hitlin, Steven, and Stephen Vaisey. 2013. "The New Sociology of Morality." *Annual Review of Sociology* 39:51–68.

Hochschild, Arlie Russell (Ed.). 1983. *The Managed Heart Commercialization of Human Feeling.* Berkeley, CA: University of California Press.

Hodgkiss, Philip. 2013. "A Moral Vision: Human Dignity in the Eyes of the Founders of Sociology." *The Sociological Review* 61(3):417–39.

Hofmann, Wilhelm, Daniel C Wisneski, Mark J Brandt, and Linda J Skitka. 2014. "Morality in Everyday Life." *Science* 345(6202):1340–43.

Hofstede, Geert H. 2001. *Culture's Consequences: Comparing Values, Behaviors, Institutions, and Organization Across Nations.* Thousand Oaks, CA: Sage.

Hookway, Nicholas. 2015. "Moral Decline Sociology: Critiquing the Legacy of Durkheim." *Journal of Sociology* 51(2):271–84.

Hout, Michael. 2008. "How Class Works: Objective and Subjective Aspects of Class Since the 1970s." In *Social Class: How Does It Work?*, edited by A. Lareau and D. Conley (pp. 25–64). New York: Russell Sage.

Hu, Shen. 2012. "China's Gini Index at 0.61, University Report Says." *Caixin Online*, http://english.caixin.com/2012-12-10/100470648.html.

Hume, David. 1978. "1739. A Treatise of Human Nature." London: John Noon.

Hunt, Pamela M. 2008. "From Festies to Tourrats: Examining the Relationship between Jamband Subculture Involvement and Role Meanings." *Social Psychology Quarterly* 71:356–78.

Hunt, Pamela M. 2010. Are You Kynd? Conformity and Deviance within the Jamband Subculture." *Deviant Behavior* 31:521–51.

Hunt, Pamela M. 2013. *Where the Music Takes You: The Social Psychology of Music Subcultures.* San Diego, CA: Cognella Academic Publishing.

Huntington, Samuel P. 1991. "Democracy's Third Wave." *Journal of Democracy* 2(2):12–34.

Ignatow, Gabriel. 2009. "Culture and Embodied Cognition: Moral Discourses in Internet Support Groups for Overeaters." *Social Forces* 88(2):643–69.

Ignatow, Gabriel. 2009. "Why the Sociology of Morality Needs Bourdieu's Habitus."
    Sociological Inquiry 79(1):98–114.
Ignatow, Gabriel. 2010. "Morality and Mind-Body Connections." In *Handbook of the
    Sociology of Morality*, edited by Steven Hitlin and Stephen Vaisey (pp. 411–24).
    New York: Springer.
Immordino-Yang, Mary Helen, Xiao-Fei Yang, and Hanna Damasio. 2016. "Cultural
    Modes of Expressing Emotions Influence How Emotions Are Experienced." *Emotion*
    16(7):1033–1039.
Inglehart, Ronald (Ed.). 1990. *Culture Shift in Advanced Industrial Society*. Princeton,
    NJ: Princeton University Press.
Inglehart, Ronald. 1995. *Inglehart, Ronald*. Ann Arbor: University of Michigan.
Inglehart, Ronald (Ed.). 1997. *Modernization and Postmodernization: Cultural, Economic,
    and Political Change in 43 Societies*. Princeton, NJ: Princeton University Press.
Inglehart, Ronald. 2006. "Mapping Global Values." *Comparative Sociology* 5(2–3):115–36.
Inglehart, Ronald, and Wayne E. Baker. 2000. "Modernization, Cultural Change, and
    the Persistance of Traditional Values." *American Sociological Review* 65(1):19–51.
Inglehart, Ronald, and Christian Welzel. 2005. *Modernization, Cultural Change, and
    Democracy*. New York: Cambridge University Press.
Izard, Carroll E. 2013. *Human Emotions*. New York: Springer Science & Business Media.
Jaffee, Sara, and Janet Shibley Hyde. 2000. "Gender Differences in Moral
    Orientation: A Meta-Analysis." *Psychological Bulletin* 126(5):703–26.
Jahoda, Gustav. 2007. *A History of Social Psychology: From the Eighteenth-Century
    Enlightenment to the Second World War*. Cambridge, England: Cambridge
    University Press.
Janoff-Bulman, Ronnie, and Nate C. Carnes. 2013. "Surveying the Moral Landscape
    Moral Motives and Group-Based Moralities." *Personality and Social Psychology
    Review* 17(3):219–36.
Joas, Hans (Ed.). 2000. *The Genesis of Values*. Cambridge, England: Polity Press.
Joas, Hans. 2013. *The Sacredness of the Person: A New Genealogy of Human Rights*.
    Washington DC: Georgetown University Press.
Joas, Hans, and Wolfgang Knobl. 2009. *Social Theory: Twenty Introductory Lectures*.
    Cambridge, England: Cambridge University Press.
Kagan, Jerome. 1994 [1984]. *The Nature of the Child*. New York: HarperCollins.
Kagan, Jerome. 2007. "A Trio of Concerns." *Perspectives on Psychological Science* 2(4):361–76.
Kagan, Jerome. 2008. "Morality and Its Development." In *Moral Psychology: The
    Neuroscience of Morality: Emotion, Brain Disorders, and Development*, edited by
    Walter Sinott-Armstrong (pp. 297–312). Cambridge, MA: MIT Press.
Kant, Immanuel. 1785. "Foundation of the Metaphysics of Morals." Indianapolis,
    IN: Bobbs-Merrill.
Kasser, Tim, Richard Koestner, and Natasha Lekes. 2002. "Early Family Experiences
    and Adult Values: A 26 Year Prospective Longitudinal Study." *Personality and Social
    Psychology Bulletin* 28(6):826–35.
Katz, Jack. 1975. "Essences as Moral Identities: Verifiability and Responsibility in
    Imputations of Deviance and Charisma." *American Journal of Sociology* 80(6):1369–90.
Katz, Jack. 1999. *How Emotions Work*. Chicago, IL: University of Chicago Press.

Kelly, Morgan. 2000. "Inequality and Crime." *The Review of Economics and Statistics* 82:530–39.

Kemper, Theodore. 2015. "Status, Power and Social Order." In *Order on the Edge of Chaos: Social Psychology and the Problem of Social Order*, edited by Edward J Lawler, Shane R Thye, and Jeongkoo Yoon (pp. 208–26). New York: Cambridge University Press.

Kennedy, Bruce P., Ichiro Kawachi, Deborah Prothrow-Stith, Kimerly Lochner, and Vanita Gupta. 1998. "Social Capital, Income Inequality, and Firearm Violent Crime." *Social Science and Medicine* 47:7–17.

Kenny, Robert Wade. 2010. "Beyond the Elementary Forms of Moral Life: Reflexivity and Rationality in Durkheim's Moral Theory." *Sociological Theory* 28(2):215–44.

Kenworthy, Lane. 2007. "Inequality and Sociology." *American Behavioral Scientist* 50:584–602.

Killen, Melanie. 2007. "Children's Social and Moral Reasoning About Exclusion." *Current Directions in Psychological Science* 16(1):32–36.

Kinder, Donald R., and Cindy D. Kam. 2009. *Us Against Them: Ethnocentric Foundations of American Opinion*. University of Chicago Press: Chicago.

Kluckhohn, C., Murray, H. A., and Schneider, D. M. (Eds.). 1953. *Personality in nature, society, and culture*, 2nd ed. Oxford, England: Knopf.

Kobayashi, Emiko, Harold Grasmick, and Gustav Friedrich. 2001. "A Cross-Cultural Study of Shame, Embarrassment, and Management Sanctions as Deterrents to Noncompliance with Organizational Rules." *Communication Research Reports* 18(2):105–17.

Kohlberg, Lawrence. 1971. "Stages of Moral Development." *Moral Education* 1:23–92.

Kohlberg, Lawrence. 1981. *The Philosophy of Moral Development, Vol 1, Moral Stges and the Idea of Justice*. New York: Harper & Row.

Kohn, Melvin L, and Carmi Schooler (Eds.). 1983. *Work and Personality: An Inquiry into the Impact of Social Stratification*. Norwood, NJ: Ablex Pub. Corp.

Kondo, Dorinne. 1990. *Crafting Selves: Power, Gender, and Discourses of Identity in a Japanese Workplace*. Chicago: University of Chicago Press.

Piff, Paul K., Michael W. Kraus, Stéphane Côté, Bonnie Hayden Cheng, and Dacher Keltner. 2010. "Having less, giving more: the influence of social class on prosocial behavior." *Journal of Personality and Social Psychology* 99(5):771–784.

Krebs, Dennis L. 2011. *The Origins of Morality: An Evolutionary Account*. New York: Oxford University Press.

Kroska Amy, and Sarah K. Harkness. 2011. "Coping with the Stigma Of Mental Illness: Empirically-Grounded Hypotheses from Computer Simulations." *Social Forces* 89(4), 1315–40.

Kroska, Amy, and Sarah K. Harkness, Lauren S. Thomas, and Ryan P. Brown. 2014. "Illness Labels and Social Distance." *Society and Mental Health* 4:215–34.

Kroska, Amy, and Sarah K. Harkness, Lauren S. Thomas, and Ryan P. Brown. 2015. "Gender, Status, and Psychiatric Labels." *Social Science Research* 54:68–79.

Kurtines, William M. 1984. "Moral Behavior as Rule-Governed Behavior: A Psychosocial Role-Theoretical Approach to Moral Behavior and Development." In *Morality, Moral*

Behavior, and Moral Development, edited by William M. Kurtines and Jacob L. Gewirtz (pp. 303–24). New York: Wiley.

Kus, Basak. 2016. "Wealth Inequality: Historical Trends and Cross-National Differences." *Sociology Compass* 10(6):518–29.

Lamont, Michèle, John Schmalzbauer, Maureen Waller, and Daniel Weber. 1996. "Cultural and Moral Boundaries in the United States: Structural Position, Geographic Location, and Lifestyle Explanations." *Poetics* 24(1):31–56.

Lareau, Annette. 2011. *Unequal Childhoods: Class, Race, and Family Life.* Berkeley, CA: University of California Press.

Lawler, Edward, Shane Thye, and Jeongkoo Yoon. 2008. "Social Exchange and the Micro Social Order." *American Sociological Review* 73:519–42.

Lawler, Edward. 2009. *Social Commitments in a Depersonalized World.* New York: Russell Sage Foundation.

Lawler, Edward. 2015. *Order on the Edge of Chaos: Social Psychology and the Problem of Social Order.* New York: Cambridge University Press.

Levine, Donald N. 2010. "Adumbrations of a Sociology of Morality in the Work of Parsons, Simmel, and Merton." In *Handbook of the Sociology of Morality*, edited by Steven Hitlin and Stephen Vaisey (pp. 57–72). New York: Springer.

Li, Jin, Lianqin Wang, and Kurt Fischer. 2004. "The Organisation Of Chinese Shame Concepts?" *Cognition and Emotion* 18(6):767–97.

Liebert, Robert M. 1984. "What Develops in Moral Development?" In *Morality, Moral Behavior, and Moral Development*, edited by William M. Kurtines and Jacob L. Gewirtz (pp. 177–92). New York: Wiley.

Link, Bruce G., Jo C. Phelan, and Mark L. Hatzenbuehler. 2014. "Stigma and Social Inequality." In *Handbook of the Social Psychology of Inequality*, edited by J. McLeod, E. J. Lawler, and M. Schwalbe (pp. 49–64). New York: Springer.

Lizardo, Omar. 2004. "The Cognitive Origins of Bourdieu's Habitus." *Journal for the Theory of Social Behavior* 34:375–401.

Lizardo, Omar, Robert Mowry, Brandon Sepulvado, Dustin S. Stoltz, Marshall A. Taylor, Justin Van Ness, and Michael Wood. 2016. "What Are Dual Process Models? Implications for Cultural Analysis in Sociology." *Sociological Theory* 34(4):287–310.

Longest, Kyle, Steven Hitlin, and Stephen Vaisey. 2013. "Position and Disposition." *Social Forces* 91(4):1499–1528.

Lough, Sinclair, Christopher M Kipps, Cate Treise, Peter Watson, James R Blair, and John R Hodges. 2006. "Social reasoning, emotion and empathy in frontotemporal dementia." *Neuropsychologia* 44(6):950–58.

Lukes, Steven. 1985. *Emile Durkheim: His Life And Work; A Historical and Critical Study*: Palo Alto, CA: Stanford University Press.

Lynch, John, George Davey Smith, Sam Harper, Marianne Hillemeier, Nancy Ross, George A. Kaplan, and Michael Wolfson. 2004. "Is Income Inequality a Determinant of Population Health? Part 1. A Systematic Review." *The Milbank Quarterly* 82:5–99.

MacKinnon, Neil J. 1994. *Symbolic Interactionism as Affect Control.* Albany, NY: State University of New York Press.

MacKinnon, Neil J. 2003. Mean Affective Ratings of 2,294 Concepts by Guelph University Undergraduates, Ontario, Canada, in 2001–3 [Computer file]. Distributed at http://www.indiana.edu/~socpsy/ACT/interact/JavaInteract.html

MacKinnon, Neil J., and David R. Heise. 2010. *Self, Identity, and Social Institutions.* New York: Palgrave Macmillan.

MacKinnon, Neil J., and Tom Langford. 1994. "The Meaning of Occupational Prestige Scores: A Social Psychological Analysis and Interpretation." *Sociological Quarterly* 35:215–45.

MacKinnon, Neil J., and Alison Luke. 2002. "Changes in Identity Attitudes as Reflections of Social and Cultural Change." *The Canadian Journal of Sociology* 27:299–338.

MacKinnon, Neil J., and Dawn T. Robinson. 2014. "Back to the Future: 25 Years of Research in Affect Control Theory." *Advances in Group Processes* 31:139–73.

Manning, Philip. 1992. *Erving Goffman and Modern Sociology.* Cambridge, England: Polity Press.

Markus, Hazel, and Shinobu Kitayama. 1991. "Culture and the Self: Implications for Cognition, Emotion, and Motivation." *Psychological review* 98:224–53.

Marsden, Peter V. 2015. "Social ORder from the Bottom Up?" In *Order on the Edge of Chaos: Social Psychology and the Problem of Social Order*, edited by Edward J Lawler, Shane R Thye, and Jeongkoo Yoon (pp. 309–22). New York: Cambridge.

Martin, John Levi. 2011. *The Explanation of Social Action,* New York: Oxford University Press.

Massey, Douglas S. 2002. "A Brief History of Human Society: The Origin and Role of Emotion in Social Life." *American Sociological Review* 67(1):1–29.

Maynard, Douglas, and Jason Turowetz. 2013. "Language Use and Social Interaction." In *Handbook of Social Psychology*, edited by John Delamater and Amanda Ward (pp. 251–79.) New York: Springer

McCaffree, Kevin. 2015. *What morality means: An interdisciplinary synthesis for the social sciences.* Springer.

McCall, Leslie, and Christine Percheski. 2010. "Income Inequality: New Trends and Research Directions." *Annual Review of Sociology* 36:329–47.

McCullough, Michael E., Shelly D. Kilpatrick, Robert A. Emmons, and David B. Larson. 2001. "Is Gratitude a Moral Affect?" *Psychological Bulletin* 127(2):249–66.

McGeer, Victoria. 2008. "Varieties of Moral Agency: Lessons from Autism (and Psychopathy)." In *Moral Psychology: The Neuroscience of Morality: Emotion, Brain Disorders, and Development*, edited by Walter Sinott-Armstrong (pp. 227–57). Cambridge, MA: MIT Press.

McLeod, Jane D., and Kathryn J. Lively. 2003. "Social Structure and Personality." In *Handbook of Social Psychology*, edited by John DeLamater (pp. 77–102). New York: Kluwer.

McLeod, Jane D., James M. Nonnemaker, and Kathleen Thiede Call. 2004. "Income Inequality, Race, and Child Well-Being: An Aggregate Analysis in the 50 United States." *Journal of Health and Social Behavior* 45:249–64.

McPherson, Miller, Lynn Smith-Lovin, and James M. Cook. 2001. "Birds of a feather: Homophily in social networks." *Annual Review of Sociology* 27(1):415–444.

Mead, George Herbert (Ed.). 1934. *Mind, Self & Society from the Standpoint of a Social Behaviorist*. Chicago, IL: The University of Chicago Press.

Menon, Usha, and Richard A. Shweder. 1994. "Kali's Tongue: Cultural Psychology and the Power of Shame in Orissa, India." In *Emotion and Culture: Empirical Studies of Mutual Influence*, edited by S. Kitayama H. R. Markus (pp. 241–82). Washington, DC: American Psychological Association.

Marmot, Michael. 2004. *Status Syndrome: How Your Social Standing Directly Affects Your Health and Life Expectancy*. London: Bloomsbury.

Mayer, Susan E. 2001. "How Did the Increase in Economic Inequality between 1970 and 1990 Affect Children's Educational Attainment?" *American Journal of Sociology* 107:1–32.

Messner, Steven F., Lawrence E. Raffalovich, and Peter Shrock. 2002. "Reassessing the Cross-National Relationship between Income Inequality and Homicide Rates: Implications of Data Quality Control in the Measurement of Income Distribution." *Journal of Quantitative Criminology* 18:377–95.

Miles, Andrew. 2014. "Addressing the Problem of Cultural Anchoring An Identity-Based Model of Culture in Action." *Social Psychology Quarterly* 77(2):210–27.

Miles, Andrew, and Stephen Vaisey. 2015. "Morality and Politics: Comparing Alternate Theories." *Social Science Research* 53(September):252–269.

Milkie, Melissa A., Catharine H. Warner, and Rashawn Ray. 2014. "Current Theorizing and Future Directions in the Social Psychology of Social Class Inequalities." In *Handbook of the Social Psychology of Inequality*, edited by J. McLeod, E. J. Lawler, and M. Schwalbe (pp. 547–73). New York, NY: Springer.

Minoura, Yasuko. 1992. "A Sensitive Period for the Incorporation of a Cultural Meaning System: A Study of Japanese Children Growing Up in the United States." *Ethos* 20(3):304–39.

Mirowsky, John. 2013. "Depression and the Sense of Control: Aging Vectors, Trajectories, and Trends." *Journal of Health and Social Behavior* 54(4):407–25.

Moll, Jorge, Ricardo de Oliveira-Souza, and Paul J. Eslinger. 2003. "Morals and the human brain: a working model." *Neuroreport* 14(3):299–305.

Moll, J., Zahn, R., de Oliveira-Souza, R., Krueger, F., and Grafman, J. (2005). "Opinion: the neural basis of human moral cognition." *Nature Reviews. Neuroscience* 6(10):799.

Moll, Jorge, Ricardo de Oliveria-Sousa, Roland Zahn, and Jordan Grafman. 2008. "The Cognitive Neuroscience of Moral Emotions." In *Moral Psychology: The Neuroscience of Morality: Emotion, Brain Disorders, and Development*, edited by Walter Sinott-Armstrong (pp. 2–17). Cambridge, MA: MIT Press.

Montada, Leo. 1993. "Understanding Oughts by Assessing Moral Reasoning or Moral Emotions." In *The Moral Self*, edited by Thomas E. Wren and Gil G. Noam. Cambridge, MA: MIT Press.

Morris, Martina, and Bruce Western. 1999. "Inequality in Earnings at the Close of the Twentieth Century." *Annual Review of Sociology* 25:623–57.

Neckerman, Kathryn M., and Florencia Torche. 2007. "Inequality: Causes and Consequences." *Annual Review of Sociology* 33:335–57.

Nevitte, Neil, and Christopher Cochrane. 2006. "Individualization in Europe and America: Connecting Religious and Moral Values." *Comparative Sociology* 5(2–3):203–30.

Nelson, Steven M. 2006. "Redefining a Bizarre Situation: Relative Concept Stability in Affect Control Theory." *Social Psychology Quarterly* 69:215–34.

Niedenthal, Paula M., June Price Tangney, and Igor Gavanski. 1994. "'If Only I Weren't' versus 'If Only I Hadn't': Distinguishing Shame and Guilt in Conterfactual Thinking." *Journal of Personality and Social Psychology* 67(4):585.

Nisbett, Richard. 2004. *The Geography of Thought: How Asians and Westerners Think Differently… and Why.* New York: Simon and Schuster.

Nisbett, Richard E., and Dov Cohen. 1996. *Culture of Honor: The Psychology of Violence in the South.* : Boulder, CO: Westview Press.

Nisbett, Richard E., Kaiping Peng, Incheol Choi, and Ara Norenzayan. 2001. "Culture and Systems of Thought: Holistic versus Analytic Cognition." *Psychological review* 108(2):291.

Norton, Michael I., and Dan Ariely. 2011. "Building a Better America—One Wealth Quintile at a Time." *Perspectives on Psychological Science* 6(1):9–12.

Nucci, Larry P. 1981. "Conceptions of Personal Issues: A Domain Distinct from Moral or Societal Concepts." *Child Development* 52(1):114–21.

Nucci, Larry P., and Elliot Turiel. 1978. "Social Interactions and the Development of Social Concepts in Preschool Children." *Child Development* 49(2):400–407.

Nunner-Winkler, Gertrud. 1984. "Two Moralities? A Critical Discussion of an Ethic of Care and Responsibility versus an Ethic of Rights and Justice." In *Morality, Moral Behavior, and Moral Development*, edited by William M. Kurtines and Jacob L. Gewirtz (pp. 348–61). New York: Wiley.

Nussbaum, Martha C. 2005. "Emotions and the Origins of Morality." In *Morality in Context*, edited by Wolfgang Edelstein and Gertrud Nunner-Winkler (pp. 61–117). Amsterdam: Elsevier.

Oishi, Shigehiro, Selin Kesebir. 2015. "Income Inequality Explains Why Economic Growth Does Not Always Translate to an Increase in Happiness." *Psychological Science* 26:1630–38.

Oishi, Shigehiro, Selin Kesebir, and Ed Diener. 2011. "Income Inequality and Happiness." *Psychological Science* 22: 1095–1100.

Oishi, Shigehiro, Ulrich Schimmack, Ed Diener, and Eunkook M. Suh. 1998. "The Measurement of Values and Individualism-Collectivism." *Personality and Social Psychology Bulletin* 24(11):1177–89.

Osgood, Charles E., William H. May, and Murray S. Miron. 1975. *Cross-Cultural Universals of Affective Meaning.* Urbana, IL: University of Illinois Press.

Osgood, Charles Egerton, George J. Suci, and Percy H. Tannenbaum. 1957. *The Measurement of Meaning.*

Osgood, Charles E., George J. Suci, and Percy Tannenbaum. 1967. *The Measurement of Meaning.* Urbana, IL: University of Illinois Press.

Ossowska, Maria. 1970. *Social Determinants of Moral Ideas.* Routledge: London.

Owens, Timothy J., and Suzanne Goodney. 2000. "Self, Identity, and the Moral Emotions Across the Life Course." In *Self and Identity Through the Life Course in Cross-Cultural Perspsective*, edited by Timothy J. Owens (pp. 33–53). Stamford, CT: JAI Press.

Oyserman, Daphna, Heather M. Coon, and Markus Kemmelmeier. 2002. "Rethinking Individualism and Collectivism: Evaluation of Theoretical Assumptions and Meta-Analyses." *Psychological Bulletin* 128(1):3–72.

Pakizeh, Ali, Jochen E. Gebauer, and Gregory R. Maio. 2007. "Basic Human Values: Inter-Value Structure in Memory." *Journal of Experimental Social Psychology* 43:458–65.

Paternoster, Raymond, and Sally Simpson. 1996. "Sanction Threats and Appeals to Morality: Testing a Rational Choice Model of Corporate Crime." *Law & Society Review* 30(3):549–84.

Patterson, Orlando. 2014. "Making Sense of Culture." *Annual Review of Sociology* 40:1–30.

Penner, Louis A., John F. Dovidio, Jane A. Piliavin, and David A. Schroeder. 2005. "Prosocial Behavior: Multilevel Perspectives." *Annual Review of Psychology* 56:365–92.

Piaget, Jean. 1960 [1932]. *The Moral Judgment of the Child*. Glencoe, IL: The Free Press.

Pickel, Andreas. 2005. "The Habitus Process: A Biopsychosocial Conception." *Journal for the Theory of Social Behavior* 35:437–61.

Pickett, Kate E., Jessica Mookherjee, and Richard G. Wilkinson. 2005. "Adolescent Birth Rates, Total Homicides, and Income Inequality in Rich Countries." *American Journal of Public Health* 95:1181–83.

Piff, Paul K, Daniel M Stancato, Stéphane Côté, Rodolfo Mendoza-Denton, and Dacher Keltner. 2012. "Higher Social Class Predicts Increased Unethical Behavior." *Proceedings of the National Academy of Sciences USA* 109(11):4086–91.

Piff, Paul K., Michael W. Kraus, Stephane Cote, Bonnie Hayden Cheng, and Dacher Keltner. 2010. "Having Less, Giving More: The Influence of Social Class on Prosocial Behavior." *Journal of Personality and Social Psychology* 99(5):771–84.

Piketty, Thomas. 2014. "Capital in the 21st Century." *Cambridge: Harvard University Press*.

Piketty, Thomas and Emmanuel Saez. 2003. "Income Inequality in the United States, 1913–1998." *The Quarterly Journal of Economics* 118:1–39.

Piliavin, Jane Allyn. 2008. "Altruism and Helping: The Evolution of a Field: The 2008 Cooley-Mead Presentation." *Social Psychology Quarterly* 72(3):209–25.

Powell, Christopher. 2010. "Four Concepts of Morality." In *Handbook of the Sociology of Morality*, edited by Steven Hitlin and Stephen Vaisey (pp. 35–56). New York: Springer.

Pratt, Nicola Christine. 2007. *Democracy and Authoritarianism in the Arab World*: Boulder, CO: Lynne Rienner Publishers.

Prinz, Jesse J. 2007. *The Emotional Construction of Morals*. New York: Oxford.

Putnam, Robert D. 2000. *Bowling Alone: The Collapse and Revival of American Community*. New York: Simon and Schuster.

Rabinovitch, Simon. 2013. "China Wealth Gap Data Stoke Scepticism." *Financial Times*, http://www.ft.com/cms/s/0/1feb0128-614a-11e2-957e-00144feab49a.html#axzz4Ddmi3P00.

Radkau, Joachim. 2011. *Max Weber: A Biography*. Cambridge, England: Polity.

Rai, Tage Shakti, and Alan Page Fiske. 2011. "Moral Psychology Is Relationship Regulation: Moral Motives for Unity, Hierarchy, Equality, and Proportionality." *Psychological Review* 118(1):57–75.

Rasmussen, Dennis C. 2016. "Adam Smith on What Is Wrong with Economic Inequality." *American Political Science Review* 110(2):342–52

Rawls, Anne Warfield. 1987. "The Interaction Order Sui Generis: Goffman's Contribution to Social Theory." *Sociological Theory* 5(2):136–49.

Rawls, Anne Warfield. 1989. "Language, Self, and Social Order: A Reformulation of Goffman and Sacks." *Human Studies* 12(1–2):147–72.

Rawls, Anne Warfield. 2010. "Social Order as Moral Order." In *Handbook of the Sociology of Morality*, edited by Steven Hitlin and Stephen Vaisey. New York: Springer.

Reskin, Barbara F. 2003. "Including Mechanisms in Our Models of Ascriptive Inequality." *American Sociological Review* 68:1–21.

Ridgeway, Cecilia L. 1991. "The Social Construction of Status Value: Gender and Other Nominal Characteristics." *Social Forces* 70: 367–86.

Ridgeway, Cecilia L. 2011. *Framed by Gender: How Gender Inequality Persists in the Modern World*. New York: Oxford University Press.

Ridgeway, Cecilia L., Kristen Backor, Yan E. Li, Justine E. Tinkler, and Kristan G. Erickson. 2009. "How Easily Does a Social Difference Become a Status Distinction? Gender Matters." *American Sociological Review* 74: 44–62.

Ridgeway, Cecilia L., and Shelley J. Correll. 2004. "Unpacking the Gender System: A Theoretical Perspective on Gender Beliefs and Social Relations." *Gender and Society* 18: 510–31.

Roccas, Sonia, and Lilach Sagiv. 2010. "Personal Values and Behavior: Taking the Cultural Context into Account." *Social and Personality Psychology Compass* 4(1):30–41.

Romney, A. Kimball, Carmella C. Moore, and Craig D. Rusch. 1997. "Cultural Universals: Measuring the Semantic Structure of Emotion Terms in English and Japanese." *Proceedings of the National Academy of Sciences* 94(10):5489–94.

Rosati, Massimo, and Raquel Weiss. 2015. "Tradition and Authenticity in Post-Conventional World: a Durkheimian Reading." *Sociologias* 17(39):110–59.

Rothstein, Bo, and Eric M. Uslaner. 2005. "All for All: Equality, Corruption and Social Trust." *World Politics* 58: 41–72.

Rozin, Paul, Laura Lowery, Sumio Imada, and Jonathan Haidt. 1999. "The CAD Triad Hypothesis: A Mapping between Three Moral Emotions (Contempt, Anger, Disgust) and Three Moral Codes (Community, Autonomy, Divinity)." *Journal of Personality and Social Psychology* 76:574–86.

Saez, Emmanuel. 2015. "Striking It Richer: The Evolution of Top Incomes in the United States (Updated with 2013 Preliminary Estimates)." https://eml.berkeley.edu/~saez/saez-UStopincomes-2013.pdf

Saez, Emmanuel, and Gabriel Zucman. 2016. "Wealth Inequality in the United States since 1913: Evidence from Capitalized Income Tax Data." *The Quarterly Journal of Economics* 131:519–78.

Sandel, Michael J. 2012. *What Money Can't Buy: The Moral Limits of Markets*. New York: Farrar, Staus and Giroux.

Sastry, Jaya, and Catherine E Ross. 1998. "Asian Ethnicity and the Sense of Personal Control." *Social Psychology Quarterly* 61(2):101–20.

Sayer, Andrew. 2005. *The Moral Significance of Class*. New York: Cambridge University Press.

Sayer, Andrew. 2011. *Why Things Matter to People: Social Science, Values, and Ethical Life*. Cambridge: Cambridge University Press.

Savolainen, Jukka. 2000. "Inequality, Welfare State, and Homicide: Further Support for the Institutional Anomie Theory." *Criminology* 38: 1021–42.

Schröder, Tobias and Wolfgang Scholl. 2009. "Affective Dynamics of Leadership: An Experimental Test of Affect Control Theory." *Social Psychology Quarterly* 72:180–97.

Schneider, Andreas. 1989. Mean Affective Ratings of 804 Concepts by West German Students in 1989 [Computer file]. Distributed at http://www.indiana.edu/~socpsy/ACT/interact/JavaInteract.html

Sewell, William H., Jr. 1992. "A Theory of Structure: Duality, Agency, and Transformation." *American Journal of Sociology* 98: 1–29.

Scheff, Thomas J. 1988. "Shame and Conformity: The Deference-Emotion System." *American Sociological Review* 53(3):395–406.

Scheff, Thomas J. 1997. *Emotions, the Social Bond, and Human Reality*. Paris: Cambridge University Press.

Scheff, Thomas J. 2000. "Shame and the Social Bond: A Sociological Theory." *Sociological Theory* 18(1):84–99.

Scheff, Thomas J. 2003. "Shame in self and society." *Symbolic Interaction* 26(2):239–262.

Schnall, Simone, Jonathan Haidt, Gerald L. Clore, and Alexander H. Jordan. 2008. "Disgust as Embodied Moral Judgment." *Personality and Social Psychology Bulletin* 34(8):1096–1109.

Schwartz, Shalom H. 1990. "Toward a Psychological Structure of Human Values: Extensions and Cross-Cultural Replications." *Journal of Personality and Social Psychology* 58:878–91.

Schwartz, Shalom H. 1992. "Universals in the Content and Structure of Values: Theoretical Advances and Empirical Tests in 20 Countries." In *Advances in Experimental Social Psychology*, edited by Mark P. Zanna. San Diego, CA: Academic Press.

Schwartz, Shalom H. 2013. "National Culture as Value Orientations: Consequences Of Value Differences and Cultural Distance." *Handbook of the Economics of Art and Culture* 2:547–86.

Schwartz, Shalom H. 2014. "Rethinking the Concept and Measurement of Societal Culture in Light of Empirical Findings." *Journal of Cross-Cultural Psychology* 45(1):5–13.

Schwartz, Shalom H., and Wolfgang Bilsky. 1987. "Toward a Psychological Structure of Human Values." *Journal of Personality and Social Psychology* 53:550–62.

Schwartz, Shalom H., Jan Cieciuch, Michele Vicchione, Eldad Davidov, Ronald Fischer, . . . Mark Konty. 2012. "Refining the Theory of Basic Individual Values." *Journal of Personality and Social Psychology* 103(4):663–88.

Schwartz, Shalom H., Gila Melech, Arielle Lehmann, Steven Burgess, Mari Harris, and Vicki Owens. 2001. "Extending the Cross-Cultural Validity of the Theory of Basic Human Values with a Different Method of Measurement." *Journal of Cross-Cultural Psychology* 32(5):519–42.

Seligman, Martin E. P., and Mihaly Csikszentmihalyi. 2014. *Positive Psychology: An Introduction*. New York: Springer.

Semuels, Alana. 2016. "The End of Welfare as We Know It." *Atlantic*.

Shadnam, Masoud. 2015. "Theorizing Morality in Context." *International Review of Sociology* 25(3):1–25.

Shamay-Tsoory, Simone G., R. Tomer, B.D. Berger, and J. Aharon-Peretz. 2003. "Characterization of Empathy Deficits Following Prefrontal Brain Damage: The

Role of the Right Ventromedial Prefrontal Cortex." *Journal of Cognitive Neuroscience* 15(3):324–37.

Shariff, Azim F., Dylan Wiwad, and Lara B. Aknin. 2016. "Income Mobility Breeds Tolerance for Income Inequality: Cross-National and Experimental Evidence." *Perspectives on Psychological Science* 11(3):373–80.

Shweder, Richard A. 1990. "In Defense of Moral Realism: Reply to Gabennesch." *Child Development* 61:2060–67.

Shweder, Richard A. 2008. "The cultural psychology of suffering: The many meanings of health in Orissa, India (and elsewhere)." *Ethos* 36(1):60–77.

Shweder, Richard A., and Jonathan Haidt. 2000. "The Cultural Psychology of the Emotions: Ancient and New." In *Handbook of Emotions*, edited by M. Lewis and J. M. Haviland-Jones (pp. 397–414). New York: Guilford.

Shweder, Richard A., Manamahan Mahapatra, and Joan Miller. 1987. "Culture and Moral Development." In *The Emergence of Morality in Young Children*, edited by Jerome Kagan and Sharon Lamb (pp. 1–83). Chicago: University of Chicago Press.

Shweder, Richard A., Nancy C. Much, Manamohan Mahapatra, and Lawrence Park. 1997. "The High Three of Morality (Autonomy, Community, Divinity) and the Big Three Explanations of Suffering." In *Morality and Health*, edited by Paul Rozin and Allan Brandt (pp. 119–69). New York: Routledge.

Siddiqi, Arjumand, Ichiro Kawachi, Lisa Berkman, S. V. Subramanian, and Clyde Hertzman. 2007. "Variation of Socioeconomic Gradients in Children's Developmental Health across Advanced Capitalist Societies: Analysis of 22 OECD Nations." *International Journal of Health Services* 37:63–87.

Silva, Jennifer M. 2013. *Coming Up Short: Working-Class Adulthood in an Age of Uncertainty*. Oxford, England: Oxford University Press.

Silventoinen, Karri, Niklas Hammar, Ebba Hedlund, Markku Koskenvuo, Tapani Ronnemaa, and Jaakko Kaprio. 2007. "Selective International Migration by Social Position, Health Behavior, and Personality." *European Journal of Public Health* 18(2):150–55.

Simmel, Georg. 1908. "Individuality and Group Structure." In *On Individuality and Social Forms*, edited by Donald N. Levine (pp. 235–248). Chicago and London: University of Chicago Press.

Smetana, Judith G. 1995. "Context, Conflict, and Constraint in Adolescent-Parent Authority Relationships." In *Morality in Everyday Life: Developmental Perspectives*, edited by Melanie Killen and Daniel Hart (pp. 225–55). New York: Cambridge University Press.

Smetana, Judith G., Melanie Killen, and Elliot Turiel. 1991. "Children's Reasoning about Interpersonal and Moral Conflicts." *Child Development* 62:629–44.

Smetana, Judith G., and Elliot Turiel. 2003. "Moral Development during Adolescence." in *Blackwell Handbook of Adolescence*, edited by Gerald R. Adams and Michael D. Berzonsky (pp. 247–68). Oxford, England: Blackwell Publishing.

Smith, Adam. 1982 [1759]. *The Theory of Moral Sentiments*. Indianapolis: Liberty Fund.

Smith, Christian. 2009. *What Is a Person?* Chicago, IL: University of Chicago Press.

Smith, Herman, W., and Yi Cai. Mean Affective Ratings of 1,146 Concepts by Shanghai Undergraduates, 1991-2002 [Computer file]. 2002. Distributed at http://www.indiana.edu/~socpsy/ACT/interact/JavaInteract.html

Smith, Herman W., and Yap MiowLin. 2006. "Guilty Americans and Shameful Chinese: An Affect Control Test of Benedict's Thesis." In *Purpose, Meaning, and Action: Control Systems Theories in Sociology*, edited by K. A. McCleland and T. J. Fararo (Pp. 213–36). New York: Palgrave MacMillan.

Smith, Herman W., Takanori Matsuno, Shuuichirou Ike, and Michio Umino. Mean Affective Ratings of 1,894 Concepts by Japanese Undergraduates, 1989–2002 [Computer file]. Distributed at http://www.indiana.edu/~socpsy/ACT/interact/JavaInteract.html

Smith-Lovin, Lynn. 1987a. "Impressions from Events." *The Journal of Mathematical Sociology* 13:35–70.

Smith-Lovin, Lynn. 1987b. "The Affect Control of Events within Settings." *The Journal of Mathematical Sociology* 13:71–101.

Smith-Lovin, Lynn. 1990. "Emotion as the Confirmation and Disconfirmation of Identity: An Affect Control Model." In *Research Agendas in the Sociology of Emotions*, edited by T. D. Kemper. New York: SUNY Press.

Smith-Lovin, Lynn, and William Douglass. 1992. "An Affect Control Analysis of Two Religious Subcultures." In *Social Perspectives on Emotions*, vol. 1, edited by V. Gecas & D. Franks (pp. 217–48). Greenwich, CT: JAI Press.

Smith-Lovin, Lynn, and David R. Heise. 1988. *Analyzing Social Interaction: Advances in Affect Control Theory*. New York: Gordon and Breach.

Snow, David A., and Peter B. Owens. 2014. "Social Movements and Social Inequality: Toward a More Balanced Assessment of the Relationship." In *Handbook of the Social Psychology of Inequality*, edited by J. McLeod, E. J. Lawler, and M. Schwalbe (pp. 657–81). New York: Springer.

Song, Myung-ja, Judith G. Smetana, and Sang Yoon Kim. 1987. "Korean Children's Conceptions of Moral and Conventional Transgressions." *Developmental Psychology* 23(4):577.

Spates, James L. 1983. "The Sociology of Values." *Annual Review of Sociology* 9:27–49.

Srivastava, Sameer B., and Mahzarin R. Banaji. 2011. "Culture, Cognition, and Collaborative Networks in Organizations." *American Sociological Review* 76(2):207–33.

Stangor, Charles, Laure Lynch, Changming Duan, and Beth Glass. 1992. "Categorization of Individuals on the Basis of Multiple Social Features." *Journal of Personality and Social Psychology* 62:207–18.

Stets, Jan E., and Michael J. Carter. 2011. "The Moral Self Applying Identity Theory." *Social Psychology Quarterly* 74(2):192–215.

Stets, Jan E., and Michael J. Carter. 2012. "A Theory of the Self for the Sociology of Morality." *American Sociological Review* 77(1):120–40.

Sunar, Diane. 2009. "Suggestions for a New Integration in the Psychology of Morality." *Social and Personality Psychology Compass* 3(4):447–74.

Sutherland, Edwin. 1947. *Principles of Criminology*. Philadelphia, PA: Lippincott.

Swidler, Ann. 1986. "Culture in Action: Symbols and Strategies." *American Sociological Review* 51(2):273–86.

Swidler, Ann. 2001. *Talk of Love: How Culture Matters*. Chicago: University of Chicago Press.

Tajfel, Henri (Ed.). 1978. *Differentiation Between Social Groups: Studies in the Social Psychology of Intergroup Relations*. London, New York: Published in cooperation with European Association of Experimental Social Psychology by Academic Press.

Tang, Mei, Zhiyan Wang, Mingyi Qian, Jun Gao, and Lili Zhang. 2008. "Transferred Shame in the Cultures of Interdependent-Self and Independent Self." *Journal of Cognition and Culture* 8(1):163–78.

Tangney, June Price, Jeff Stuewig, and Debra J. Mashek. 2007. "Moral Emotions and Moral Behavior." *Annual Review of Psychology* 58:345–72.

Tappan, Mark B. 1997. "Language, Culture, and Moral Development: A Vygotskian Perspective." *Developmental Review* 17:78–100.

Taylor, Charles (Ed.). 1989. *Sources of the Self: The Making of the Modern Identity*. Cambridge, MA: Harvard University Press.

Tetlock, Phillip E., Orie V. Kristel, S. Beth Elson, Melanie C. Green, and Jennifer S. Lerner. 2000. "The Psychology of the Unthinkable: Taboo Trade-Offs, Forbidden Base Rates, and Heretical Counterfactuals." *Journal of Personality and Social Psychology* 78(5):853–70.

Thacher, David. 2016. "The Perception of Value: Adam Smith on the Moral Role of Social Research." *European Journal of Social Theory* 19(1):94–110.

Thomassen, Lisa. 2002. "An Alcoholic Is Good and Sober: Sentiment Change in AA." *Deviant Behavior: An Interdisciplinary Journal* 23:177–200.

Triandis, Harry (Ed.). 1995. *Individualism and Collectivism*. Boulder, CO: Westview Press.

Tronto, Joan C. 1993. *Moral Boundaries: A Political Argument for an ethic of Care*. New York: Routledge.

Tugendhat, Ernst. 1993. "The Role of Identity in the Constitution of Morality." In *The Moral Self*, edited by Thomas E. Wren and Gil G. Noam (pp. 3–15). New Baskerville, MA: MIT Press.

Turiel, Elliot. 1983. *The Development of Social Knowledge: Moralty and Convention*. Cambridge, England: Cambridge University Press.

Turiel, Elliot. 1994. "Morality, Authoritarianism, and Personal Agency in Cultural Contexts." In *Personality and Intelligence*, edited by Robert J. Sternberg and Patricia Ruzgis (pp. 271–99). Cambridge, England: Cambridge University Press.

Turiel, Elliot. 2002. *The Culture of Morality: Social Development, Context, and Conflict*. New York: Cambridge University Press.

Turiel, Elliot, Carolyn Hildebrandt, Cecilia Wainryb, and Herbert D Saltzstein. 1991. "Judging Social Issues: Difficulties, Inconsistencies, and Consistencies." *Monographs of the Society for Research in Child Development* 56(2).

Turiel, Elliot, M. Killen, and Charles C. Helwig. 1987. "Morality: Its Structure, Functions and Vagarities." In *The Emergence of Morality in Young Children*, edited by Jerome Kagan and S. Lamb (Pp. 155–243). Chicago, IL: University of Chicago Press.

Turner, Jonathan H. 2007. *Human Emotions: A Sociological Theory*. New York: Routledge.

Turner, Jonathan H. 2010. "Natural Selection and the Evolution of Morality in Human Societies." In *Handbook of the Sociology of Morality*, edited by Steven Hitlin and Stephen Vaisey (pp. 125–45). New York: Springer.

Turner, Jonathan H. 2015. "The Evolutionary Biology and Sociology of Social Order." In *Order on the Edge of Chaos: Social Psychology and the Problem of Social Order*, edited by Edward J Lawler, Shane R Thye, and Jeongkoo Yoon (pp. 1842). New York: Cambridge University Press.

Turner, Jonathan H., and Jan E. Stets. 2006a. "Moral Emotions." In *Handbook of the Sociology of Emtoions*, edited by J. E. Stets and J. H. Turner (pp. 544–66). New York: Springer.

Turner, Jonathan H., and Jan E. Stets. 2006b. "Sociological Theories of Human Emotions." *Annual Review of Sociology* 32:25–52.

Turner, Ralph H. 1976. "The Real Self: From Institution to Impulse." *American Journal of Sociology* 84:1–23.

Twenge, Jean M. 2006. *Generation Me: Why Today's Young Americans are More Confident, Assertive, Entitled—and More Miserable—than Ever Before*. New York: Free Press.

Twenge, Jean M., Sara Konrath, Joshua D. Foster, W. Keith Campbell, and Brad J. Bushman. 2008. "Egos Inflating Over Time: A Cross-Temporal Meta-Analysis of the Narcissistic Personality Inventory." *Journal of Personality* 76(4):875–902.

United Nations, Department of Economic and Social Affairs. 2015. "Trends in International Migrant Stock: Migrants by Destination and Origin." http://www.un.org/en/development/desa/population/migration/data/estimates2/estimates15.shtml

Uslaner, Eric M. 2002. *The Moral Foundations of Trust*. Cambridge, England: Cambridge University Press.

Vaisey, Stephen. 2009. "Motivation and Justification: A Dual-Process Model of Culture in Action." *American Journal of Sociology* 114(6):1675–715.

Vaisey, Stephen, and Andrew Miles. 2014. "Tools from Moral Psychology for Measuring Personal Moral Culture." *Theory & Society* 43(3–4):311–332.

Vagero, Denny, and Olle Lundberg. 1989. "Health Inequalities in Britain and Sweden." *The Lancet* 334:35–36.

Van Leeuwen, Florian, and Justin H Park. 2009. "Perceptions of Social Dangers, Moral Foundations, and Political Orientation." *Personality and Individual Differences* 47(3):169–73.

Volscho, Thomas W., and Nathan J. Kelly. 2012. "The Rise of the Super-Rich: Power Resources, Taxes, Financial Markets, and the Dynamics of the Top 1 Percent, 1949–2008." *American Sociological Review* 77:679–99.

Walker, Janet S. 2000. "Choosing Biases, Using Power, and Practicing Resistance: Moral Development in a World Without Certainty." *Human Development* 43:135–56.

Walker, Lawrence J. 2006. "Gender and Morality." In *Handbook of Moral Development*, edited by Melanie Killen and Judith Smetana (pp. 93–115). Mahwah, NJ: Lawrence Erlbaum Associates.

Walker, Lawrence J., and R. C. Pitts. 1998. "Naturalistic Conceptions of Moral Maturity." *Developmental Psychology* 34:403–19.

Walmsley, R. 2014. "World Prison Population List, London: Kings College London International Centre for Prison Studies.

Weber, Max. 1930 [1905]. *The Protestant Ethic and the Spirit of Capitalism*. New York: Scribner's.

Western, Bruce. 2006. *Punishment and Inequality in America*. New York: Russell Sage Foundation.

Western, Bruce, Deirdre Bloome, and Christine Percheski. 2008. "Inequality among American Families with Children, 1975 to 2005." *American Sociological Review* 73:903–20.

Wiessner, Polly. 2002. "The Vines of Complexity: Egalitarian Structures and the Institutionalization of Inequality among the Enga." *Current Anthropology* 43:233–69.

Wiggins, Beverly, and David R. Heise, 1987. "Expectations, Intentions, and Behavior: Some Tests of Affect Control Theory." *The Journal of Mathematical Sociology* 13:153–69.

Wilkins, Amy C., Stefanie Mollborn, and Boróka Bó. 2014. "Constructing Difference." In *Handbook of the Social Psychology of Inequality*, edited by J. McLeod, E. J. Lawler, and M. Schwalbe (pp. 125–54). New York: Springer.

Wilkinson, Richard G. 2004. "Why Is Violence More Common Where Inequality Is Greater?" *Annals of the New York Academy of Sciences* 1036:1–12.

Wilkinson, Richard G., and Kate E. Pickett. 2006. "Income Inequality and Population Health: A Review and Explanation of the Evidence." *Social Science and Medicine* 62: 1768–84.

Wilkinson, Richard, and Kate Pickett. 2011. *The Spirit Level: Why Greater Equality Makes Societies Stronger.* New York: Bloomsbury Publishing.

Willer, Robb. 2009. "Groups Reward Individual Sacrifice: The Status Solution to the Collective Action Problem." *American Sociological Review* 74:23–43.

Willer, Robb, Matthew Feinberg, Kyle Irwin, Michael Schultz, and Brent Simpson. 2010. "The Trouble with Invisible Men: How Reputational Concenrs Motivate Generosity." In *Handbook of the Sociology of Morality*, edited by Steven Hitlin and Stephen Vaisey (pp. 315–30). New York: Springer.

Wimmer, Andreas. 2013. *Ethnic Boundary Making: Institutions, Power, Networks.* New York: Oxford.

Winchester, Daniel. 2008. "Embodying the Faith: Religious Practice and the Making of a Muslim Moral Habitus." *Social Forces* 86(4):2008.

Wolf, Achim, Ron Gray, and Seena Fazel. 2014. "Violence as a Public Health Problem: An Ecological Study of 169 Countries." *Social Science and Medicine* 104: 220–27.

Wong, Ying, and Jeanne Tsai. 2007. "Cultural Models of Shame and Guilt." In *The self-conscious emotions: Theory and research*, edited by Jessica L. Tracy, Richard W. Robins, and June Price Tangney (pp. 209–23). New York: Guilford Press.

Woodard, Colin. 2016. *American Character: A History of the Epic Struggle Between Individual Liberty and the Common Good.* New York: Viking.

Xie, Yu, and Xiang Zhou. "Income Inequality in Today's China." *Proceedings of the National Academy of Sciences USA* 111(19),6928–33.

Young, Alford A. 2004. *The Minds of Marginalized Black Men: Making Sense of Mobility, Opportunity, and Future Life Chances.* Princeton, NJ: Princeton University Press.

Youniss, James, and Miranda Yates. 1999. "Youth Service and Moral-Civic Identity: A Case for Everyday Morality." *Educational Psychology Review* 11(4):361–76.

Zerubavel, Eviatar. 1997. *Social Mindscapes: An Invitation To Cognitive Sociology.* Caimbridge, MA: Harvard University Press.

Zigon, Jarrett. 2008. *Morality: An Anthropological Perspective.* Oxford, England: Berg.

Tables and figures are indicated by an italic "*t*" and "*f*" following the page number.